History of the Conquest of Peru

𝔐onte𝔷uma 𝔈dition

THE WORKS OF WILLIAM H. PRESCOTT

TWENTY-TWO VOLUMES

Vol. V

Montezuma Edition

HISTORY OF THE

Conquest of Peru

BY

WILLIAM H. PRESCOTT

EDITED BY

WILFRED HAROLD MUNRO

PROFESSOR OF EUROPEAN HISTORY IN BROWN UNIVERSITY

AND COMPRISING THE NOTES OF THE EDITION BY
JOHN FOSTER KIRK

Congestæ cumulantur opes, orbisque rapinas
Accipit.
            CLAUDIAN, In Ruf., lib. i. v. 194

So color de religion
Van á buscar plata y oro
Del encubierto tesoro.
      LOPE DE VEGA, El Nuevo Mundo, Jorn. I

VOL. I

PHILADELPHIA AND LONDON
J. B. LIPPINCOTT COMPANY

EDITOR'S PREFACE

WHEN, in 1847, the announcement was made that William Hickling Prescott had published a new work dealing with the history of the Spanish conquests in the New World, the booksellers in both England and America were amazed at the orders that poured in upon them.

Mr. Prescott had concentrated public attention upon himself ten years before by his " History of the Reign of Ferdinand and Isabella," and had secured by that work the foremost place among the American historians. The " History of the Conquest of Mexico," put forth in 1843, made his reputation international and placed him in the front rank of the historical writers of the nineteenth century. His second work startled the reading public. A wonderful story was told in a strangely fascinating way. Never before had the magnificent barbarism which the Spaniards encountered been adequately described. Never had an author been more successful in riveting attention upon his hero than was Prescott in the case of Hernando Cortés. Every reader made the goal of the great Spaniard his own. No man could lay his volume down until he found himself domiciled with Cortés in the " Halls of the Montezumas," amid the smoking ruins of the Aztec capital.

And now in the " History of the Conquest of
Peru " a still more astounding tale was told, a story
of marvels at which the world could only gasp, of
wealth that almost paralyzed the imagination. A
succession of such fascinating pen-pictures was
drawn as few writers of any country had ever presented to mankind. No such commanding figure
as that of Cortés focussed the attention, but the
interest was held so completely that the reader
turned his last leaf with even more regret than
when he closed the last volume of the " Conquest
of Mexico."

How did Mr. Prescott produce this effect?

In the first place, the Inca civilization was even
more interesting than the Aztec had been. Men
were amazed to learn that among the savages of
the Andes a government rivalling in some respects
the most prosperous in Europe had been developed. The horrible features of the Aztec state—
the wars regularly entered into that living victims
might be secured for sacrifices and for future cannibal repasts—were happily lacking. No such
blots stained the escutcheon of the Incas. Men
saw a government so paternal that poverty was
unknown, so provident that famines were actually
eliminated, so beneficent that conquered nations
soon rejoiced to be governed by the successors of
Manco Capac. Not even Venice at the height of
its prosperity was more successful in dealing with
subject states.

The agricultural development was more perfect
than that of most European countries in the sixteenth century. Mountains that in the Iberian

peninsula would have been left in their primeval barrenness were here terraced almost to their summits and were made to produce such crops as the Spaniards had never before seen. Other regions that remained in their native state were covered with immense flocks of strange animals which when domesticated were made to carry upon their backs the commerce of the nation. These creatures, the llamas, furnished when shorn the material from which the garments of the people were made. They could also be depended upon to furnish such a food supply as was found nowhere else in America.

The traffic of a great empire was carried on over roads that extorted the admiration of the skilled engineers of Europe. Upon these great arteries of communication stations were built at frequent intervals, and at these stations were magazines filled with supplies for the use of the armies of the Inca, as well as for the ordinary travelling public.

Into this land of smiling plenty came a band of adventurers whose sole object was to secure wealth. They manifested the same contempt for hardship and danger, the same indifference concerning the numbers of their opponents, the same heroic endurance, which had for generations distinguished the soldiers of Spain. But they were for the most part men of no standing in their native land—inferior in everything but valor to those who followed the standard of the Conqueror of Mexico. Rarely has a general had to deal with more unruly followers, rarely have soldiers

followed a more unprincipled leader than was
Francisco Pizarro.*

The victories won by the invaders over armies
far outnumbering their own do not greatly surprise us. Civilization always conquers barbarism
when the issues are fairly joined, and in this case
the advantage in weapons was all on the side of
the Spaniards. We know from the beginning
what the result of the struggle will be. But we are
not prepared for the astounding wealth in gold
and silver that fell into the hands of the conquerors. Accustomed though men are to contemplate the enormous fortunes of the twentieth century, the ransom exacted from the captive Inca
still dazzles the imagination.

With the execution of the Peruvian leader and
the distribution of the treasure his orders had
brought together, the interest in the story does not
end. With most readers it becomes more intense.
What will be the effect upon this band of brigands
of the enormous wealth so unexpectedly acquired?
Will those whom only constant danger has held
together, whom only the fear of annihilation in
that hostile land has kept from flying at each
others' throats, remain longer subject to discipline
now that their end has been attained? Almost immediately discord arises. Fierce brawls enrage the
soldiers. The chiefs are unable to live in harmony.
The conquerors divide into two hostile camps. The
land is rent with civil wars. First Almagro is sent

* The judgment passed by scientists upon his character, when the
opportunity for examining his cranial development was afforded
them, is recorded in a note in the first chapter of the third volume
of this work.

to his death. Then Pizarro falls, struck down by
the men of Chili. Will even the royal authority of
the far distant Spanish king be powerful enough
to bring about peace? The colonial policy Spain
had thus far followed is of no avail at this crisis.
Viceroys whose powers were hedged about with so
many petty restrictions were quite unable to cope
with such desperate men. When, as in the case of
Vaca de Castro, they developed great ability, and
were gradually gaining the mastery, others were
sent to supersede them lest they should become too
powerful for the home government to control.
There were no trained subordinates upon whom
the newcomers could rely. Each viceroy had to
devise his own scheme for asserting and maintaining authority.

Sympathy goes forth occasionally to the men
with whom fortune seems to deal unfairly, as in
the case of young Almagro. Later Gonzalo
Pizarro chains for a time our reluctant regard.
The uncanny figure of old Carbajal, with the wind
blowing the hairs from off his head, fascinates us
completely. He holds our attention from the
moment he rides forth to take part in his first
battle. Reprobate, monster of cruelty though he
is, there is no more picturesque figure in the
pages of American history, and Prescott never
achieved a greater success than in his delineation
of the character of this sarcastic old warrior. The
song he hummed in moments of greatest danger
is always sounding in our ears. But even Carbajal's wisdom and valor and military skill cannot
secure permanent power for his chief, and we

become convinced at last that while one of the Pizarro family lives peace cannot be restored to Peru.

When we have reached this conclusion, Prescott brings Gasca upon the scene. With a few masterstrokes he sketches for us his early life, predisposes us in his favor before he allows him to leave the shores of Spain, and makes us realize that the Spanish king has at last mastered the situation by giving absolute power to this humble ecclesiastic. We know that the " President of the Royal Audience " will eventually bring order out of chaos. His wisdom is equal to all emergencies, his patience is inexhaustible, his courage never falters, his tact never fails. From his vantage-ground in Panama he removes the most dangerous obstacles, and in the fulness of time sails for the coast of Peru. The country is already his own. Slowly but surely he surmounts difficulties that to others had proved insuperable. One by one he removes the most discordant elements from the distracted land. Everywhere peace follows in his footsteps. " After the dark and turbulent spirits with which we have hitherto been occupied it is refreshing to dwell on a character like that of Gasca."

With the work of the great President accomplished, Prescott wisely ends his story. No dramatist could have brought his plot to a more felicitous conclusion.

WILFRED H. MUNRO.

BROWN UNIVERSITY, February 25, 1905.

PREFACE

THE most brilliant passages in the history of Spanish adventure in the New World are undoubtedly afforded by the conquests of Mexico and Peru,—the two states which combined with the largest extent of empire a refined social polity and considerable progress in the arts of civilization. Indeed, so prominently do they stand out on the great canvas of history that the name of the one, notwithstanding the contrast they exhibit in their respective institutions, most naturally suggests that of the other; and when I sent to Spain to collect materials for an account of the Conquest of Mexico I included in my researches those relating to the Conquest of Peru.

The larger part of the documents, in both cases, was obtained from the same great repository,—the archives of the Royal Academy of History at Madrid; a body specially intrusted with the preservation of whatever may serve to illustrate the Spanish colonial annals. The richest portion of its collection is probably that furnished by the papers of Muñoz. This eminent scholar, the historiographer of the Indies, employed nearly fifty years of his life in amassing materials for a history of Spanish discovery and conquest in America. For this, as he acted under the authority of the government, every facility was afforded him; and public offices and private depositories, in all the

principal cities of the empire, both at home and
throughout the wide extent of its colonial possessions, were freely opened to his inspection. The
result was a magnificent collection of manuscripts,
many of which he patiently transcribed with his
own hand. But he did not live to reap the fruits
of his persevering industry. The first volume of
his work, relating to the voyages of Columbus, was
scarcely finished when he died; and his manuscripts, at least that portion of them which have
reference to Mexico and Peru, were destined to
serve the uses of another, an inhabitant of that
New World to which they related.

Another scholar, to whose literary stores I am
largely indebted, is Don Martin Fernandez de
Navarrete, late Director of the Royal Academy of
History. Through the greater part of his long
life he was employed in assembling original documents to illustrate the colonial annals. Many of
these have been incorporated in his great work,
" Coleccion de los Viages y Descubrimientos,"
which, although far from being completed after
the original plan of its author, is of inestimable
service to the historian. In following down the
track of discovery, Navarrete turned aside from
the conquests of Mexico and Peru, to exhibit the
voyages of his countrymen in the Indian seas.
His manuscripts relating to the two former countries he courteously allowed to be copied for me.
Some of them have since appeared in print, under
the auspices of his learned coadjutors, Salvà and
Baranda, associated with him in the Academy;
but the documents placed in my hands formed a

most important contribution to my materials for the present history.

The death of this illustrious man, which occurred some time after the present work was begun, has left a void in his country not easy to be filled; for he was zealously devoted to letters, and few have done more to extend the knowledge of her colonial history. Far from an exclusive solicitude for his own literary projects, he was ever ready to extend his sympathy and assistance to those of others. His reputation as a scholar was enhanced by the higher qualities which he possesed as a man,—by his benevolence, his simplicity of manners, and unsullied moral worth. My own obligations to him are large; for from the publication of my first historical work, down to the last week of his life, I have constantly received proofs from him of his hearty and most efficient interest in the prosecution of my historical labors; and I now the more willingly pay this well-merited tribute to his deserts, that it must be exempt from all suspicion of flattery.

In the list of those to whom I have been indebted for materials I must also include the name of M. Ternaux-Compans, so well known by his faithful and elegant French versions of the Muñoz manuscripts; and that of my friend Don Pascual de Gayangos, who, under the modest dress of translation, has furnished a most acute and learned commentary on Spanish-Arabian history,—securing for himself the foremost rank in that difficult department of letters, which has been illumined by the labors of a Masdeu, a Casiri, and a Conde.

To the materials derived from these sources I have added some manuscripts of an important character from the library of the Escorial. These, which chiefly relate to the ancient institutions of Peru, formed part of the splendid collection of Lord Kingsborough, which has unfortunately shared the lot of most literary collections, and been dispersed, since the death of its noble author. For these I am indebted to that industrious bibliographer, Mr. O. Rich, now resident in London. Lastly, I must not omit to mention my obligations, in another way, to my friend Charles Folsom, Esq., the learned librarian of the Boston Athenæum, whose minute acquaintance with the grammatical structure and the true idiom of our English tongue has enabled me to correct many inaccuracies into which I had fallen in the composition both of this and of my former works.

From these different quarters I have accumulated a large amount of manuscripts, of the most various character and from the most authentic sources; royal grants and ordinances, instructions of the court, letters of the emperor to the great colonial officers, municipal records, personal diaries and memoranda, and a mass of private correspondence of the principal actors in this turbulent drama. Perhaps it was the turbulent state of the country which led to a more frequent correspondence between the government at home and the colonial officers. But, whatever be the cause, the collection of manuscript materials in reference to Peru is fuller and more complete than that which relates to Mexico; so that there is scarcely a nook or corner so obscure, in the path of the adventurer, that some light has not been thrown on it by the written correspondence of the period. The historian has rather had occasion to complain of the *embarras des richesses;* for in the multiplicity of contradictory testimony it is not always easy to detect the truth, as the multiplicity of cross-lights is apt to dazzle and bewilder the eye of the spectator.

The present History has been conducted on the same general plan with that of the Conquest of Mexico. In an Introductory Book I have endeavored to portray the institutions of the Incas, that the reader may be acquainted with the character and condition of that extraordinary race before he enters on the story of their subjugation. The remaining books are occupied with the narrative of the Conquest. And here the subject, it must be allowed, notwithstanding the opportunities it presents for the display of character, strange romantic incident, and picturesque scenery, does not afford so obvious advantages to the historian as the Conquest of Mexico. Indeed, few subjects can present a parallel with that, for the purposes either of the historian or the poet. The natural development of the story, there, is precisely what would be prescribed by the severest rules of art. The conquest of the country is the great end always in the view of the reader. From the first landing of the Spaniards on the soil, their subsequent adventures, their battles and negotiations, their ruinous retreat, their rally and final siege, all tend to this grand result, till the long series is

closed by the downfall of the capital. In the
march of events, all moves steadily forward to this
consummation. It is a magnificent epic, in which
the unity of interest is complete.

In the " Conquest of Peru," the action, so far as
it is founded on the subversion of the Incas, ter-
minates long before the close of the narrative.
The remaining portion is taken up with the fierce
feuds of the Conquerors, which would seem, from
their very nature, to be incapable of being gathered round a central point of interest. To secure
this, we must look beyond the immediate overthrow
of the Indian empire. The conquest of the natives
is but the first step, to be followed by the conquest
of the Spaniards—the rebel Spaniards—themselves, till the supremacy of the crown is permanently established over the country. It is not till
this period that the acquisition of this transatlantic
empire can be said to be completed; and by fixing
the eye on this remoter point the successive steps of
the narrative will be found leading to one great
result, and that unity of interest preserved which is
scarcely less essential to historic than dramatic
composition. How far this has been effected in
the present work must be left to the judgment of
the reader.

No history of the Conquest of Peru, founded on
original documents and aspiring to the credit
of a classic composition, like the " Conquest of
Mexico " by Solis, has been attempted, so far as I
am aware, by the Spaniards. The English possess
one of high value, from the pen of Robertson,
whose masterly sketch occupies its due space in his

great work on America. It has been my object to
exhibit this same story in all its romantic details;
not merely to portray the characteristic features of
the Conquest, but to fill up the outline with the
coloring of life, so as to present a minute and
faithful picture of the times. For this purpose,
I have, in the composition of the work, availed myself freely of my manuscript materials, allowed
the actors to speak as much as possible for themselves, and especially made frequent use of their
letters; for nowhere is the heart more likely to dis-
close itself than in the freedom of private correspondence. I have made liberal extracts from
these authorities in the notes, both to sustain the
text, and to put in a printed form those productions of the eminent captains and statesmen of the
time, which are not very accessible to Spaniards
themselves.

M. Amédée Pichot, in the Preface to the French
translation of the " Conquest of Mexico," infers
from the plan of the composition that I must have
carefully studied the writings of his countryman
M. de Barante. The acute critic does me but
justice in supposing me familiar with the principles of that writer's historical theory, so ably
developed in the Preface to his " Ducs de Bour-
gogne." And I have had occasion to admire the
skilful manner in which he illustrates this theory
himself, by constructing out of the rude materials
of a distant time a monument of genius that trans-
ports us at once into the midst of the Feudal Ages,
—and this without the incongruity which usually
attaches to a modern-antique. In like manner I

B

have attempted to seize the characteristic expression of a distant age and to exhibit it in the freshness of life. But in an essential particular I have deviated from the plan of the French historian. I have suffered the scaffolding to remain after the building has been completed. In other words, I have shown to the reader the steps of the process by which I have come to my conclusions. Instead of requiring him to take my version of the story on trust, I have endeavored to give him a reason for my faith. By copious citations from the original authorities, and by such critical notices of them as would explain to him the influences to which they were subjected, I have endeavored to put him in a position for judging for himself, and thus for revising, and, if need be, reversing, the judgments of the historian. He will, at any rate, by this means, be enabled to estimate the difficulty of arriving at truth amidst the conflict of testimony; and he will learn to place little reliance on those writers who pronounce on the mysterious past with what Fontenelle calls " a frightful degree of certainty,"—a spirit the most opposite to that of the true philosophy of history.

Yet it must be admitted that the chronicler who records the events of an earlier age has some obvious advantages in the store of manuscript materials at his command,—the statements of friends, rivals, and enemies furnishing a wholesome counterpoise to each other,—and also in the general course of events, as they actually occurred, affording the best commentary on the true motives of the parties. The actor, engaged in the heat of the strife, finds his view bounded by the circle around him, and his vision blinded by the smoke and dust of the conflict; while the spectator, whose eye ranges over the ground from a more distant and elevated point, though the individual objects may lose somewhat of their vividness, takes in at a glance all the operations of the field. Paradoxical as it may appear, truth founded on contemporary testimony would seem, after all, as likely to be attained by the writer of a later day as by contemporaries themselves.

Before closing these remarks, I may be permitted to add a few of a personal nature. In several foreign notices of my writings, the author has been said to be blind; and more than once I have had the credit of having lost my sight in the composition of my first history. When I have met with such erroneous accounts, I have hastened to correct them. But the present occasion affords me the best means of doing so; and I am the more desirous of this as I fear some of my own remarks, in the Prefaces to my former histories, have led to the mistake.

While at the University, I received an injury in one of my eyes, which deprived me of the sight of it. The other, soon after, was attacked by inflammation so severely that for some time I lost the sight of that also; and, though it was subsequently restored, the organ was so much disordered as to remain permanently debilitated, while twice in my life, since, I have been deprived of the use of it for all purposes of reading and writing, for several years together. It was during one of these periods that I received from Madrid the materials for the "History of Ferdinand and Isabella," and in my disabled condition, with my transatlantic treasures lying around me, I was like one pining from hunger in the midst of abundance. In this state, I resolved to make the ear, if possible, do the work of the eye. I procured the services of a secretary, who read to me the various authorities; and in time I became so far familiar with the sounds of the different foreign languages (to some of which, indeed, I had been previously accustomed by a residence abroad) that I could comprehend his reading without much difficulty. As the reader proceeded, I dictated copious notes; and when these had swelled to a considerable amount they were read to me repeatedly, till I had mastered their contents sufficiently for the purposes of composition. The same notes furnished an easy means of reference to sustain the text.

Still another difficulty occurred, in the mechanical labor of writing, which I found a severe trial to the eye. This was remedied by means of a writing-case, such as is used by the blind, which enabled me to commit my thoughts to paper without the aid of sight, serving me equally well in the dark as in the light. The characters thus formed made a near approach to hieroglyphics; but my secretary became expert in the art of deciphering, and a fair copy—with a liberal allowance for unavoidable blunders—was transcribed for the use of the printer. I have described the process with more minuteness, as some curiosity has been repeatedly expressed in reference to my *modus operandi*

under my privations, and the knowledge of it
may be of some assistance to others in similar
circumstances.

Though I was encouraged by the sensible progress of my work, it was necessarily slow. But in
time the tendency to inflammation diminished, and
the strength of the eye was confirmed more and
more. It was at length so far restored that I could
read for several hours of the day, though my labors
in this way necessarily terminated with the day-
light. Nor could I ever dispense with the services
of a secretary, or with the writing-case; for, contrary to the usual experience, I have found writing
a severer trial to the eye than reading,—a remark,
however, which does not apply to the reading of
manuscript; and to enable myself, therefore, to
revise my composition more carefully, I caused a
copy of the " History of Ferdinand and Isabella "
to be printed for my own inspection before it was
sent to the press for publication. Such as I have
described was the improved state of my health during the preparation of the " Conquest of Mexico; "
and, satisfied with being raised so nearly to a level
with the rest of my species, I scarcely envied the
superior good fortune of those who could prolong
their studies into the evening and the later hours
of the night.

But a change has again taken place during the
last two years. The sight of my eye has become
gradually dimmed, while the sensibility of the
nerve has been so far increased that for several
weeks of the last year I have not opened a volume,
and through the whole time I have not had the use

of it, on an average, for more than an hour a day.
Nor can I cheer myself with the delusive expectation that, impaired as the organ has become from
having been tasked, probably, beyond its strength,
it can ever renew its youth, or be of much service
to me hereafter in my literary researches. Whether
I shall have the heart to enter, as I had proposed,
on a new and more extensive field of historical
labor, with these impediments, I cannot say. Perhaps long habit, and a natural desire to follow up
the career which I have so long pursued, may make
this, in a manner, necessary, as my past experience
has already proved that it is practicable.

From this statement—too long, I fear, for his
patience—the reader who feels any curiosity about
the matter will understand the real extent of my
embarrassments in my historical pursuits. That
they have not been very light will be readily admitted, when it is considered that I have had but a
limited use of my eye in its best state, and that
much of the time I have been debarred from the
use of it altogether. Yet the difficulties I have had
to contend with are very far inferior to those which
fall to the lot of a blind man. I know of no historian now alive who can claim the glory of having
overcome such obstacles, but the author of " La
Conquête de l'Angleterre par les Normands; "
who, to use his own touching and beautiful language, " has made himself the friend of darkness,"
and who, to a profound philosophy that requires
no light but that from within, unites a capacity for
extensive and various research, that might well
demand the severest application of the student.

The remarks into which I have been led at such length will, I trust, not be set down by the reader to an unworthy egotism, but to their true source, a desire to correct a misapprehension to which I may have unintentionally given rise myself, and which has gained me the credit with some—far from grateful to my feelings, since undeserved—of having surmounted the incalculable obstacles which lie in the path of the blind man.

Boston, April 2, 1847.

GENERAL CONTENTS

BOOK I
INTRODUCTION—VIEW OF THE CIVILIZATION OF THE INCAS

BOOK II
DISCOVERY OF PERU

BOOK III
CONQUEST OF PERU

BOOK IV
CIVIL WARS OF THE CONQUERORS

BOOK V
SETTLEMENT OF THE COUNTRY

APPENDIX

CONTENTS OF VOL. I

BOOK I

INTRODUCTION—VIEW OF THE CIVILIZATION OF THE INCAS

CHAPTER I

PHYSICAL ASPECT OF THE COUNTRY — SOURCES OF PERUVIAN CIVILIZATION — EMPIRE OF THE INCAS — ROYAL FAMILY — NOBILITY

CHAPTER II

ORDERS OF THE STATE—PROVISIONS FOR JUSTICE—DIVISION OF
LANDS—REVENUES AND REGISTERS—GREAT ROADS AND POSTS
—MILITARY TACTICS AND POLICY

CHAPTER V

PERUVIAN SHEEP—GREAT HUNTS—MANUFACTURES—MECHANI-
CAL SKILL—ARCHITECTURE—CONCLUDING REFLECTIONS

BOOK II

DISCOVERY OF PERU

CHAPTER I

ANCIENT AND MODERN SCIENCE—ART OF NAVIGATION—MARITIME
DISCOVERY — SPIRIT OF THE SPANIARDS — POSSESSIONS IN THE
NEW WORLD—RUMORS CONCERNING PERU

CHAPTER II

FRANCISCO PIZARRO—HIS EARLY HISTORY—FIRST EXPEDITION TO
THE SOUTH—DISTRESSES OF THE VOYAGERS—SHARP ENCOUN-
TERS—RETURN TO PANAMA—ALMAGRO'S EXPEDITION

CHAPTER III

THE FAMOUS CONTRACT—SECOND EXPEDITION—RUIZ EXPLORES
THE COAST—PIZARRO'S SUFFERINGS IN THE FOREST—ARRIVAL
OF NEW RECRUITS — FRESH DISCOVERIES AND DISASTERS —
PIZARRO ON THE ISLE OF GALLO

CHAPTER IV

INDIGNATION OF THE GOVERNOR—STERN RESOLUTION OF PIZARRO —PROSECUTION OF THE VOYAGE—BRILLIANT ASPECT OF TUM-BEZ—DISCOVERIES ALONG THE COAST—RETURN TO PANAMA— PIZARRO EMBARKS FOR SPAIN

c

LIST OF ILLUSTRATIONS

·

BOOK I

INTRODUCTION

VIEW OF THE CIVILIZATION OF THE INCAS

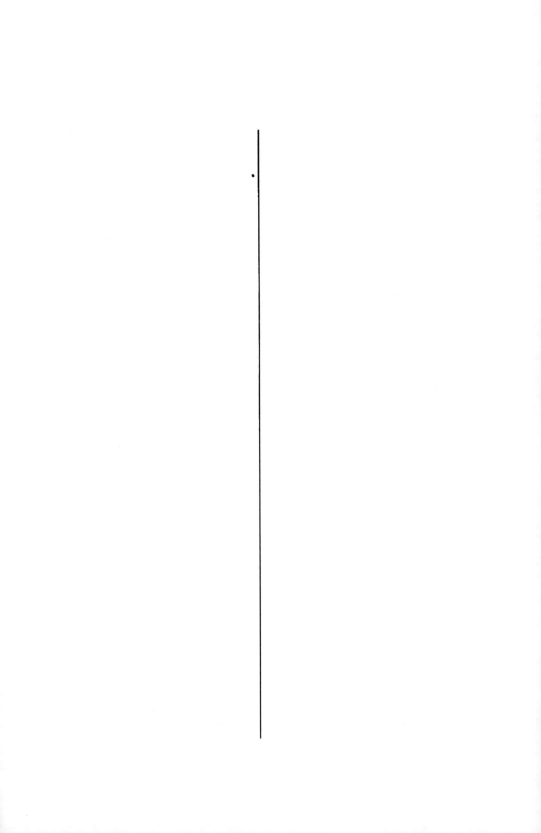

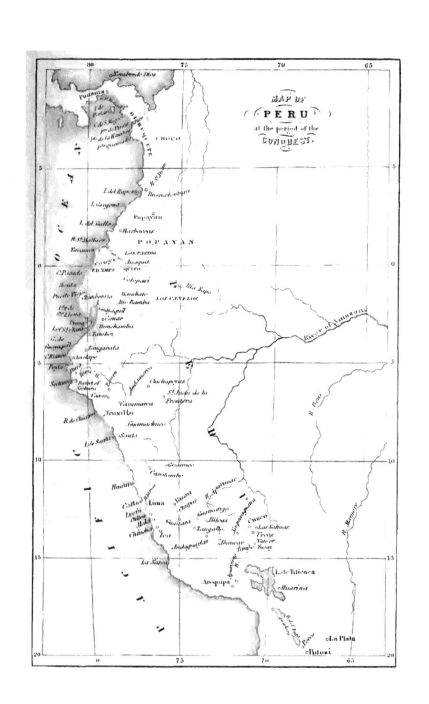

MAP OF
PERU
at the period of the
CONQUEST.

CONQUEST OF PERU

CHAPTER I

OF the numerous nations which occupied the great American continent at the time of its discovery by the Europeans, the two most advanced in power and refinement were undoubtedly those of Mexico and Peru. But, though resembling one another in extent of civilization, they differed widely as to the nature of it; and the philosophical student of his species may feel a natural curiosity to trace the different steps by which these two nations strove to emerge from the state of barbarism and place themselves on a higher point in the scale of humanity. In a former work I have endeavored to exhibit the institutions and character of the ancient Mexicans, and the story of their conquest by the Spaniards. The present will be devoted to the Peruvians; and if their history shall be found to present less strange anomalies and striking contrasts than that of the Aztecs, it may interest us quite as much by the pleasing picture it offers of a well-regulated government and sober habits of industry under the patriarchal sway of the Incas.

3

The empire of Peru, at the period of the Spanish invasion, stretched along the Pacific from about the second degree north to the thirty-seventh degree of south latitude; a line, also, which describes the western boundaries of the modern republics of Ecuador, Peru, Bolivia, and Chili. Its breadth cannot so easily be determined; for, though bounded everywhere by the great ocean on the west, towards the east it spread out, in many parts, considerably beyond the mountains, to the confines of barbarous states, whose exact position is undetermined, or whose names are effaced from the map of history. It is certain, however, that its breadth was altogether disproportioned to its length.[1]

The topographical aspect of the country is very remarkable. A strip of land, rarely exceeding twenty leagues in width, runs along the coast, and is hemmed in through its whole extent by a colossal range of mountains, which, advancing from the straits of Magellan, reaches its highest elevation—indeed, the highest on the American continent—about the seventeenth degree south,[2] and,

[1] Sarmiento, Relacion, MS., cap. 65.*—Cieza de Leon, Cronica del Peru (Anvers, 1554), cap. 41 —Garcilasso de la Vega, Commentarios Reales (Lisboa, 1609), Parte 1, lib 1, cap. 8 —According to the last authority, the empire, in its greatest breadth, did not exceed one hundred and twenty leagues. But Garcilasso's geography will not bear criticism.

[2] According to Malte-Brun, it is under the equator that we meet with the loftiest summits of this chain. (Universal Geography, Eng. trans, book 86) But more recent measurements have shown this to be between fifteen and seventeen degrees south, where the

* [In regard to the real authorship of the work erroneously attributed by Prescott to Juan de Sarmiento, see infra, p. 178, note. —K.]

after crossing the line, gradually subsides into hills of inconsiderable magnitude, as it enters the Isthmus of Panamá. This is the famous Cordillera of the Andes, or "copper mountains," [3] as termed by the natives, though they might with more reason have been called "mountains of gold." Arranged sometimes in a single line, though more frequently in two or three lines running parallel or obliquely to each other, they seem to the voyager on the ocean but one continuous chain; while the huge volcanoes, which to the inhabitants of the table-land look like solitary and independent masses, appear to him only like so many peaks of the same vast and magnificent range. So immense is the scale on which Nature works in these regions that it is only when viewed from a great distance that the spectator can in any degree comprehend the relation of the several parts to the stupendous whole. Few of the works of Nature, indeed, are calculated to produce impressions of higher sublimity than the aspect of this coast, as it is gradually unfolded to the eye of the mariner sailing on the distant waters of the

Nevado de Sorata rises to the enormous height of 25,250 feet, and the Illimani to 24,300 *

[a] At least, the word *anta*, which has been thought to furnish the etymology of *Andes*, in the Peruvian tongue, signified "copper." †
Garcilasso, Com. Real., Parte 1, lib. 5, cap. 14

* [According to the latest authorities the Nevado de Sorata, or Illampu, is 21,484 feet in height Wiener, who with two companions scaled Illimani in 1877, calculated its highest point to be 20,692 feet above the sea.—M.]

† [But this etymology has not been generally accepted, and it is in fact highly improbable. The real derivation, as Humboldt remarks, is "lost in the obscurity of the past."—K.]

Pacific; where mountain is seen to rise above
mountain, and Chimborazo, with its glorious
canopy of snow, glittering far above the clouds,
crowns the whole as with a celestial diadem.[4] *

The face of the country would appear to be
peculiarly unfavorable to the purposes both of
agriculture and of internal communication. The
sandy strip along the coast, where rain rarely falls,
is fed only by a few scanty streams, that furnish
a remarkable contrast to the vast volumes of water
which roll down the eastern sides of the Cordilleras into the Atlantic. The precipitous steeps of
the sierra, with its splintered sides of porphyry
and granite, and its higher regions wrapped in
snows that never melt under the fierce sun of the
equator, unless it be from the desolating action of
its own volcanic fires, might seem equally unpropitious to the labors of the husbandman. And all
communication between the parts of the long-
extended territory might be thought to be pre-
cluded by the savage character of the region,
broken up by precipices, furious torrents, and

[4] Humboldt, Vues des Cordillères et Monumens des Peuples in-
digènes de l'Amérique (Paris, 1810), p. 106.—Malte-Brun, book 88.
—The few brief sketches which M de Humboldt has given of the
scenery of the Cordilleras, showing the hand of a great painter, as
well as of a philosopher, make us regret the more that he has not
given the results of his observations in this interesting region as
minutely as he has done in respect to Mexico

* [The summit of Chimborazo, until his time deemed inaccessible,
was twice reached by Whymper, once in 1879 and again in the succeeding year. His accurate measurements determined its height to
be 20,496 It is, therefore, not so high a mountain as Illampu or
Illimani. (See preceding note) Aconcagua, in Chili, is almost 2000
feet higher. Whymper, Travels among the Great Andes of the
Equator (1892), is the best authority on Andean mountains.—M.]

impassable *quebradas*,*—those hideous rents in the mountain-chain, whose depths the eye of the terrified traveller, as he winds along his aërial pathway, vainly endeavors to fathom.[5] Yet the industry, we might also say the genius, of the Indian was sufficient to overcome all these impediments of Nature.

By a judicious system of canals and subterraneous aqueducts, the waste places on the coast were refreshed by copious streams, that clothed them in fertility and beauty. Terraces were raised upon the steep sides of the Cordillera; and, as the different elevations had the effect of difference of latitude, they exhibited in regular gradation every variety of vegetable form, from the stimulated growth of the tropics to the temperate products of a northern clime; while flocks of *llamas*—the Peruvian sheep—wandered with their shepherds over the broad, snow-covered wastes on the crests of the sierra, which rose beyond the limits of cultivation. An industrious population settled along the lofty regions of the plateaus, and towns and hamlets, clustering amidst orchards and wide-spreading gardens, seemed suspended in the air far above the ordinary elevation of the clouds.[6] Intercourse

[5] "These crevices are so deep," said M de Humboldt, with his usual vivacity of illustration, "that if Vesuvius or the Puy de Dôme were seated in the bottom of them, they would not rise above the level of the ridges of the neighboring sierra." Vues des Cordillères, p. 9

[6] The plains of Quito are at the height of between nine and ten thousand feet above the sea. (See Condamine, Journal d'un Voyage

* [The term "quebrada," the participle of the verb quebrar, to break, admirably describes the terrific rents where the mountains seem literally to have been broken apart.—M.]

was maintained between these numerous settlements by means of the great roads which traversed the mountain-passes and opened an easy communication between the capital and the remotest extremities of the empire.

The source of this civilization is traced to the valley of Cuzco, the central region of Peru, as its name implies.[7] The origin of the Peruvian empire, like the origin of all nations, except the very few which, like our own, have had the good fortune to date from a civilized period and people, is lost in the mists of fable, which, in fact, have settled as darkly round its history as round that of any nation, ancient or modern, in the Old World. According to the tradition most familiar to the European scholar, the time was when the ancient races of the continent were all plunged in deplorable barbarism; when they worshipped nearly every object in nature indiscriminately, made war their pastime, and feasted on the flesh of their slaughtered captives. The Sun, the great luminary and parent of mankind, taking compassion on their degraded condition, sent two of his children, Manco Capac and Mama Oello Huaco, to gather the natives into communities and teach them the arts of civilized life. The celestial pair, brother and sister, husband and wife, advanced along the high plains in the neighborhood of Lake Titicaca to about the sixteenth degree south. They bore with them a golden wedge, and were directed

à l'Équateur (Paris, 1751), p. 48.) Other valleys or plateaus in this vast group of mountains reach a still higher elevation.

[7] "*Cuzco*, in the language of the Incas," says Garcilasso, "signifies *navel*." Com. Real., Parte 1, lib. 1, cap. 18

to take up their residence on the spot where the sacred emblem should without effort sink into the ground. They proceeded accordingly but a short distance, as far as the valley of Cuzco, the spot indicated by the performance of the miracle, since there the wedge speedily sank into the earth and disappeared forever. Here the children of the Sun established their residence, and soon entered upon their beneficent mission among the rude inhabitants of the country; Manco Capac teaching the men the arts of agriculture, and Mama Oella [8] initiating her own sex in the mysteries of weaving and spinning. The simple people lent a willing ear to the messengers of Heaven, and, gathering together in considerable numbers, laid the foundations of the city of Cuzco. The same wise and benevolent maxims which regulated the conduct of the first Incas [9] descended to their successors,

[8] *Mama*, with the Peruvians, signified "mother." (Garcilasso, Com. Real , Parte 1, lib. 4, cap. 1.) The identity of this term with that used by Europeans is a curious coincidence. It is scarcely more so, however, than that of the corresponding word *papa*, which with the ancient Mexicans denoted a priest of high rank; reminding us of the *papa*, "pope," of the Italians With both, the term seems to embrace in its most comprehensive sense the paternal relation, in which it is more familiarly employed by most of the nations of Europe. Nor was the use of it limited to modern times, being applied in the same way both by Greeks and Romans; "Πάππα Φίλε," says Nausikaa, addressing her father, in the simple language which the modern versifiers have thought too simple to render literally

[9] *Inca* signified *king* or *lord* Capac meant *great* or *powerful* It was applied to several of the successors of Manco, in the same manner as the epithet *Yupanqui*, signifying *rich in all virtues*, was added to the names of several Incas. (Cieza de Leon, Cronica, cap. 41.—Garcilasso, Com Real., Parte I, lib 2, cap. 17.) The good qualities commemorated by the cognomens of most of the Peruvian princes afford an honorable, though not altogether unsuspicious, tribute to the excellence of their characters.

and under their mild sceptre a community gradually extended itself along the broad surface of the table-land, which asserted its superiority over the surrounding tribes. Such is the pleasing picture of the origin of the Peruvian monarchy, as portrayed by Garcilasso de la Vega, the descendant of the Incas, and through him made familiar to the European reader.[10]

But this tradition is only one of several current among the Peruvian Indians, and probably not the one most generally received. Another legend speaks of certain white and bearded men, who, advancing from the shores of Lake Titicaca, established an ascendency over the natives and imparted to them the blessings of civilization. It may remind us of the tradition existing among the Aztecs in respect to Quetzalcoatl, the good deity, who with a similar garb and aspect came up the great plateau from the east on a like benevolent mission to the natives. The analogy is the more remarkable as there is no trace of any communication with, or even knowledge of, each other to be found in the two nations.[11]

[10] Com Real, Parte 1, lib 1, cap. 9–16.

[11] These several traditions, all of a very puerile character, are to be found in Ondegardo, Relacion Segunda, MS.,—Sarmiento, Relacion, MS., cap. 1,—Cieza de Leon, Cronica, cap. 105,—Conquista i Poblacion del Piru, MS,—Declaracion de los Presidente é Oydores de la Audiencia Reale del Peru, MS.,—all of them authorities contemporary with the Conquest. The story of the bearded white men finds its place in most of their legends.*

* [Such legends will not be considered "puerile," nor will their similarity with those of remote races seem inexplicable, when they are viewed in their true light, as embodying conceptions of nature formed by the human mind in the early stages of its development Thus considered, "the very myths," as Mr. Tylor remarks, " that

The date usually assigned for these extraordinary events was about four hundred years before the coming of the Spaniards, or early in the twelfth century.[12] But, however pleasing to the imagination, and however popular, the legend of Manco Capac, it requires but little reflection to show its improbability, even when divested of supernatural accompaniments. On the shores of Lake Titicaca extensive ruins exist at the present day, which the Peruvians themselves acknowledge to be of older date than the pretended advent of the Incas, and to have furnished them with the models of their architecture.[13] The date of their

[12] Some writers carry back the date five hundred, or even five hundred and fifty, years before the Spanish invasion. (Balboa, Histoire du Pérou, chap i —Velasco, Histoire du Royaume de Quito, tom. i p. 81 —Ambo auct. ap Relations et Mémoires originaux pour servir à l'Histoire de la Découverte de l'Amérique, par Ternaux-Compans (Paris, 1840)) In the Report of the Royal Audience of Peru, the epoch is more modestly fixed at two hundred years before the Conquest. Dec. de la Aud. Real, MS.

[13] "Otras cosas ay mas que dezir deste Tiaguanaco, que passo por no detenerme: concluyēdo que yo para mi tengo esta antigualla por la mas antigua de todo el Peru Y assi se tiene que antes q̄ los Ingas reynassen con muchos tiempos estavan hechos algunos edificios destos: porque yo he oydo afirmar a Indios, que los Ingas hizieron los edificios grandes del Cuzco por la forma que vieron tener la muralla o pared que se vee en este pueblo" (Cieza de Leon, Cronica, cap 105) See also Garcilasso (Com. Real, Parte 1, lib. 3, cap 1), who gives an account of these remains, on the authority of a Spanish ecclesiastic, which might compare, for the marvellous,

were discarded as lying fables, prove to be sources of history in ways that their makers and transmitters little dreamed of." The Peruvian traditions seem, in particular, to deserve a closer investigation than they have yet received Besides the authorities cited by Prescott, the relations of Christoval de Molina and the Indian Salcamayhua, translated by Mr. Markham, are entitled to mention, both for the minuteness and the variations with which they present the leading features of the same oft-repeated nature-myth.—K.]

appearance, indeed, is manifestly irreconcilable with their subsequent history. No account assigns to the Inca dynasty more than thirteen princes before the Conquest.* But this number is alto-

with any of the legends of his order. Other ruins of similar traditional antiquity are noticed by Herrera (Historia general de los Hechos de los Castellanos en las Islas y Tierra Firme del Mar Océano (Madrid, 1730), dec. 6, lib. 6, cap. 9). McCulloh, in some sensible reflections on the origin of the Peruvian civilization, adduces, on the authority of Garcilasso de la Vega, the famous temple of Pachacamac, not far from Lima, as an example of architecture more ancient than that of the Incas. (Researches, Philosophical and Antiquarian, concerning the Aboriginal History of America (Baltimore, 1829), p. 405.) This, if true, would do much to confirm the views in our text. But McCulloh is led into an error by his blind guide, Rycaut, the translator of Garcilasso, for the latter does not speak of the temple as existing before the time of the Incas, but before the time when the country was conquered by the Incas. Com. Real., Parte 1, lib. 6, cap. 30.

* [The list of Incas commonly accepted at the present time comprises eighteen names, as follows:

1. Manco Capac		about 1250
2 Sinchi Rocca		about 1260
3 Lloque Yupanqui		about 1280
4 Mayta Capac		about 1300
5. Capac Yupanqui		about 1320
6 Inca Rocca		about 1340
7 Yahuar-huaccac		about 1360
8 Viracocha		about 1380
9 Inca Urco		about 1400
10 Pachacutec Inca Yupanqui		about 1400
11 Tupac Yupanqui		about 1439
12 Huayna Capac		about 1475
13. Huascar (Inti Casi Huallpa)		1523
14 Atahuallpa		1532
15 Manco Capac Yupanqui		1533
16 Sayri Tupac		1544
17. Cusi Titu Yupanqui		1560
18 Tupac Amaru		1571

Markham always writes the name Capac, " Ccapac." " The first C is a gutteral far back in the throat; the second, on the roof of the mouth." Urco's name is not always included in the list, as he was deposed and his reign was short. In the reigns of Pachacutec and of Yupanqui his son, the events dealt with in the drama " Ollenta" are placed (see note, page 141) Perhaps the ordinary reader may prefer to call Yahuar-huaccac by his last two names,

gether too small to have spread over four hundred years, and would not carry back the foundations of the monarchy, on any probable computation, beyond two centuries and a half,—an antiquity not incredible in itself, and which, it may be remarked, does not precede by more than half a century the alleged foundation of the capital of Mexico. The fiction of Manco Capac and his sister-wife was devised, no doubt, at a later period, to gratify the vanity of the Peruvian monarchs, and to give additional sanction to their authority by deriving it from a celestial origin.*

viz., Inca Yupanqui. His first name, "weeping blood," probably refers to some malady. Atahuallpa was an usurper, as will appear later in this work. Capac signifies rich; Sinchi, strong, Lloque, left-handed; Mayta, where; Yupanqui, you will count; Tupac, royal splendor; Huayna, youth; Huascar, chain. Viracocha Inca means king and God; Pachacutec, he who changes the world. The etymology of Manco Rocca and Atahuallpa is not clear. Sayri is tobacco, Cusi means joy, and Amaru a serpent.—M.]

* [This theory of the origin of the story is scarcely more plausible or philosophical than that of Garcilasso de la Vega, who conjectures that Manco Capac "may have been some Indian of good understanding, prudence, and judgment, who appreciated the great simplicity of those nations, and saw the necessity they had for instruction and teaching in natural life. He may have invented a fable with sagacity and astuteness, that he might be respected, saying that he and his wife were children of the Sun, who had come from Heaven, and that their Father had sent them to teach and do good to the people . . The belief in the fable of the Ynca's origin would be confirmed by the benefits and privileges he conferred on the Indians, until they at last firmly believed that he was the Child of the Sun, come from Heaven." (Markham's trans., i 94) Mr Markham pronounces "all this sensible enough," and it at least indicates the true spirit, if not the right method, of investigation. But a wider comparison of popular traditions has led to a general rejection, in such cases as the present, of the idea of conscious invention—whether as idle fable or designed imposture—to account for their origin The only question in regard to such a story is whether it is to be considered as purely mythical or as the mythical adapta-

We may reasonably conclude that there existed in the country a race advanced in civilization before the time of the Incas; and, in conformity with nearly every tradition, we may derive this race from the neighborhood of Lake Titicaca; [14] a conclusion strongly confirmed by the imposing architectural remains which still endure, after the lapse of so many years, on its borders. Who this race were, and whence they came, may afford a tempting theme for inquiry to the speculative anti-

[14] Among other authorities for this tradition, see Sarmiento, Relacion, MS , cap. 3, 4,—Herrera, Hist general, dec. 5, lib. 3, cap. 6, —Conq. i Pob. del Piru, MS.,—Zarate, Historia del Descubrimiento y de la Conquista del Peru, lib. 1, cap. 10, ap. Barcia, Historiadores primitivos de las Indias occidentales (Madrid, 1749), tom. 3.—In most, not all, of the traditions, Manco Capac is recognized as the name of the founder of the Peruvian monarchy, though his history and character are related with sufficient discrepancy.

tion or development of an historical fact. In this instance Dr. Brinton takes the latter view, asserting that Manco Capac was "a real character," "first of the historical Incas," "the Rudolph of Hapsburg of their reigning family," who "flourished about the eleventh century," and to whom "tradition has transferred a portion of the story of Viracocha," the Peruvian deity. (Myths of the New World, 179) Mr. Tylor, on the other hand, after noticing the legend of the Muyscas, a neighboring people, in which Bochica and Huythaca are evident personifications of the sun and moon, says, "Like to this in meaning, though different in fancy, is the civilization-myth of the Incas. . . . In after-ages the Sun and Moon were still represented in rule and religion by the Inca and his sister-wife, continuing the mighty race of Manco Capac and Mama Oello. But the two great ancestors returned when their earthly work was done, to become, what we may see they had never ceased to be, the sun and moon themselves " (Primitive Culture, i. 319.) It would not be inconsistent with a full acceptance of this theory to consider all such myths as veiling the real existence of men of superior endowments, to whom civilization must everywhere have owed its earliest developments; but to link them with the actual history of these personages would require very different evidence from what exists in the present or any similar case.—K.]

quarian.   But it is a land of darkness that lies far beyond the domain of history.[15]

The same mists that hang round the origin of

[15] Mr. Ranking,

> "Who can deep mysteries unriddle
> As easily as thread a needle,"

finds it "highly probable that the first Inca of Peru was a son of the Grand Khan Kublai"[1] (Historical Researches on the Conquest of Peru, etc., by the Moguls (London, 1827), p. 170.) The coincidences are curious, though we shall hardly jump at the conclusion of the adventurous author. Every scholar will agree with Humboldt in the wish that "some learned traveller would visit the borders of the lake of Titicaca, the district of Callao, and the high plains of the Tiahuanaco, the theatre of the ancient American civilization." (Vues des Cordillères, p. 199) And yet the architectural monuments of the aborigines, hitherto brought to light, have furnished few materials for a bridge of communication across the dark gulf that still separates the Old World from the New.*

* [The regions mentioned by Humboldt were visited in 1847 by a French savant, M Angrand, who brought away carefully-prepared plans of many of the ruins, of which a description is given by Desjardins (Le Pérou avant la Conquête espagnole), tending to confirm the conclusions drawn from previous sources of information, that a civilization, superior to that of the Incas, had passed away long before the period of the Spanish conquest. A work announced as in the press, by Mr. Hutchinson, formerly English consul in Peru, may be expected to give the fruits of more recent explorations But it may be safely predicted that no discoveries that may be made will ever establish the fact of a communication at some remote period between the two hemispheres. It may be doubted, indeed, whether the whole inquiry, so persistently pursued, has not sprung from an illusion. Had the Eastern Continent been discovered by a voyager from the Western, it would perhaps have been assumed that the latter had furnished those swarms which afterwards passed through Asia into Europe, and that here was the original seat of the human family and the spot where culture had first begun to dawn. Mr James S Wilson's discovery, on the coast of Ecuador, of articles of pottery and of gold, "in a stratum of mould beneath the sea-level, and covered by several feet of clay," proves, according to Murchison, that "within the human period the lands on the west coast of equatorial America were depressed and submerged; and that after the accumulation of marine clays above the terrestrial relics the whole coast was elevated to its present position." If, then, the existence not only of the human race, but of human art,

the Incas continue to settle on their subsequent annals; and so imperfect were the records em-

in America, antedates the present conformation of the continent, how futile must be every attempt to connect its early history with that of Egypt or of India! *—K.]

* [Mr Hutchinson (Two Years in Peru, ii. p. 224) writes, "The reader who has accompanied me to this will see that from my explorations along the coast of Peru I cannot believe that a single item of Inca civilization is manifested in the archæological remains that exist in such profusion there. I confine my observations simply to the coast district, which shows only what the Incas have undone— not what they did." Again he writes, "I believe the mounds, huacas, cemeteries, and fortresses already mentioned by me are of an age hundreds, if not thousands, of years anterior to the period of the Incas—of whose connection with the valley of the Rimac we have no reliable historical proof whatever." (Ibid, ii. p. 255.) "That the Incas conquered the seaboard valleys I admit; that we have any reliable historical proof of their ever having occupied those valleys I emphatically deny" (p 260). Mr. Hutchinson could find in 1873 no traces ("not a single yard") of the Inca roads in the coast districts, "the level country between the Andes and the Ocean," in a diligent search at every place he visited from Arica to San José, a coast distance of more than a thousand miles.

E. G. Squier published in 1877 Peru: Incidents of Travel and Exploration in the Land of the Incas, a work which Mr. Markham truly pronounces to be, "On the whole, the most valuable result of antiquarian researches in Peru that has ever been presented to the public" Mr. Squier was a skilled archæologist when he began his explorations in Peru. He was devoid of historical prejudices, and his single aim was to make trustworthy additions to historical knowledge. His conclusion was, that civilization went on with almost equal steps in all parts of South America where the conditions were favorable to its advancement—that the superiority of the Incas was more apparent than real, more the outgrowth of new conditions and relationships than of anything innate The Incas were able as warriors to establish their great empire, because under most propitious circumstances they had first developed capacity as statesmen When their supremacy was acknowledged, it was inevitable that, in after centuries, all the great traditional achievements of the races they had conquered should be blended and incorporated with their own. It would at length become impossible to determine where the history of one race ended and that of the composite race began In this way the contradictions in legendary Peruvian history, which so vex the righteous souls of minor historical writers, may be accounted for. "The legendary history of the various prin-

ployed by the Peruvians, and so confused and contradictory their traditions, that the historian finds no firm footing on which to stand till within a century of the Spanish conquest.[16] At first, the

[16] A good deal within a century, to say truth. Garcilasso and Sarmiento, for example, the two ancient authorities in highest repute, have scarcely a point of contact in their accounts of the earlier Peruvian princes, the former representing the sceptre as gliding down in peaceful succession from hand to hand through an unbroken dynasty, while the latter garnishes his tale with as many conspiracies, depositions, and revolutions as belong to most barbarous and, unhappily, most civilized communities. When to these two are added the various writers, contemporary and of the succeeding age, who have treated of the Peruvian annals, we shall find ourselves in such a conflict of traditions that criticism is lost in conjecture. Yet this uncertainty as to historical events fortunately does not extend to the history of arts and institutions which were in existence on the arrival of the Spaniards.

cipalities which went to make up the Inca Empire is one thing, and that of the empire itself is quite another The former is very ancient, going back, probably, as far into antiquity as that of any other people on the globe; while the latter is comparatively modern" (p. 571). "There are some, not to say many, traces in Peru of an early and comparatively rude past Combined with the stupendous and elaborate remains of Tiahuanuco—remains as elaborate and admirable as those of Assyria, of Egypt, Greece, or Rome—there are others that are almost exact counterparts of those of Stonehenge or Carnac, in Brittany, to which is assigned the remotest place in monumental history. The rude sun-circles of Sillustani, under the very shadow of some of the most elaborate and, architecturally, the most wonderful works of aboriginal America, are indistinguishable counterparts of the sun-circles of England, Denmark, and Tartary" (p. 575) Because few traces of early Peruvian towns remain, we must not judge that Inca civilization was young. Population was redundant. Everything that cumbered the arable ground had to be swept away that sustenance might be provided for the swarming peoples In no country in the world was the utilization of every square foot of ground more necessary. Under those circumstances ancient landmarks were swept out of existence,—as they are in the United States to-day when they block the wheels of progress. "I assert the existence in Peru of monuments coincident in character, if not in time, with those which the unanimous verdict of science gives to the earliest of what we call the Old World. . . . All that can now safely be said is that these

progress of the Peruvians seems to have been slow, and almost imperceptible. By their wise and temperate policy they gradually won over the neighboring tribes to their dominion, as these latter became more and more convinced of the benefits of a just and well-regulated government. As they grew stronger, they were enabled to rely more directly on force; but, still advancing under cover of the same beneficent pretexts employed by their predecessors, they proclaimed peace and civilization at the point of the sword. The rude nations of the country, without any principle of cohesion among themselves, fell one after another before the victorious arm of the Incas. Yet it was not till the middle of the fifteenth century that the famous Topa Inca Yupanqui, grandfather of the monarch who occupied the throne at the coming of the Spaniards, led his armies across the terrible desert of Atacama, and, penetrating to the southern region of Chili, fixed the permanent boundary of his dominions at the river Maule. His son, Huayna Capac, possessed of ambition and military talent fully equal to his father's, marched along the Cordillera towards the north, and, pushing his conquests across the equator, added the powerful kingdom of Quito to the empire of Peru.[17]

[17] Sarmiento, Relacion, MS., cap. 57, 64.—Conq. i Pob. del Piru, MS.—Velasco, Hist. de Quito, p 59.—Dec. de la Aud. Real, MS

monuments are old, very old; but how old we cannot, at least at present, ascertain And, further, that there is no valid evidence that within any period known to human records the progenitors of the Peruvians reached their country from abroad, or that their civilization was imparted to them by any other race" (p. 576).—M.]

The ancient city of Cuzco, meanwhile, had been gradually advancing in wealth and population, till it had become the worthy metropolis of a great and flourishing monarchy. It stood in a beautiful valley on an elevated region of the plateau, which among the Alps would have been buried in eternal snows, but which within the tropics enjoyed a genial and salubrious temperature. Towards the north it was defended by a lofty eminence, a spur of the great Cordillera; and the city was traversed by a river, or rather a small stream, over which bridges of timber, covered with heavy slabs of stone, furnished an easy means of communication with the opposite banks. The streets were long and narrow, the houses low, and those of the poorer sort built of clay and reeds. But Cuzco was the royal residence and was adorned with the ample dwellings of the great nobility; and the massy fragments still incorporated in many of the modern edifices bear testimony to the size and solidity of the ancient.[18]

—Garcilasso, Com. Real, Parte 1, lib. 7, cap 18, 19; lib. 8, cap. 5-8.—The last historian, and, indeed, some others, refer the conquest of Chili to Yupanqui, the father of Topa Inca. The exploits of the two monarchs are so blended together by the different annalists as in a manner to confound their personal identity.

[18] Garcilasso, Com. Real., Parte 1, lib. 7, cap 8-11.—Cieza de Leon, Cronica, cap. 92.—" El Cuzco tuuo gran manera y calidad, deuio ser fundada por gente de gran ser Auia grandes calles, saluo q̃ erã angostas, y las casas hechas de piedra pura cõ tan lindas junturas, q̃ illustra el antiguedad del edificio, pues estauan piedras tan grãdes muy bien assentadas " (Ibid, ubi supra) Compare with this Miller's account of the city as existing at the present day: " The walls of many of the houses have remained unaltered for centuries. The great size of the stones, the variety of their shapes, and the inimitable workmanship they display, give to the city that interesting air of antiquity and romance which fills the mind with pleasing

The health of the city was promoted by spacious openings and squares, in which a numerous population from the capital and the distant country assembled to celebrate the high festivals of their religion. For Cuzco was the " Holy City; " [19] and the great temple of the Sun, to which pilgrims resorted from the farthest borders of the empire, was the most magnificent structure in the New World, and unsurpassed, probably, in the costliness of its decorations by any building in the Old.

Towards the north, on the sierra or rugged eminence already noticed, rose a strong fortress,* the

though painful veneration." Memoirs of Gen Miller in the Service of the Republic of Peru (London, 1829, 2d ed.), vol. ii. p. 225.

[19] "La Imperial Ciudad de Cozco, que la adoravan los Indios, como á Cosa Sagrada " Garcilasso, Com. Real., Parte 1, lib. 3, cap 20.—Also Ondegardo, Rel. Seg., MS.

* [Sacsahuaman, Fill thee, falcon! or Gorge thyself, hawk! was the name the Incas gave to this fortress. In Chapter XXIII. of Squier's Peru may be found an admirable account of it. Mr. Squier thinks that Sacsahuaman "will remain as long as the Pyramids shall last, or Stonehenge or the Colosseum shall endure," so perfect is its masonry. He calls attention to an error of statement in Prescott's text. Where the approaches were less difficult the fortress was protected by three, *not two,* lines of walls. This error is the more remarkable because Garcilasso, on whom Prescott so confidently relies, expressly mentions three walls. The stones were brought from neighboring quarries. Similar masses of limestone are scattered over the plateau near the fortress. Two distinct well-graded roads still remain, leading to the quarries, a mile or less distant. There was no need to go fifteen leagues for material when an abundant supply was so near at hand. Mr. Squier also measured many of the stones. The largest one was twenty-seven feet high, fourteen broad, and twelve thick Those fifteen by twelve by ten were quite common. Like the Colosseum, Sacsahuaman has for centuries been used as a quarry whence frugal, not to say thievish, builders have most easily secured building material. The famous " Piedra Cansada," or " Tired Stone," of which Garcilasso speaks (Com. Real., Parte 1, lib. 7, cap. 29), which was dragged by cables in the hands of more than twenty thousand Indians, and which

remains of which at the present day, by their vast size, excite the admiration of the traveller.[20] It was defended by a single wall of great thickness, and twelve hundred feet long on the side facing the city, where the precipitous character of the ground was of itself almost sufficient for its defence. On the other quarter, where the approaches were less difficult, it was protected by two other semicircular walls of the same length as the preceding. They were separated a considerable distance from one another and from the fortress; and the intervening ground was raised so that the walls afforded a breastwork for the troops stationed there in times of assault. The fortress consisted of three towers, detached from one another. One was appropriated to the Inca, and was garnished with the sumptuous decorations befitting a royal residence rather than a military post. The other two were held by the garrison, drawn from the Peruvian nobles, and commanded by an officer of the blood royal; for the position was of too great importance to be intrusted to inferior hands. The hill was excavated below the towers, and several

[20] See, among others, the Memoirs, above cited, of Gen. Miller, which contain a minute and very interesting notice of modern Cuzco. (Vol. ii. p. 223, et seq) Ulloa, who visited the country in the middle of the last century, is unbounded in his expressions of admiration. Voyage to South America, Eng trans. (London, 1806), book vii. ch. 12.

once, slipping down a hill, killed three or four thousand of the men who were guiding it, is, according to Squier, "an enormous mass of a thousand tons or more, and certainly was never moved ever so slightly by human power" The largest stone in the fortress is estimated to weigh three hundred and sixty-one tons. The structure was completed only a short time before the coming of the Spaniards.—M]

subterraneous galleries communicated with the city and the palaces of the Inca.[21]

The fortress, the walls, and the galleries were all built of stone, the heavy blocks of which were not laid in regular courses, but so disposed that the small ones might fill up the interstices between the great. They formed a sort of rustic work, being rough-hewn except towards the edges, which were finely wrought; and, though no cement was used, the several blocks were adjusted with so much exactness and united so closely that it was impossible to introduce even the blade of a knife between them.[22] Many of these stones were of vast size; some of them being full thirty-eight feet long, by eighteen broad, and six feet thick.[23] *

We are filled with astonishment when we consider that these enormous masses were hewn from their native bed and fashioned into shape by a peo-

[21] Betanzos, Suma y Narracion de los Yngas, MS., cap. 12.—Garcilasso, Com. Real., Parte 1, lib. 7, cap. 27–29.—The demolition of the fortress, begun immediately after the Conquest, provoked the remonstrance of more than one enlightened Spaniard, whose voice, however, was impotent against the spirit of cupidity and violence. See Sarmiento, Relacion, MS., cap 48.

[22] Ibid., ubi supra.—Inscripciones, Medallas, Templos, Edificios, Antiguedades, y Monumentos del Peru, MS   This manuscript, which formerly belonged to Dr Robertson, and which is now in the British Museum, is the work of some unknown author, somewhere probably about the time of Charles III.,—a period when, as the sagacious scholar to whom I am indebted for a copy of it remarks, a spirit of sounder criticism was visible in the Castilian historians.

[23] Acosta, Naturall and Morall Historie of the East and West Indies, Eng. trans. (London, 1604), lib. 6, cap. 14.—He measured the stones himself.—See also Garcilasso, Com. Real., loc cit.

* [Prescott is in error here. By referring to Acosta one may see that the stone he measured was at Tiahuanaco Acosta exaggerates immensely when he says, "there are many of greater size in the fortress of Cuzco."—M.]

ple ignorant of the use of iron; that they were brought from quarries, from four to fifteen leagues distant,[24] without the aid of beasts of burden; were transported across rivers and ravines, raised to their elevated position on the sierra, and finally adjusted there with the nicest accuracy, without the knowledge of tools and machinery familiar to the European. Twenty thousand men are said to have been employed on this great structure, and fifty years consumed in the building.[25] However this may be, we see in it the workings of a despotism which had the lives and fortunes of its vassals at its absolute disposal, and which, however mild in its general character, esteemed these vassals, when employed in its service, as lightly as the brute animals for which they served as a substitute.

The fortress of Cuzco was but part of a system of fortifications established throughout their dominions by the Incas. This system formed a prominent feature in their military policy; but before entering on this latter it will be proper to give the reader some view of their civil institutions and scheme of government.

The sceptre of the Incas, if we may credit their

[24] Cieza de Leon, Cronica, cap 93.—Ondegardo, Rel. Seg. MS—Many hundred blocks of granite may still be seen, it is said, in an unfinished state, in a quarry near Cuzco.

[25] Sarmiento, Relacion, MS, cap. 48—Ondegardo, Rel Seg. MS—Garcilasso, Com Real, Parte 1, lib 7, cap. 27, 28—The Spaniards, puzzled by the execution of so great a work with such apparently inadequate means, referred it all, in their summary way, to the Devil, an opinion which Garcilasso seems willing to indorse. The author of the Antig y Monumentos del Peru, MS, rejects this notion with becoming gravity.

historian, descended in unbroken succession from father to son, through their whole dynasty. Whatever we may think of this, it appears probable that the right of inheritance might be claimed by the eldest son of the *Coya,* or lawful queen, as she was styled, to distinguish her from the host of concubines who shared the affections of the sovereign.[26] The queen was further distinguished, at least in later reigns, by the circumstance of being selected from the sisters of the Inca, an arrangement which, however revolting to the ideas of civilized nations, was recommended to the Peruvians by its securing an heir to the crown of the pure heaven-born race, uncontaminated by any mixture of earthly mould.[27]

In his early years, the royal offspring was intrusted to the care of the *amautas,* or " wise men,"

[26] Sarmiento, Relacion, MS., cap. 7.—Garcilasso, Com. Real., Parte 1, lib. 1, cap. 26.—Acosta speaks of the eldest brother of the Inca as succeeding in preference to the son (lib. 6, cap. 12) He may have confounded the Peruvian with the Aztec usage. The Report of the Royal Audience states that a brother succeeded in default of a son. Dec. de la Aud. Real., MS.

[27] " *Et soror et conjux.*" According to Garcilasso, the heir-apparent *always* married a sister. (Com. Real., Parte 1, lib. 4, cap. 9) Ondegardo notices this as an innovation at the close of the fifteenth century. (Relacion Primera, MS.) The historian of the Incas, however, is confirmed in his extraordinary statement by Sarmiento. Relacion, MS., cap 7.*

* [" The sister-marriage of the Incas," remarks Mr. Tylor, " had in their religion at once a meaning and a justification,"—as typifying, namely, the supposed relation of the sun and moon, like the Egyptian Osiris and Isis. (Primitive Culture, i 261.) It may, however, indicate also different ideas from those of our race in regard to consanguinity. See Morgan, Systems of Consanguinity and Affinity of the Human Family (Smithsonian Contributions). —K]

as the teachers of Peruvian science were called, who instructed him in such elements of knowledge as they possessed, and especially in the cumbrous ceremonial of their religion, in which he was to take a prominent part. Great care was also bestowed on his military education, of the last importance in a state which, with its professions of peace and good will, was ever at war for the acquisition of empire.

In this military school he was educated with such of the Inca nobles as were nearly of his own age; for the sacred name of Inca—a fruitful source of obscurity in their annals—was applied indifferently to all who descended by the male line from the founder of the monarchy.[28] At the age of sixteen the pupils underwent a public examination, previous to their admission to what may be called the order of chivalry. This examination was conducted by some of the oldest and most illustrious Incas. The candidates were required to show their prowess in the athletic exercises of the warrior; in wrestling and boxing, in running such long courses as fully tried their agility and strength, in severe fasts of several days' duration, and in mimic combats, which, although the weapons were blunted, were always attended with wounds, and sometimes with death. During this trial, which lasted thirty days, the royal neophyte fared no better than his comrades, sleeping on the bare ground, going unshod, and wearing a mean attire,—a mode of life, it was supposed, which might tend to inspire him with more sympathy with

[28] Garcilasso, Com. Real., Parte 1, lib. 1, cap. 26.

the destitute. With all this show of impartiality, however, it will probably be doing no injustice to the judges to suppose that a politic discretion may have somewhat quickened their perceptions of the real merits of the heir-apparent.

At the end of the appointed time, the candidates selected as worthy of the honors of their barbaric chivalry were presented to the sovereign, who condescended to take a principal part in the ceremony of inauguration. He began with a brief discourse, in which, after congratulating the young aspirants on the proficiency they had shown in martial exercises, he reminded them of the responsibilities attached to their birth and station, and, addressing them affectionately as " children of the Sun," he exhorted them to imitate their great progenitor in his glorious career of beneficence to mankind. The novices then drew near, and, kneeling one by one before the Inca, he pierced their ears with a golden bodkin; and this was suffered to remain there till an opening had been made large enough for the enormous pendants which were peculiar to their order, and which gave them, with the Spaniards, the name of *orejones*.[29]   This ornament was so

[29] From *oreja*, " ear "—" Los caballeros de la sangre Real tenian orejas horadadas, y de ellas colgando grandes rodetes de plata y oro: llamaronles por esto los *orejones* los Castellanos la primera vez que los vieron." (Montesinos, Memorias antiguas historiales del Peru, MS., lib. 2, cap. 6.)   The ornament, which was in the form of a wheel, did not depend from the ear, but was inserted in the gristle of it, and was as large as an orange   " La hacen tan ancha como una gran rosca de naranja; los Señores i Principales traian aquellas roscas de oro fino en las orejas." (Conq. i Pob. del Piru, MS.—Also Garcilasso, Com. Real., Parte 1, cap 22)   " The larger the hole," says one of the old Conquerors. " the more of a gentleman ! "   Pedro Pizarro, Descub. y Conq , MS

massy in the ears of the sovereign that the cartilage was distended by it nearly to the shoulder, producing what seemed a monstrous deformity in the eyes of the Europeans, though, under the magical influence of fashion, it was regarded as a beauty by the natives.

When this operation was performed, one of the most venerable of the nobles dressed the feet of the candidates in the sandals worn by the order, which may remind us of the ceremony of buckling on the spurs of the Christian knight. They were then allowed to assume the girdle or sash around the loins, corresponding with the *toga virilis* of the Romans, and intimating that they had reached the season of manhood. Their heads were adorned with garlands of flowers, which, by their various colors, were emblematic of the clemency and goodness that should grace the character of every true warrior; and the leaves of an evergreen plant were mingled with the flowers, to show that these virtues should endure without end.[30] The prince's head was further ornamented by a fillet, or tasselled fringe, of a yellow color, made of the fine threads of the vicuña wool, which encircled the forehead as the peculiar insignia of the heir-apparent. The great body of the Inca nobility next made their appearance, and, beginning with those nearest of kin, knelt down before the prince and did him homage as successor to the crown. The whole assembly then moved to the great square of the capital, where songs and dances and other public

[30] Garcilasso, Com. Real., Parte 1, lib. 6, cap. 27.

festivities closed the important ceremonial of the
huaracu.[31]

The reader will be less surprised by the resemblance which this ceremonial bears to the inauguration of a Christian knight in the feudal ages,
if he reflects that a similar analogy may be traced
in the institutions of other people more or less
civilized, and that it is natural that nations occupied with the one great business of war should
mark the period when the preparatory education
for it was ended, by similar characteristic ceremonies.

Having thus honorably passed through his or-
deal, the heir-apparent was deemed worthy to sit
in the councils of his father, and was employed in
offices of trust at home, or, more usually, sent on
distant expeditions to practise in the field the les-
sons which he had hitherto studied only on the
mimic theatre of war. His first campaigns were
conducted under the renowned commanders who
had grown gray in the service of his father, until,
advancing in years and experience, he was placed
in command himself, and, like Huayna Capac, the
last and most illustrious of his line, carried the
banner of the rainbow, the armorial ensign of his
house, far over the borders, among the remotest
tribes of the plateau.

The government of Peru was a despotism, mild
in its character, but in its form a pure and unmiti-

---

[31] Garcilasso, Com. Real., Parte 1, lib. 6, cap. 24–28 —According
to Fernandez, the candidates wore white shirts, with something like
a cross embroidered in front! (Historia del Peru (Sevilla, 1571),
Parte 2, lib. 3, cap. 6.) We may fancy ourselves occupied with
some chivalrous ceremonial of the Middle Ages.

gated despotism. The sovereign was placed at an immeasurable distance above his subjects. Even the proudest of the Inca nobility, claiming a descent from the same divine original as himself, could not venture into the royal presence, unless barefoot, and bearing a light burden on his shoulders in token of homage.[32] As the representative of the Sun, he stood at the head of the priesthood, and presided at the most important of the religious festivals.[33] He raised armies, and usually commanded them in person. He imposed taxes, made laws, and provided for their execution by the appointment of judges, whom he removed at pleasure. He was the source from which every thing flowed,—all dignity, all power, all emolument. He was, in short, in the well-known phrase of the European despot, "himself the state."[34]

[32] Zarate, Conq del Peru, lib. 1, cap. 11.—Sarmiento, Relacion, MS , cap. 7.—" Porque verdaderamente á lo que yo he averiguado toda la pretension de los Ingas fue una subjeccion en toda la gente, qual yo nunca he oido decir de ninguna otra nacion en tanto grado, que por muy principal que un Señor fuese, dende que entrava cerca del Cuzco en cierta señal que estava puesta en cada camino de quatro que hay, havia dende alli de venir cargado hasta la presencia del Inga, y alli dejava la carga y hacia su obediencia." Ondegardo, Rel. Prim , MS.

[33] It was only at one of these festivals, and hardly authorizes the sweeping assertion of Carli that the royal and sacerdotal authority were blended together in Peru. We shall see, hereafter, the important and independent position occupied by the high-priest. " Le Sacerdoce et l'Empire étoient divisés au Mexique; au lieu qu'ils étoient réunis au Pérou, comme au Tibet et à la Chine, et comme il le fut à Rome, lorsqu' Auguste jetta les fondemens de l'Empire, en y réunissant le Sacerdoce ou la dignité de Souverain Pontife" Lettres Américaines (Paris, 1788), trad Franç, tom. i let. 7.

[34] " Porque el Inga dava á entender que era hijo del Sol, con este titulo se hacia adorar, i governava principalmente en tanto grado que nadie se le atrevia, i su palabra era ley, i nadie osaba ir contra su palabra ni voluntad; aunque obiese de matar cient mill Indios,

The Inca asserted his claims as a superior being by assuming a pomp in his manner of living well calculated to impose on his people. His dress was of the finest wool of the vicuña, richly dyed, and ornamented with a profusion of gold and precious stones. Round his head was wreathed a turban of many-colored folds, called the *llautu,* with a tasselled fringe, like that worn by the prince, but of a scarlet color, while two feathers of a rare and curious bird, called th*e coraquenque,* placed upright in it, were the distinguishing insignia of royalty. The birds from which these feathers were obtained were found in a desert country among the mountains; and it was death to destroy or to take them, as they were reserved for the exclusive purpose of supplying the royal headgear. Every succeeding monarch was provided with a new pair of these plumes, and his credulous subjects fondly believed that only two individuals of the species had ever existed to furnish the simple ornament for the diadem of the Incas.[35]

Although the Peruvian monarch was raised so far above the highest of his subjects, he condescended to mingle occasionally with them, and took great pains personally to inspect the condition of the humbler classes.* He presided at some

no havia ninguno en su Reino que le osase decir que no lo hiciese." Conq i Pob del Piru, MS.

[35] Garcilasso, Com Real , Parte I, lib 1, cap. 22; lib. 6, cap. 28. —Cieza de Leon, Cronica, cap. 114.—Acosta, lib. 6, cap. 12.

* [Fiske, Discovery of America, ii. p 335, is confident that there was a council to assist the Inca in his government. "Ollanta," a drama, hereafter to be noticed, presents the Inca in a light to which we are not accustomed —M]

of the religious celebrations, and on these occasions entertained the great nobles at his table, when he complimented them, after the fashion of more civilized nations, by drinking the health of those whom he most delighted to honor.[36]

But the most effectual means taken by the Incas for communicating with their people were their progresses through the empire. These were conducted, at intervals of several years, with great state and magnificence. The sedan, or litter, in which they travelled, richly emblazoned with gold and emeralds, was guarded by a numerous escort. The men who bore it on their shoulders were provided by two cities, specially appointed for the purpose. It was a post to be coveted by no one, if, as is asserted, a fall was punished with death.[37] *

[36] One would hardly expect to find among the American Indians this social and kindly custom of our Saxon ancestors,—now fallen somewhat out of use, in the capricious innovations of modern fashion. Garcilasso is diffuse in his account of the forms observed at the royal table. (Com. Real., Parte 1, lib. 6, cap. 23) The only hours of eating were at eight or nine in the morning, and at sunset, which took place at nearly the same time, in all seasons, in the latitude of Cuzco The historian of the Incas admits that, though temperate in eating, they indulged freely in their cups, frequently prolonging their revelry to a late hour of the night Ibid , Parte 1, lib 6, cap 1.

[37] "In lecticâ, aureo tabulato constratâ, humeris ferebant; in summâ, ea erat observantia, vt vultum ejus intueri maxime incivile putarent, et inter baiulos, quicunque vel leviter pede offenso hæsitaret, e vestigio interficerent" Levinus Apollonius, De Peruviæ Regionis Inventione, et Rebus in eâdem gestis (Antverpiæ, 1567), fol. 37.—Zarate, Conq del Peru, lib. 1, cap. 11.—According to this writer, the litter was carried by the nobles; one thousand of whom were specially reserved for the humiliating honor. Ubi supra

* [According to Polo de Ondegardo, "those who performed special services were exempted from other classes of tribute There is an example of this in the province of Lucanas, where the people were trained to carry the litter of the Ynca, and had the art of

They travelled with ease and expedition, halting at the *tambos*, or inns, erected by government along the route, and occasionally at the royal palaces, which in the great towns afforded ample accommodations to the whole of the monarch's retinue. The noble roads which traversed the table-land were lined with people, who swept away the stones and stubble from their surface, strewing them with sweet-scented flowers, and vying with each other in carrying forward the baggage from one village to another. The monarch halted from time to time to listen to the grievances of his subjects, or to settle some points which had been referred to his decision by the regular tribunals. As the princely train wound its way along the mountain-passes, every place was thronged with spectators eager to catch a glimpse of their sovereign; and when he raised the curtains of his litter and showed himself to their eyes, the air was rent with acclamations as they invoked blessings on his head.[38] Tradition long commemorated the spots at which he halted, and the simple people of the country held them in

[38] The acclamations must have been potent indeed, if, as Sarmiento tells us, they sometimes brought the birds down from the sky! "De esta manera eran tan temidos los Reyes que si salian por el Reyno y permitian alzar algun paño de los que iban en las andas para dejarse ver de sus vasallos, alzaban tan gran alarido que hacian caer las aves de lo alto donde iban volando á ser tomados á manos" (Relacion, MS., cap. 10) The same author has given in another place a more credible account of the royal progresses, which the Spanish reader will find extracted in Appendix No. 1.

going with a very even and equal pace" See Markham's Rites and Laws of the Yncas, p. 168 Hakluyt Soc Pub. The other district whence the litter-bearers came was Soras.—M.]

reverence as places consecrated by the presence of an Inca.[39]

The royal palaces were on a magnificent scale, and, far from being confined to the capital or a few principal towns, were scattered over all the provinces of their vast empire.[40] The buildings were low, but covered a wide extent of ground. Some of the apartments were spacious, but they were generally small, and had no communication with one another, except that they opened into a common square or court. The walls were made of blocks of stone of various sizes, like those described in the fortress of Cuzco, rough-hewn, but carefully wrought near the line of junction, which was scarcely visible to the eye. The roofs were of wood or rushes, which have perished under the rude touch of time, that has shown more respect for the walls of the edifices.* The whole seems to have been characterized by solidity and strength, rather than by any attempt at architectural elegance.[41]

[39] Garcilasso, Com. Real, Parte 1, lib. 3, cap. 14; lib. 6, cap. 3. —Zarate, Conq del Peru, lib 1, cap 11.

[40] Velasco has given some account of several of these palaces situated in different places in the kingdom of Quito. Hist. de Quito, tom. i. pp. 195–197.

[41] Cieza de Leon, Cronica, cap. 44.—Antig y Monumentos de Peru, MS —See, among others, the description of the remains still existing of the royal buildings at Callo, about ten leagues south of Quito, by Ulloa, Voyage to South America, book 6, ch. 11, and since, more carefully, by Humboldt, Vues des Cordillères, p 197.

* [In Squier's Peru, pp. 393–395, may be found an account of one of the most remarkable monuments of antiquity in Peru This structure, the Sondor-huasi, "retains its original thatched roof after a lapse of over three hundred years, showing us how much skill and beauty, as well as utility, may be achieved and displayed even in a roof of thatch"—M]

But whatever want of elegance there may have been in the exterior of the imperial dwellings, it was amply compensated by the interior, in which all the opulence of the Peruvian princes was ostentatiously displayed. The sides of the apartments were thickly studded with gold and silver ornaments. Niches, prepared in the walls, were filled with images of animals and plants curiously wrought of the same costly materials; and even much of the domestic furniture, including the utensils devoted to the most ordinary menial services, displayed the like wanton magnificence! [42] With these gorgeous decorations were mingled richly-colored stuffs of the delicate manufacture of the Peruvian wool, which were of so beautiful a texture that the Spanish sovereigns, with all the luxuries of Europe and Asia at their command, did not disdain to use them. [43] The royal household consisted of a throng of menials, supplied by the neighboring towns and villages, which, as in Mexico, were bound to furnish the monarch with fuel and other necessaries for the consumption of the palace.

[42] Garcilasso, Com. Real, Parte 1, lib. 6, cap. 1.—"Tanto que todo el servicio de la Casa del Rey así de cantaras para su vino, *como de cozina*, todo era oro y plata, y esto no en un lugar y en una parte lo tenia, sino en muchas." (Sarmiento, Relacion, MS., cap. 11) See also the flaming accounts of the palaces of Bilcas, to the west of Cuzco, by Cieza de Leon, as reported to him by Spaniards who had seen them in their glory. (Cronica, cap. 89.) The niches are still described by modern travellers as to be found in the walls. (Humboldt, Vues des Cordillères, p. 197)

[43] "La ropa de la cama toda era de mantas, y freçadas de lana de Vicuña, que es tan fina, y tan regalada, que entre otras cosas preciadas de aquellas Tierras, se las han traido para la cama del Rey Don Phelipe Segundo." Garcilasso, Com. Real, Parte 1, lib. 6, cap. 1.

But the favorite residence of the Incas was at Yucay, about four leagues distant from the capital. In this delicious valley, locked up within the friendly arms of the sierra, which sheltered it from the rude breezes of the cast, and refreshed by gushing fountains and streams of running water, they built the most beautiful of their palaces. Here, when wearied with the dust and toil of the city, they loved to retreat, and solace themselves with the society of their favorite concubines, wandering amidst groves and airy gardens, that shed around their soft, intoxicating odors and lulled the senses to voluptuous repose. Here, too, they loved to indulge in the luxury of their baths, replenished by streams of crystal water which were conducted through subterraneous silver channels into basins of gold. The spacious gardens were stocked with numerous varieties of plants and flowers that grew without effort in this *temperate* region of the tropics, while parterres of a more extraordinary kind were planted by their side, glowing with the various forms of vegetable life skilfully imitated in gold and silver! Among them the Indian corn, the most beautiful of American grains, is particularly commemorated, and the curious workmanship is noticed with which the golden ear was half disclosed amidst the broad leaves of silver, and the light tassel of the same material that floated gracefully from its top.[44]

[44] Garcilasso, Com Real., Parte 1, lib. 5, cap. 26; lib. 6, cap. 2. —Sarmiento, Relacion, MS., cap. 24.—Cieza de Leon, Cronica, cap. 94.—The last writer speaks of a cement, made in part of liquid

If this dazzling picture staggers the faith of the reader, he may reflect that the Peruvian mountains teemed with gold; that the natives understood the art of working the mines, to a considerable extent; that none of the ore, as we shall see hereafter, was converted into coin, and that the whole of it passed into the hands of the sovereign for his own exclusive benefit, whether for purposes of utility or ornament. Certain it is that no fact is better attested by the Conquerors themselves, who had ample means of information, and no motive for misstatement. The Italian poets, in their gorgeous pictures of the gardens of Alcina and Morgana, came nearer the truth than they imagined.

Our surprise, however, may reasonably be excited when we consider that the wealth displayed by the Peruvian princes was only that which each had amassed individually for himself. He owed nothing to inheritance from his predecessors. On the decease of an Inca, his palaces were abandoned; all his treasures, except what were employed in his obsequies, his furniture and apparel, were suffered to remain as he left them, and his mansions, save one, were closed up forever. The new sovereign was to provide himself with every thing new for his royal state. The reason of this was the popular belief that the soul of the departed monarch would return after a time to re-animate his body on earth; and they wished that he should find everything to

gold, as used in the royal buildings of Tambo, a valley not far from Yucay' (Ubi supra.) We may excuse the Spaniards for demolishing such edifices,—if they ever met with them.

which he had been used in life prepared for his reception.[45]

When an Inca died, or, to use his own language, "was called home to the mansions of his father, the Sun," [46] his obsequies were celebrated with great pomp and solemnity. The bowels were taken from the body and deposited in the temple of Tampu, about five leagues from the capital. A quantity of his plate and jewels was buried with them, and a number of his attendants and favorite concubines, amounting sometimes, it is said, to a thousand, were immolated on his tomb.[47] Some of them showed the natural repugnance to the sacrifice occasionally manifested by the victims of a similar superstition in India. But these were probably the menials and more humble attendants; since the women have been known, in more than

[45] Acosta, lib. 6, cap. 12.—Garcilasso, Com Real., Parte 1, lib. 6, cap 4

[46] The Aztecs, also, believed that the soul of the warrior who fell in battle went to accompany the Sun in his bright progress through the heavens. (See Conquest of Mexico, book 1, chap 3.)

[47] Conq i Pob del Piru, MS —Acosta, lib. 5, cap. 6.—Four thousand of these victims, according to Sarmiento,*—we may hope it is an exaggeration,—graced the funeral obsequies of Huayna Capac, the last of the Incas before the coming of the Spaniards. Relacion, MS., cap 65

* [It is possible that Cieza de Leon (Sarmiento) may have been somewhat wild in statement here In the same chapter he states that when Huayna Capac died, "the lamentations were so great that the shouting rose up to the clouds, and the noise so stupefied the birds that they fell from a great height to the ground" Another statement in the same chapter—that the Indians told the writer that they buried the Inca in the river Ancasmayu, diverting it from its course to make the tomb—recalls the burial of Alaric the Visigoth in the bed of the river Busento. See Markham's translation of the Second Part of the Chronicles of Peru (chap. lxviii.) in the publications of the Hakluyt Society.—M.]

one instance, to lay violent hands on themselves, when restrained from testifying their fidelity by this act of conjugal martyrdom. This melancholy ceremony was followed by a general mourning throughout the empire. At stated intervals, for a year, the people assembled to renew the expressions of their sorrow; processions were made, displaying the banner of the departed monarch; bards and minstrels were appointed to chronicle his achievements, and their songs continued to be rehearsed at high festivals in the presence of the reigning monarch,—thus stimulating the living by the glorious example of the dead.[48]

The body of the deceased Inca was skilfully embalmed, and removed to the great temple of the Sun at Cuzco. There the Peruvian sovereign, on entering the awful sanctuary, might behold the effigies of his royal ancestors, ranged in opposite files,*—the men on the right, and their queens on the left, of the great luminary which blazed in refulgent gold on the walls of the temple. The bodies, clothed in the princely attire which they had been accustomed to wear, were placed on chairs of gold, and sat with their heads inclined downward, their hands placidly crossed over their bosoms, their countenances exhibiting their natural dusky hue,— less liable to change than the fresher coloring of a European complexion,—and their hair of raven

[48] Cieza de Leon, Cronica, cap. 62.—Garcilasso, Com. Real., Parte I, lib. 6, cap. 5.—Sarmiento, Relacion, MS., cap. 8.

* [These effigies, ranged as they were in chronological order, must have been of immense assistance to the annalists in recalling the history of the nation.—M.]

black, or silvered over with age, according to the period at which they died! It seemed like a company of solemn worshippers fixed in devotion,— so true were the forms and lineaments to life. The Peruvians were as successful as the Egyptians in the miserable attempt to perpetuate the existence of the body beyond the limits assigned to it by nature.[49]

They cherished a still stranger illusion in the

[49] Ondegardo, Rel Prim, MS.—Garcilasso, Com, Real., Parte 1, lib. 5, cap 29 —The Peruvians secreted these mummies of their sovereigns after the Conquest, that they might not be profaned by the insults of the Spaniards Ondegardo, when *corregidor* of Cuzco, discovered five of them, three male and two female The former were the bodies of Viracocha, of the great Tupac Inca Yupanqui, and of his son Huayna Capac Garcilasso saw them in 1560. They were dressed in their regal robes, with no insignia but the *llautu* on their heads They were. in a sitting posture, and, to use his own expression, "perfect as life, without so much as a hair or an eyebrow wanting." As they were carried through the streets, decently shrouded with a mantle, the Indians threw themselves on their knees, in sign of reverence, with many tears and groans and were still more touched as they beheld some of the Spaniards themselves doffing their caps in token of respect to departed royalty.* (Ibid, ubi supra) The bodies were subsequently removed to Lima; and Father Acosta, who saw them there some twenty years later, speaks of them as still in perfect preservation.

* [When, in 1881, the recently discovered mummies of twenty or more Egyptian kings and queens were taken from the tomb where they had lain for so many centuries, and were placed upon steamers to be carried along the Nile to Cairo, "for more than fifty miles below Thebes the villagers turned out en masse, not merely to stare at the piled decks as the steamers went by, but to show respect to the illustrious dead. Women with dishevelled hair running along the banks and shrieking the death-wail, men ranged in solemn silence and firing their guns in the air, greeted the Pharaohs as they passed. Never, assuredly, did history repeat itself more strangely than when Rameses and his peers, after more than three thousand years of sepulture, were borne along the Nile with funeral honors." Amelia B. Edwards, "Lying in State in Cairo," Harper's Mag., July, 1882 —M.]

attentions which they continued to pay to these insensible remains, as if they were instinct with life. One of the houses belonging to a deceased Inca was kept open and occupied by his guard and attendants, with all the state appropriate to royalty. On certain festivals, the revered bodies of the sovereigns were brought out with great ceremony into the public square of the capital. Invitations were sent by the captains of the guard of the respective Incas to the different nobles and officers of the court; and entertainments were provided in the names of their masters, which displayed all the profuse magnificence of their treasures,—and "such a display," says an ancient chronicler, "was there in the great square of Cuzco, on this occasion, of gold and silver plate and jewels, as no other city in the world ever witnessed." [50] The banquet was served by the menials of the respective households, and the guests partook of the melancholy cheer in the presence of the royal phantom with the same attention to the forms of courtly etiquette as if the living monarch had presided! [51]

[50] "Tenemos por muy cierto que ni en Jerusalem, Roma, ni en Persia, ni en ninguna parte del mundo por ninguna Republica ni Rey de el, se juntaba en un lugar tanta riqueza de Metales de oro y Plata y Pedreria como en esta Plaza del Cuzco; quando estas fiestas y otras semejantes se hacian." Sarmiento, Relacion, MS, cap 27.

[51] Idem, Relacion, MS, cap 8, 27.—Ondegardo, Rel. Seg., MS.— It was only, however, the great and good princes that were thus honored, according to Sarmiento, "whose souls the silly people fondly believed, on account of their virtues, were in heaven, although, in truth," as the same writer assures us, "they were all the time burning in the flames of hell"! "Digo los que haviendo sido en vida buenos y valerosos, generosos con los Indios en les hacer

The nobility of Peru consisted of two orders, the first and by far the most important of which was that of the Incas, who, boasting a common descent with their sovereign, lived, as it were, in the reflected light of his glory. As the Peruvian monarchs availed themselves of the right of polygamy to a very liberal extent, leaving behind them families of one or even two hundred children,[52] the nobles of the blood royal, though comprehending only their descendants in the male line, came in the course of years to be very numerous.[53] They were divided into different lineages, each of which traced its pedigree to a different member of the royal dynasty, though all terminated in the divine founder of the empire.

They were distinguished by many exclusive and very important privileges; they wore a peculiar dress, spoke a dialect, if we may believe the chron-

mercedes, perdonadores de injurias, porque á estos tales canonizaban en su ceguedad por Santos y honrraban sus huesos, sin entender que las animas ardian en los Ynfiernos y creian que estaban en el Cielo." Ibid, ubi supra.

[52] Garcilasso says over three hundred! (Com. Real, Parte 1, lib. 3, cap. 19.) The fact, though rather startling, is not incredible, if, like Huayna Capac, they counted seven hundred wives in their seraglio See Sarmiento, Relacion, MS., cap. 7.

[53] Garcilasso mentions a class of Incas *por privilegio*, who were allowed to possess the name and many of the immunities of the blood royal, though only descended from the great vassals that first served under the banner of Manco Capac * (Com Real, Parte 1, lib. 1, cap. 22.) This important fact, to which he often refers, one would be glad to see confirmed by a single authority.

* [Garcilasso himself had really no right to the name Inca, as he was descended in the female line " The name was applied to all who were descendants in the male, but not in the female, line" Com Real, Parte 1, lib 1, cap. 26.—M.]

icler, peculiar to themselves,[54] and had the choicest portion of the public domain assigned for their support. They lived, most of them, at court, near the person of the prince, sharing in his counsels, dining at his board, or supplied from his table. They alone were admissible to the great offices in the priesthood. They were invested with the command of armies and of distant garrisons, were placed over the provinces, and, in short, filled every station of high trust and emolument.[55] Even the laws, severe in their general tenor, seem not to have been framed with reference to them; and the people, investing the whole order with a portion of the sacred character which belonged to the sovereign, held that an Inca noble was incapable of crime.[56]

The other order of nobility was the *Curacas*, the caciques of the conquered nations, or their

[54] "Los Incas tuvieron otra Lengua particular, que hablavan entre ellos, que no la entendian los demàs Indios, ni les era licito aprenderla, como Lenguage Divino. Esta me escriven del Perù, que se ha perdido totalmente; porque como pereciò la Republica particular de los Incas, pereciò tambien el Lenguage dellos." Garcilasso, Com. Real., Parte 1, lib. 7, cap. 1.*

[55] "Una sola gente hallo yo que era exenta, que eran los Ingas del Cuzco y por alli al rededor de ambas parcialidades, porque estos no solo no pagavan tributo, pero aun comian de lo que traian al Inga de todo el reino, y estos eran por la mayor parte los Governadores en todo el reino, y por donde quiera que iban se les hacia mucha honrra." Ondegardo, Rel. Prim., MS

[56] Garcilasso, Com Real, Parte 1, lib. 2, cap 15

* [Meyen (Ueber die Ureinbewohner von Peru) decides that the Incas had no dialect peculiar to themselves. Markham, after examining the eleven words specified by Garcilasso as belonging to the court language, decides that they are ordinary Quichua words, and concurs with Hervas and von Humboldt in the conclusion that this court language had no real existence. Narrative and Critical History of America, i. 241 —M.]

descendants. They were usually continued by the government in their places, though they were required to visit the capital occasionally, and to allow their sons to be educated there as the pledges of their loyalty. It is not easy to define the nature or extent of their privileges. They were possessed of more or less power, according to the extent of their patrimony and the number of their vassals. Their authority was usually transmitted from father to son, though sometimes the successor was chosen by the people.[57] They did not occupy the highest posts of state, or those nearest the person of the sovereign, like the nobles of the blood. Their authority seems to have been usually local, and always in subordination to the territorial jurisdiction of the great provincial governors, who were taken from the Incas.[58]

It was the Inca nobility, indeed, who constituted the real strength of the Peruvian monarchy. Attached to their prince by ties of consanguinity, they had common sympathies and, to a considerable extent, common interests with him. Distinguished by a peculiar dress and insignia, as well as by language and blood, from the rest of the community, they were never confounded with the other tribes and nations who were incorporated into the

[57] In this event, it seems, the successor named was usually presented to the Inca for confirmation. (Dec. de la Aud Real, MS.) At other times the Inca himself selected the heir from among the children of the deceased Curaca. "In short," says Ondegardo, "there was no rule of succession so sure, but it might be set aside by the supreme will of the sovereign" Rel. Prim, MS.

[58] Garcilasso, Com Real, Parte 1, lib. 4, cap. 10—Sarmiento, Relacion, MS., cap. 11—Dec. de la Aud. Real, MS.—Cieza de Leon, Cronica, cap 93—Conq. i Pob. del Piru, MS.

great Peruvian monarchy. After the lapse of centuries they still retained their individuality as a peculiar people. They were to the conquered races of the country what the Romans were to the barbarous hordes of the Empire or the Normans to the ancient inhabitants of the British Isles. Clustering around the throne, they formed an invincible phalanx to shield it alike from secret conspiracy and open insurrection. Though living chiefly in the capital, they were also distributed throughout the country in all its high stations and strong military posts, thus establishing lines of communication with the court, which enabled the sovereign to act simultaneously and with effect on the most distant quarters of his empire. They possessed, moreover, an intellectual pre-eminence, which, no less than their station, gave them authority with the people. Indeed, it may be said to have been the principal foundation of their authority. The crania of the Inca race show a decided superiority over the other races of the land in intellectual power; [59] and it cannot be denied

[59] Dr. Morton's valuable work contains several engravings of both the Inca and the common Peruvian skull, showing that the facial angle in the former, though by no means great, was much larger than that in the latter, which was singularly flat and deficient in intellectual character. Crania Americana (Philadelphia, 1829).*

* [It is hardly possible that Dr. Morton ever saw any crania of the Inca race Rivero (Peruvian Antiquities, p 40, trans.) says, "With the exception of the mummies of the four emperors which were carried to Lima . . . and the remains of which it has been impossible to discover up to this day, the sepulchres of the others are unknown, as well as of the nobility descended from them." Professor Wyman has this to say in his "Observations on Crania," in the fourth annual report of the Peabody Museum of American

that it was the fountain of that peculiar civilization and social polity which raised the Peruvian
monarchy above every other state in South America. Whence this remarkable race came,* and what

Archæology and Ethnology (fifty-six Peruvian skulls had been presented to the Museum by E. G. Squier):

"The Peruvian crania present the two modes of artificial distor-
tion commonly seen; those from Chulpas, or burial-towers, and
other places in the neighborhood of Lake Titicaca being lengthened,
while those from nearly all the other localities are broadened and
shortened by the flattening of the occiput They are, on the whole,
massive and heavy. . . . We find nothing in these crania which
sustains the view once admitted, but afterwards abandoned, by Dr
Morton, and more recently revived by Mr. John H. Blake and Dr.
Daniel Wilson, in regard to the existence of *naturally* long Peruvian skulls." Dr Wilson thinks the form must be natural, because
in crania artificially distorted the retention of anything like normal
symmetry of proportion is impossible. Professor Wyman, however,
finds entirely symmetrical crania which yet show unequivocal marks
of circular pressure. The crania come from several localities, but
in most respects are alike. "The average capacity of the fifty-six
crania measured agrees very closely with that indicated by Morton
and Meigs, viz., twelve hundred and thirty cubic centimetres, or
seventy-five cubic inches, which is considerably less than that of the
barbarous tribes of America, and almost exactly that of the Aus-
tralians and Hottentots as given by Morton and Meigs, and smaller
than that derived from a larger number of measurements by Davis
Thus we have in this particular a race which has established a complex civil and religious polity, and made great progress in the useful
and fine arts,—as its pottery, textile fabrics, wrought metals, highways and aqueducts, colossal architectural structures, and court of
almost imperial splendor prove,—on the same level, as regards the
quantity of brain, with a race whose social and religious conditions
are among the most degraded exhibited by the human race"

"All this goes to show, and cannot be too much insisted upon,
that the relative capacity of the skull is to be considered merely as
an anatomical and not as a physiological characteristic, and unless
the quality of the brain can be represented at the same time as the
quantity, brain measurements cannot be assumed as an indication
of the intellectual position of races any more than of individuals."
—M]

* [The wildest speculations on this point have not been those of
early writers, unguided by any principles of philological or ethno-
logical science, and accustomed to regard the Hebrew Scriptures

was its early history, are among those mysteries
that meet us so frequently in the annals of the

as the sole fountain of knowledge in regard to the origin and diffusion of the human race   Modern research in matters of language
and mythology, while dispelling many illusions and furnishing a
key to many riddles, has opened a field in which the imagination,
equipped with a quasi-scientific apparatus, finds a wider range
than ever before. The discoveries of the Abbé Brasseur de Bour-
bourg in regard to the origin of the Mexican civilization have been
matched by those of a Peruvian scholar, Dr. Vincente Fidel Lopez,
who, in a work entitled Les Races aryennes du Pérou (Paris, 1871),
has brought forward a vast array of arguments to prove that the
dominant race in Peru was an offshoot of the great Indo-European
family, transplanted at some remote period to the American soil,
and not connected by blood with any of its other occupants. This
theory is based on a comparison of languages, of architectural and
other remains, and of institutions and ideas The Quichua language,
it is admitted, differs in *form* from all the recognized Aryan
tongues. Like the other American languages, it is *polysynthetic*,
though Dr. Lopez, who makes no distinction between the two terms,
calls it *agglutinative*, classing it with the dialects of the Turanian
family. But many philologists hold that there must have been a
period when the oldest Aryan tongues were destitute of inflexions
and employed the same modes of expression as the Chinese and
other monosyllabic languages. There is therefore a "missing link,"
which is supplied by the Quichua, this being agglutinative in form
but Aryan in substance The latter point is established by the
identity of its leading roots with those of the Sanscrit: that is to
say, there are *kas*, *tas*, and *vas*, with meanings capable of being
distorted into some similarity, in both. The argument in regard to
architecture, pottery, etc , is of a more familiar kind, having been
long since adduced in support of various conjectures. The mytho-
logical hypotheses are more amusing. Dr. Lopez holds, with M.
Brasseur, that all myths are identical; but while the latter insists
that their common significance is geological, the former contends
that it is astronomical A single example will illustrate the method
by which the author establishes his points. The most ancient Peruvian deity, as Dr Lopez believes, was *Ati*, the representative of the
waning moon, identical with the *Ate* of the Homeric mythology.
Another step brings us to Hevate,—properly 'Εξ-ἀτῇ *of* or *by*
Ate,—and a third to Athene—Ati-inna—and Minerva, both names
signifying the same thing, viz., *force de la lune*. Lest it should be
supposed that such conjectures have sprung from the remoteness
and isolation in which, as Dr. Lopez complains, the Peruvian
scholar is placed, it may be proper to mention that he has been

New World, and which time and the antiquary
have as yet done little to explain.

anticipated and even outstripped in his leading ideas by some
German savants, who, by a similar etymological process, have iden-
tified both the Peruvians and the Aztecs as Celts. "Aber woher
kamen diese Kelten?" asks one of these enthusiastic explorers.
"Denn dass es Kelten gewesen sind, kann nicht mehr zweifelhaft
sein." And he answers his own inquiry by showing the probability
that they were Irish, "the last pagan remains of that people," who
rescued their old druidical worship from the inroads of Christianity,
and having carried it across the ocean,—whether stopping at Green-
lánd on the way or not he is unable to decide,—planted it on the
Andes, "that is to say, *the beautiful land,* from *an,* pleasant, beautiful, and *des,* land." Frenzel, Der Belus oder Sonnendienst auf
den Anden, oder Kelten in America (Leipzig, 1867).—K.]

CHAPTER II

ORDERS OF THE STATE—PROVISIONS FOR JUSTICE—
DIVISION OF LANDS—REVENUES AND REGISTERS—
GREAT ROADS AND POSTS—MILITARY TACTICS AND
POLICY

IF we are surprised at the peculiar and original features of what may be called the Peruvian aristocracy, we shall be still more so as we descend to the lower orders of the community and see the very artificial character of their institutions,—as artificial as those of ancient Sparta, and, though in a different way, quite as repugnant to the essential principles of our nature. The institutions of Lycurgus, however, were designed for a petty state, while those of Peru, although originally intended for such, seemed, like the magic tent in the Arabian tale, to have an indefinite power of expansion, and were as well suited to the most flourishing condition of the empire as to its infant fortunes. In this remarkable accommodation to change of circumstances we see the proofs of a contrivance that argues no slight advance in civilization.

The name of Peru was not known to the natives. It was given by the Spaniards, and originated, it is said, in a misapprehension of the Indian name of " river." [1] However this may be, it is certain

---

[1] Pelu, according to Garcilasso, was the Indian name for "river," and was given by one of the natives in answer to a question put to him by the Spaniards, who conceived it to be the name of the country. (Com. Real., Parte 1, lib. 1, cap. 6.) Such blunders have led

48

that the natives had no other epithet by which to designate the large collection of tribes and nations who were assembled under the sceptre of the Incas, than that of *Tavantinsuyu*, or " four quarters of the world." [2] This will not surprise a citizen of the United States, who has no other name by which to class himself among nations than what is borrowed from a quarter of the globe.[3] The king-

to the names of many places both in North and South America. Montesinos, however, denies that there is such an Indian term for " river " * (Mem. antiguas, MS., lib 1, cap. 2.) According to this writer, Peru was the ancient *Ophir*, whence Solomon drew such stores of wealth, and which, by a very *natural* transition, has in time been corrupted into *Phiru, Piru, Peru!* The first book of the Memorias, consisting of thirty-two chapters, is devoted to this precious discovery.†

[2] Ondegardo, Rel. Prim., MS.—Garcilasso, Com. Real., Parte 1, lib. 2, cap. 11.

[3] Yet an *American* may find food for his vanity in the reflection that the name of a quarter of the globe, inhabited by so many civilized nations, has been exclusively conceded to him.—Was it conceded or assumed? ‡

* [This statement would appear to be correct, and Garcilasso's etymology must be rejected on that, if on no other ground. More probable derivations are those given by Pascual de Andagoya,—from *Birú*, the name of a province first visited by Gaspar de Morales and Francisco Pizarro,—and by Father Blas Valera—from the Quichua word *Pirua*, a granary Garcilasso's objection, that the spelling *Piru* was a later and corrupt form, would, even if well founded, be of little moment.—K.]

† [A recent writer, forgetting, as Montesinos seems also to have done, that *Peru* was not the native name for the country, suggests its connection with *Persia*—itself a mere corruption—as an argument in support of the Aryan origin of the Quichuans!—K]

‡ [This comparison, which seems quite out of place, might be supposed to imply that the Peruvian word translated " four quarters of the world" bore a similar meaning to that conveyed by the English phrase. But Garcilasso himself explains it as indicating merely the four cardinal points, by which divisions of territory, as well as architectural arrangements and even social organizations, were so commonly regulated among primitive nations The extent to which this was carried in America, and the consequent impor-

dom, conformably to its name, was divided into
four parts, distinguished each by a separate title,
and to each of which ran one of the four great
roads that diverged from Cuzco, the capital or
navel of the Peruvian monarchy. The city was in
like manner divided into four quarters; and the
various races which gathered there from the distant
parts of the empire lived each in the quarter nearest to its respective province. They all continued
to wear their peculiar national costume, so that it
was easy to determine their origin; and the same
order and system of arrangement prevailed in the
motley population of the capital as in the great
provinces of the empire. The capital, in fact, was
a miniature image of the empire.[4]

The four great provinces were each placed under
a viceroy or governor, who ruled over them with
the assistance of one or more councils for the different departments. These viceroys resided, some
portion of their time, at least, in the capital, where
they constituted a sort of council of state to the
Inca.[5] The nation at large was distributed into

[4] Garcilasso, Com. Real., Parte 1, lib. 2, cap. 9, 10.—Cieza de
Leon, Cronica, cap. 93.—The capital was further divided into two
parts, the Upper and Lower town, founded, as pretended, on the
different origin of the population; a division recognized also in
the inferior cities. Ondegardo, Rel. Seg., MS.

[5] Dec. de la Aud. Real, MS.—Garcilasso, Com. Real., Parte 1,
lib. 2, cap. 15.—For this account of the councils I am indebted to
Garcilasso, who frequently fills up gaps that have been left by his
fellow-laborers. Whether the filling up will, in all cases, bear the
touch of time as well as the rest of his work, one may doubt.

tance and sacredness attached to the number four, as exemplified
in many myths and traditions, have been pointed out with great
fulness of research and illustration by Dr. Brinton, in his *Myths
of the New World.*—K.]

decades, or small bodies of ten; and every tenth
man, or head of a decade, had supervision of the
rest,—being required to see that they enjoyed the
rights and immunities to which they were entitled,
to solicit aid in their behalf from government,
when necessary, and to bring offenders to justice.
To this last they were stimulated by a law that
imposed on them, in case of neglect, the same
penalty that would have been incurred by the
guilty party.   With this law hanging over his
head, the magistrate of Peru, we may well believe,
did not often go to sleep on his post.[6]

The people were still further divided into bodies
of fifty, one hundred, five hundred, and a thousand, each with an officer having general supervision over those beneath, and the higher ones possessing, to a certain extent, authority in matters
of police.   Lastly, the whole empire was distributed into sections or departments of ten thousand
inhabitants, with a governor over each, from the
Inca nobility, who had control over the *curacas* and
other territorial officers in the district.   There were,
also, regular tribunals of justice, consisting of
magistrates in each of the towns or small communities, with jurisdiction over petty offences,
while those of a graver character were carried before superior judges, usually the governors or
rulers of the districts.   These judges all held their
authority and received their support from the

[6] Dec. de la Aud. Real, MS.—Montesinos, Mem. antiguas, MS,
lib. 2, cap. 6.—Ondegardo, Rel Prim, MS.—How analogous is the
Peruvian to the Anglo-Saxon division into hundreds and tithings!
But the Saxon law which imposed only a fine on the district in case
of a criminal's escape was more humane.

crown, by which they were appointed and removed at pleasure. They were obliged to determine every suit in five days from the time it was brought before them; and there was no appeal from one tribunal to another. Yet there were important provisions for the security of justice.* A committee of visitors patrolled the kingdom at certain times to investigate the character and conduct of the magistrates; and any neglect or violation of duty was punished in the most exemplary manner. The inferior courts were also required to make monthly returns of their proceedings to the higher ones, and these made reports in like manner to the viceroys; so that the monarch, seated in the centre of his dominions, could look abroad, as it were, to their most distant extremities, and review and rectify any abuses in the administration of the law.[7]

The laws were few and exceedingly severe. They related almost wholly to criminal matters. Few other laws were needed by a people who had no money, little trade, and hardly anything that could be called fixed property. The crimes of theft, adultery, and murder were all capital; though it was wisely provided that some extenu-

[7] Dec. de la Aud. Real, MS.—Ondegardo, Rel Prim et Seg, MSS —Garcilasso, Com Real, Parte 1, lib 2, cap 11-14—Montesinos, Mem antiguas, MS, lib. 2, cap. 6—The accounts of the Peruvian tribunals by the early authorities are very meagre and unsatisfactory. Even the lively imagination of Garcilasso has failed to supply the blank.

* [In this we see something analogous to the "missi dominici" of Charlemagne; so in the laws specified below we see not a few resemblances to the codes of the various Barbarians who eventually overthrew the power of the Roman empire in the west of Europe —M.]

ating circumstances might be allowed to mitigate
the punishment.[8]   Blasphemy against the Sun, and
malediction of the Inca,—offences, indeed, of the
same complexion,—were also punished with death.
Removing landmarks, turning the water away
from a neighbor's land into one's own, burning a
house, were all severely punished.   To burn a
bridge was death.   The Inca allowed no obstacle
to those facilities of communication so essential to
the maintenance of public order.   A rebellious city
or province was laid waste, and its inhabitants ex-
terminated.   Rebellion against the " Child of the
Sun " was the greatest of all crimes.[9]

The simplicity and severity of the Peruvian
code may be thought to infer a state of society
but little advanced, which had few of those complex interests and relations that grow up in a
civilized community, and which had not proceeded
far enough in the science of legislation to econo-
mize human suffering by proportioning penalties
to crimes.   But the Peruvian institutions must be
regarded from a different point of view from

[8] Ondegardo, Rel Prim , MS.—Herrera, Hist. general, dec. 5,
lib. 4, cap 3 —Theft was punished less severely if the offender had
been really guilty of it to supply the necessities of life   It is a
singular circumstance that the Peruvian law made no distinction
between fornication and adultery, both being equally punished with
death   Yet the law could hardly have been enforced, since prosti-
tutes were assigned, or at least allowed, a residence in the suburbs
of the cities. See Garcilasso, Com. Real , Parte 1, lib 4, cap 34.

[9] Sarmiento, Relacion, MS , cap 23 —" I los traidores entre ellos
llamava *aucaes*, i esta palabra es la mas abiltada de todas quantas
pueden decir aun Indio del Pirú, que quiere decir traidor á su
Señor." (Conq i Pob del Pirú, MS)   " En las rebeliones y alza-
mientos se hicieron los castigos tan asperos, que algunas veces aso-
laron las provincias de todos los varones de edad sin quedar ninguno." Ondegardo, Rel. Prim., MS.

that in which we study those of other nations. The laws emanated from the sovereign, and that sovereign held a divine commission and was possessed of a divine nature. To violate the law was not only to insult the majesty of the throne, but it was sacrilege. The slightest offence, viewed in this light, merited death; and the gravest could incur no heavier penalty.[10] Yet in the infliction of their punishments they showed no unnecessary cruelty; and the sufferings of the victim were not prolonged by the ingenious torments so frequent among barbarous nations.[11]

These legislative provisions may strike us as very defective, even as compared with those of the semi-civilized races of Anahuac, where a gradation of courts, moreover, with the right of appeal, afforded a tolerable security for justice. But in a country like Peru, where but few criminal causes were known, the right of appeal was of less consequence. The law was simple, its application easy; and, where the judge was honest, the case was as likely to be determined correctly on the first hearing as on the second. The inspection of the board of visitors, and the monthly returns of the tribunals, afforded no slight guarantee for their

[10] " El castigo era riguroso, que por la mayor parte era de muerte, por liviano que fuese el delito; porque decian, que no los castigavan por el delito que avian hecho, ni por la ofensa agena, sino por aver quebrantado el mandamiento, y rompido la palabra del Inca, que lo respetavan como á Dios." Garcilasso, Com. Real, Parte 1, lib. 2, cap. 12

[11] One of the punishments most frequent for minor offences was to carry a stone on the back. A punishment attended with no suffering but what arises from the disgrace attached to it is very justly characterized by McCulloh as a proof of sensibility and refinement. Researches, p. 361.

integrity. The law which required a decision within five days would seem little suited to the complex and embarrassing litigation of a modern tribunal. But, in the simple questions submitted to the Peruvian judge, delay would have been useless; and the Spaniards, familiar with the evils growing out of long-protracted suits, where the successful litigant is too often a ruined man, are loud in their encomiums of this swift-handed and economical justice.[12] *

The fiscal regulations of the Incas, and the laws respecting property, are the most remarkable features in the Peruvian polity. The whole territory of the empire was divided into three parts, one for the Sun, another for the Inca, and the last for the people. Which of the three was the largest is doubtful. The proportions differed materially in different provinces. The distribution, indeed, was made on the same general principle, as each new conquest was added to the monarchy; but the proportion varied according to the amount of population, and the greater or less amount of

---

[12] The Royal Audience of Peru under Philip II.—there cannot be a higher authority—bears emphatic testimony to the cheap and efficient administration of justice under the Incas: " De suerte que los vicios eran bien castigados y la gente estaba bien sujeta y obediente; y aunque en las dichas penas havia esceso, redundaba en buen govierno y policia suya, y mediante ella eran aumentados. . . . Porque los Yndios alababan la governacion del Ynga, y aun los Españoles que algo alcanzan de ella, es porque todas las cosas susodichas se determinaban sin hacerles costas." Dec. de la Aud Real, MS.

* [The Spaniards were so impressed with the evils of litigation, that in some of their colonies the admission of lawyers into the country was strictly forbidden —M.]

land consequently required for the support of the inhabitants.[13]

The lands assigned to the Sun furnished a revenue to support the temples and maintain the costly ceremonial of the Peruvian worship and the multitudinous priesthood. Those reserved for the Inca went to support the royal state, as well as the numerous members of his household and his kindred, and supplied the various exigencies of government. The remainder of the lands was divided, *per capita*, in equal shares among the people. It was provided by law, as we shall see hereafter, that every Peruvian should marry at a certain age. When this event took place, the community or district in which he lived furnished him with a dwelling, which, as it was constructed of humble materials, was done at little cost. A lot of land was then assigned to him sufficient for his own maintenance and that of his wife. An additional portion was granted for every child, the amount allowed for a son being the double of that for a daughter. The division of the soil was renewed every year, and the possessions of the tenant were increased or diminished according to the numbers in his family.[14] The same arrangement was observed with

[13] Acosta, lib. 6, cap. 15 —Garcilasso, Com. Real , Parte 1, lib. 5, cap. 1.—" Si estas partes fuesen iguales, o qual fuese mayor, yo lo he procurado averiguar, y en unas es diferente de otras, y finalm^te yo tengo entendido que se hacia conforme á la disposicion de la tierra y á la calidad de los Indios." Ondegardo, Rel Prim , MS.

[14] Ondegardo, Rel. Prim., MS.—Garcilasso, Com Real., Parte 1, lib. 5, cap. 2.—The portion granted to each new-married couple, according to Garcilasso, was a *fanega* and a half of land A similar quantity was added for each male child that was born, and half of the quantity for each female. The *fanega* was as much land as

reference to the curacas, except only that a domain was assigned to them corresponding with the superior dignity of their stations.[15]

A more thorough and effectual agrarian law than this cannot be imagined. In other countries where such a law has been introduced, its operation, after a time, has given way to the natural order of events, and, under the superior intelligence and thrift of some and the prodigality of others, the usual vicissitudes of fortune have been allowed to take their course and restore things to their natural inequality. Even the iron law of Lycurgus ceased to operate after a time, and melted away before the spirit of luxury and avarice. The nearest approach to the Peruvian constitution was probably in Judea, where, on the recurrence of the great national jubilee, at the close of every half-century, estates reverted to their original proprietors. There was this important difference in Peru; that not only did the lease, if we may so call it; terminate with the year, but during that period the tenant had no power to alienate or to add to his

could be planted with a hundred-weight of Indian corn. In the fruitful soil of Peru, this was a liberal allowance for a family

[15] Ibid, Parte 1, lib 5, cap. 3.—It is singular that, while so much is said of the Inca sovereign, so little should be said of the Inca nobility, of their estates, or the tenure by which they held them. Their historian tells us that they had the best of the lands, wherever they resided, besides the interest which they had in those of the Sun and the Inca, as children of the one and kinsmen of the other. He informs us, also, that they were supplied from the royal table when living at court (lib. 6, cap. 3). But this is very loose language The student of history will learn, on the threshold, that he is not to expect precise, or even very consistent, accounts of the institutions of a barbarous age and people from contemporary annalists.

possessions. The end of the brief term found him in precisely the same condition that he was in at the beginning. Such a state of things might be supposed to be fatal to any thing like attachment to the soil, or to that desire of improving it which is natural to the permanent proprietor, and hardly less so to the holder of a long lease. But the practical operation of the law seems to have been otherwise; and it is probable that, under the influence of that love of order and aversion to change which marked the Peruvian institutions, each new partition of the soil usually confirmed the occupant in his possession, and the tenant for a year was converted into a proprietor for life.

The territory was cultivated wholly by the people. The lands belonging to the Sun were first attended to. They next tilled the lands of the old, of the sick, of the widow and the orphan, and of soldiers engaged in actual service; in short, of all that part of the community who, from bodily infirmity or any other cause, were unable to attend to their own concerns. The people were then allowed to work on their own ground, each man for himself, but with the general obligation to assist his neighbor when any circumstance—the burden of a young and numerous family, for example—might demand it.[16] Lastly, they cultivated the lands of the Inca. This was done with great ceremony, by the whole population in a body. At break of day they were summoned together by

[16] Garcilasso relates that an Indian was hanged by Huayna Capac for tilling the ground of a curaca, his near relation, before that of the poor. The gallows was erected on the curaca's own land. Com. Real., Parte 1, lib. 5, cap 2.

proclamation from some neighboring tower or eminence, and all the inhabitants of the district, men,
women, and children, appeared dressed in their
gayest apparel, bedecked with their little store of
finery and ornaments, as if for some great jubilee.
They went through the labors of the day with the
same joyous spirit, chanting their popular ballads
which commemorated the heroic deeds of the Incas,
regulating their movements by the measure of the
chant, and all mingling in the chorus, of which
the word *hailli*, or "triumph," was usually the
burden. These national airs had something soft
and pleasing in their character, that recommended
them to the Spaniards; and many a Peruvian song
was set to music by them after the Conquest, and
was listened to by the unfortunate natives with
melancholy satisfaction, as it called up recollec-
tions of the past, when their days glided peace-
fully away under the sceptre of the Incas.[17]

A similar arrangement prevailed with respect to
the different manufactures as to the agricultural
products of the country. The flocks of llamas, or
Peruvian sheep, were appropriated exclusively to
the Sun and to the Inca.[18] Their number was immense. They were scattered over the different

[17] Garcilasso, Com. Real., Parte 1, lib. 5, cap. 1-3 —Ondegardo,
Rel. Seg., MS.
[18] Ondegardo, Rel. Prim., MS.—Yet sometimes the sovereign
would recompense some great chief, or even some one among the
people, who had rendered him a service, by the grant of a small
number of llamas,—never many. These were not to be disposed
of or killed by their owners, but descended as common property
to their heirs. This strange arrangement proved a fruitful source
of litigation after the Conquest Ibid, ubi supra *

* [For a more complete account of the llamas, see chap. v.—M.]

provinces, chiefly in the colder regions of the country, where they were intrusted to the care of experienced shepherds, who conducted them to different pastures according to the change of season. A large number was every year sent to the capital for the consumption of the court, and for the religious festivals and sacrifices. But these were only the males, as no female was allowed to be killed. The regulations for the care and breeding of these flocks were prescribed with the greatest minuteness, and with a sagacity which excited the admiration of the Spaniards, who were familiar with the management of the great migratory flocks of merinos in their own country.[19]

At the appointed season they were all sheared, and the wool was deposited in the public magazines. It was then dealt out to each family in such quantities as sufficed for its wants, and was consigned to the female part of the household, who were well instructed in the business of spinning and weaving. When this labor was accomplished, and the family was provided with a coarse but warm covering, suited to the cold climate of the mountains,—for in the lower country cotton, furnished in like manner by the crown, took the place, to a certain extent, of wool,—the people were required to labor for the Inca. The quantity of the cloth needed, as well as the peculiar kind and quality of the fabric, was first determined at Cuzco. The work was then apportioned among

[19] See especially the account of the Licentiate Ondegardo, who goes into more detail than any contemporary writer concerning the management of the Peruvian flocks. Rel Seg, MS.

the different provinces. Officers appointed for the purpose superintended the distribution of the wool, so that the manufacture of the different articles should be intrusted to the most competent hands.[20] They did not leave the matter here, but entered the dwellings from time to time, and saw that the work was faithfully executed. This domestic inquisition was not confined to the labors for the Inca. It included, also, those for the several families; and care was taken that each household should employ the materials furnished for its own use in the manner that was intended, so that no one should be unprovided with necessary apparel.[21] In this domestic labor all the female part of the establishment was expected to join. Occupation was found for all, from the child five years old to the aged matron not too infirm to hold a distaff. No one, at least none but the decrepit and the sick, was allowed to eat the bread of idleness in Peru. Idleness was a crime in the eye of the law, and, as such, severely punished; while industry was publicly commended and stimulated by rewards.[22]

The like course was pursued with reference to the other requisitions of the government. All the mines in the kingdom belonged to the Inca. They were wrought exclusively for his benefit, by per-

---

[20] Ondegardo, Rel. Prim. et Seg, MSS —The manufacture of cloths for the Inca included those for the numerous persons of the blood royal, who wore garments of a finer texture than was permitted to any other Peruvian Garcilasso, Com. Real., Parte 1, lib. 5, cap. 6.

[21] Ondegardo, Rel Seg, MS.—Acosta, lib. 6, cap. 15.

[22] Ondegardo, Rel. Seg., MS.—Garcilasso, Com. Real., Parte 1, lib. 5, cap. 11.

sons familiar with this service and selected from the districts where the mines were situated.[23] Every Peruvian of the lower class was a husbandman, and, with the exception of those already specified, was expected to provide for his own support by the cultivation of his land. A small portion of the community, however, was instructed in mechanical arts,—some of them of the more elegant kind, subservient to the purposes of luxury and ornament. The demand for these was chiefly limited to the sovereign and his court; but the labor of a larger number of hands was exacted for the execution of the great public works which covered the land. The nature and amount of the services required were all determined at Cuzco by commissioners well instructed in the resources of the country and in the character of the inhabitants of different provinces.[24]

This information was obtained by an admirable regulation, which has scarcely a counterpart in the annals of a semi-civilized people. A register was kept of all the births and deaths throughout the country, and exact returns of the actual population were made to the government every year, by

[23] Garcilasso would have us believe that the Inca was indebted to the curacas for his gold and silver, which were furnished by the great vassals as presents. (Com. Real, Parte 1, lib. 5, cap 7.) This improbable statement is contradicted by the Report of the Royal Audience, MS., by Sarmiento (Relacion, MS, cap 15), and by Ondegardo (Rel. Prim, MS.), who all speak of the mines as the property of the government and wrought exclusively for its benefit. From this reservoir the proceeds were liberally dispensed in the form of presents among the great lords, and still more for the embellishment of the temples

[24] Garcilasso, Com Real, Parte 1, lib. 5, cap. 13–16.—Ondegardo, Rel. Prim. et Seg., MSS.

means of the *quipus*, a curious invention, which will be explained hereafter.[25] * At certain intervals, also, a general survey of the country was made, exhibiting a complete view of the character of the soil, its fertility, the nature of its products, both agricultural and mineral,—in short, of all that constituted the physical resources of the empire.[26] Furnished with these statistical details, it was easy for the government, after determining the amount of requisitions, to distribute the work among the respective provinces best qualified to execute it. The task of apportioning the labor was assigned to the local authorities, and great care was taken that it should be done in such a manner that, while the most competent hands were selected, the weight should not fall disproportionately on any.[27]

The different provinces of the country furnished persons peculiarly suited to different employments, which, as we shall see hereafter, usually descended from father to son. Thus, one district supplied those most skilled in working the mines,

[25] Montesinos, Mem. antiguas, MS, lib 2, cap. 6—Pedro Pizarro, Relacion del Descubrimiento y Conquista de los Reynos del Perú, MS.—"Cada provincia, en fin del año, mandava asentar en los quipos, por la cuenta de sus nudos, todos, los hombres que habian muerto en ella en aquel año, y por el consiguiente los que habian nacido, y por principio del año que entraba, venian con los quipos al Cuzco." Sarmiento, Relacion, MS., cap. 16.

[26] Garcilasso, Com. Real., Parte 1, lib. 2, cap 14.

[27] Ondegardo, Rel. Prim., MS—Sarmiento, Rel. MS., cap. 15.— "Presupuesta y entendida la dicha division que el Inga tenia hecha de su gente, y orden que tenia puesta en el govierno de ella, era muy facil haverla en la division y cobranza de los dichos tributos; porque era claro y cierto lo que á cada uno cabia sin que hubiese desigualdad ni engaño." Dec de la Aud. Real., MS.

* [See chap. iv.—M.]

another the most curious workers in metals or in wood, and so on.[28]   The artisan was provided by government with the materials; and no one was required to give more than a stipulated portion of his time to the public service.   He was then succeeded by another for the like term; and it should be observed that all who were engaged in the employment of the government—and the remark applies equally to agricultural labor—were maintained, for the time, at the public expense.[29] By this constant rotation of labor it was intended that no one should be overburdened, and that each man should have time to provide for the demands of his own household.   It was impossible—in the judgment of a high Spanish authority—to improve on the system of distribution, so carefully was it accommodated to the condition and comfort of the artisan.[30]   The security of the working-classes seems to have been ever kept in view in the regulations of the government; and these were so discreetly arranged that the most wearing and unwholesome labors, as those of the mines, occasioned no detriment to the health of the laborer; a striking contrast to his subsequent condition under the Spanish rule.[31]

[28] Sarmiento, Relacion, MS., cap 15 —Ondegardo, Rel. Seg., MS
[29] Ondegardo, Rel. Prim., MS —Garcilasso, Com. Real , Parte 1, lib. 5, cap. 5.
[30] " Y tambien se tenia cuenta que el trabajo que pasavan fuese moderado, y con el menos riesgo que fuese posible. . . . Era tanta la orden que tuvieron estos Indios, que á mi parecer aunque mucho se piense en ello seria dificultoso mejorarla conocida su condicion y costumbres." Ondegardo, Rel. Prim., MS.
[31] " The working of the mines," says the President of the Council of the Indies, " was so regulated that no one felt it a hardship,

A part of the agricultural produce and manufactures was transported to Cuzco, to minister to the immediate demands of the Inca and his court. But far the greater part was stored in magazines scattered over the different provinces. These spacious buildings, constructed of stone, were divided between the Sun and the Inca, though the greater share seems to have been appropriated by the monarch. By a wise regulation, any deficiency in the contributions of the Inca might be supplied from the granaries of the Sun.[32] But such a necessity could rarely have happened; and the providence of the government usually left a large surplus in the royal depositories, which was removed to a third class of magazines, whose design was to supply the people in seasons of scarcity, and, occasionally, to furnish relief to individuals whom sickness or misfortune had reduced to poverty; thus in a manner justifying the assertion of a Castilian document, that a large portion of the revenues of the Inca found its way back again, through one channel or another, into the hands of the people.[33] These magazines were found by the Spaniards, on their arrival, stored with all the

much less was his life shortened by it" (Sarmiento, Relacion, MS., cap. 16.) It is a frank admission for a Spaniard

[32] Garcilasso, Com. Real., Parte 1, lib. 5, cap 34.—Ondegardo, Rel. Prim., MS.—" E asi esta parte del Inga no hay duda sino que de todas tres era la mayor, y en los depositos se parece bien que yó visité muchos en diferentes partes, é son mayores é mas largos que nó los de su religion sin comparasion." Idem, Rel Seg., MS.

[33] " Todos los dichos tributos y servicios que el Inga imponia y llevaba como dicho es eran con color y para efecto del govierno y pro comun de todos, asi como lo que se ponia en depositos todo se combertia y distribuia entre los mismos naturales." Dec. de la Aud. Real., MS

various products and manufactures of the country,—with maize, *coca, quinua,* woollen and cotton
stuffs of the finest quality, with vases and utensils
of gold, silver, and copper, in short, with every
article of luxury or use within the compass of
Peruvian skill.[34] * The magazines of grain, in
particular, would frequently have sufficed for
the consumption of the adjoining district for
several years.[35] An inventory of the various
products of the country, and the quarters whence
they were obtained, was every year taken by the
royal officers and recorded by the *quipucamayus*
on their registers, with surprising regularity and
precision.† These registers were transmitted to
the capital and submitted to the Inca, who could
thus at a glance, as it were, embrace the whole results of the national industry and see how far they

[34] Acosta, lib. 6, cap. 15.—"No podre decir," says one of the Conquerors, "los depositos. Vide de rropas y de todos generos de
rropas y vestidos que en este reino se hacian y vsavan que faltava
tiempo para vello y entendimiento para comprender tanta cosa,
muchos depositos de barretas de cobre para las minas y de costales
y sogas de vasos de palo y platos del oro y plata que aqui se hallo
hera cosa despanto." Pedro Pizarro, Descub. y Conq., MS

[35] For ten years, sometimes, if we may credit Ondegardo, who
had every means of knowing: "É ansi cuando nó era menester se
estaba en los depositos é habia algunas vezes comida de diez años
. . Los cuales todos se hallaron llenos cuando llegaron los Españoles desto y de todas las cosas necesarias para la vida humana."
Rel. Seg, MS.

* [Never had a nation provided more surely for its own conquest
by the swords of an invading army. Pizarro and his men experienced little hardship and suffered little opposition in comparison
with Cortés and his companions —M]

† [It is not remarkable that all the features of the Peruvian institutions should have been so minutely reported by the Spanish
writers. There was nothing of the kind in Spain, and the conquerors were simply astounded by what they saw.—M.]

corresponded with the requisitions of the government.[36]

Such are some of the most remarkable features of the Peruvian institutions relating to property, as delineated by writers who, however contradictory in the details, have a general conformity of outline. These institutions are certainly so remarkable that it is hardly credible they should ever have been enforced throughout a great empire and for a long period of years. Yet we have the most unequivocal testimony to the fact from the Spaniards, who landed in Peru in time to witness their operation; some of whom, men of high judicial station and character, were commissioned by the government to make investigations into the state of the country under its ancient rulers.

The impositions on the Peruvian people seem to have been sufficiently heavy. On them rested the whole burden of maintaining not only their own order, but every other order in the state. The members of the royal house, the great nobles, even the public functionaries, and the numerous body of the priesthood, were all exempt from taxation.[37] The whole duty of defraying the expenses of the government belonged to the people. Yet this was not materially different from the condition of things formerly existing in most parts of Europe, where the various privileged classes claimed exemption—not always with success, in-

---

[36] Ondegardo, Rel Prim , MS —" Por tanta orden é cuenta que seria dificultoso creerlo ni darlo á entender como ellos lo tienen en su cuenta é por registros é por menudo lo manifestaron que se pudiera por estenso " Idem, Rel Seg., MS.

[37] Garcilasso, Com. Real., Parte 1, lib 5, cap. 15.

deed—from bearing part of the public burdens. The great hardship in the case of the Peruvian was that he could not better his condition.* His labors were for others, rather than for himself. However industrious, he could not add a rood to his own possessions, nor advance himself one hair's breadth in the social scale. The great and universal motive to honest industry, that of bettering one's lot, was lost upon him. The great law of human progress was not for him. As he was born, so he was to die. Even his time he could not properly call his own. Without money, with little property of any kind, he paid his taxes in labor.[38] No wonder that the government should have dealt with sloth as a crime. It was a crime against the state, and to be wasteful of time was, in a manner, to rob the exchequer. The Peruvian, laboring all his life for others, might be compared to the convict in a treadmill, going the same dull round of incessant toil, with the consciousness that, however profitable the results to the state, they were nothing to him.

But this is the dark side of the picture. If no man could become rich in Peru, no man could become poor. No spendthrift could waste his substance in riotous luxury. No adventurous schemer could impoverish his family by the spirit of speculation. The law was constantly directed to enforce a steady industry and a sober management of his affairs. No mendicant was tolerated in Peru. When a man was reduced by poverty or misfor-

[38] "Solo el trabajo de las personas era el tributo que se dava, porque ellos no poseian otra cosa." Ondegardo, Rel. Prim., MS.

* [No more could the serf in mediæval France.—M.]

tune (it could hardly be by fault), the arm of
the law was stretched out to minister relief; not
the stinted relief by private charity, nor that which
is doled out, drop by drop, as it were, from the
frozen reservoirs of " the parish," but in generous
measure, bringing no humiliation to the object of
it, and placing him on a level with the rest of his
countrymen.[39]

No man could be rich, no man could be poor, in
Peru; but all might enjoy, and did enjoy, a com-
petence. Ambition, avarice, the love of change,
the morbid spirit of discontent, those passions
which most agitate the minds of men, found no
place in the bosom of the Peruvian. The very
condition of his being seemed to be at war with
change. He moved on in the same unbroken circle
in which his fathers had moved before him, and
in which his children were to follow. It was the
object of the Incas to infuse into their subjects
a spirit of passive obedience and tranquillity,—a
perfect acquiescence in the established order of

[39] " Era tanta la orden que tenia en todos sus Reinos y provincias,
que no consentia haver ningun Indio pobre ni menesteroso, porque
havia orden i formas para ello sin que los pueblos reciviesen vexa-
cion ni molestia, porque el Inga lo suplia de sus tributos." (Conq
i Pob. del Piru, MS) The Licentiate Ondegardo sees only a device
of Satan in these provisions of the Peruvian law, by which the old,
the infirm, and the poor were rendered, in a manner, independent
of their children and those nearest of kin, on whom they would
naturally have leaned for support; no surer way to harden the
heart, he considers, than by thus disengaging it from the sympathies
of humanity; and no circumstance has done more, he concludes,
to counteract the influence and spread of Christianity among the
natives (Rel. Seg., MS) The views are ingenious; but in a
country where the people had no property, as in Peru, there would
seem to be no alternative for the supernumeraries but to receive
support from government or to starve.

things. In this they fully succeeded. The Spaniards who first visited the country are emphatic in their testimony that no government could have been better suited to the genius of the people, and no people could have appeared more contented with their lot or more devoted to their government.[40]

Those who may distrust the accounts of Peruvian industry will find their doubts removed on a visit to the country. The traveller still meets, especially in the central regions of the table-land, with memorials of the past, remains of temples, palaces, fortresses, terraced mountains, great military roads, aqueducts, and other public works, which, whatever degree of science they may display in their execution, astonish him by their number, the massive character of the materials, and the grandeur of the design. Among them, perhaps the most remarkable are the great roads, the broken remains of which are still in sufficient preservation to attest their former magnificence. There were many of these roads, traversing different parts of the kingdom; but the most considerable were the two which extended from Quito to Cuzco, and, again diverging from the capital, continued in a southerly direction towards Chili.

One of these roads passed over the grand plateau, and the other along the lowlands on the borders of the ocean. The former was much the more difficult achievement from the character of the country. It was conducted over pathless sierras buried in snow; galleries were cut for

<hr>

[40] Acosta, lib. 6, cap. 12, 15.—Sarmiento, Relacion, MS., cap. 10.

leagues through the living rock; rivers were crossed by means of bridges that swung suspended in the air; precipices were scaled by stairways hewn out of the native bed; ravines of hideous depth were filled up with solid masonry: in short, all the difficulties that beset a wild and mountainous region, and which might appall the most courageous engineer of modern times, were encountered and successfully overcome. The length of the road, of which scattered fragments only remain, is variously estimated at from fifteen hundred to two thousand miles; and stone pillars, in the manner of European mile-stones, were erected at stated intervals of somewhat more than a league, all along the route. Its breadth scarcely exceeded twenty feet.[41] It was built of heavy flags of freestone, and, in some parts at least, covered with a bituminous cement, which time has made harder than the stone itself. In some places, where the ravines had been filled up with masonry, the mountain-torrents, wearing on it for ages, have gradually eaten a way through the base, and left the superincumbent mass—such is the cohesion of the materials—still spanning the valley like an arch![42]

[41] Dec. de la Aud Real, MS.—"Este camino hecho por valles ondos y por sierras altas, por montes de nieve, por tremedales de agua y por peña viva y junto á rios furiosos por estas partes y hallano y empredrado por las laderas, bien sacado por las sierras, deshechado, por las peñas socavado, por junto á los Rios sus paredes, entre nieves con escalones y descanso, por todas partes limpio barrido descombrado, lleno de aposentos, de depositos de tesoros, de Templos del Sol, de Postas que havia en este camino." Sarmiento, Relacion, MS., cap. 60.

[42] "On avait comblé les vides et les ravins par de grandes masses de maçonnerie. Les torrents qui descendent des hauteurs après des

Over some of the boldest streams it was necessary to construct suspension-bridges, as they are

pluies abondantes avaient creusé les endroits les moins solides, et
s'étaient frayé une voie sous le chemin, le laissant ainsi suspendu en
l'air comme un pont fait d'une seule pièce." (Velasco, Hist. de
Quito, tom. i. p. 206) This writer speaks from personal observation, having examined and measured different parts of the road,
in the latter part of the last century. The Spanish scholar will find
in Appendix No. 2 an animated description of this magnificent
work and of the obstacles encountered in the execution of it, in a
passage borrowed from Sarmiento, who saw it in the days of the
Incas.*

* [Very few traces of the Inca roads are now to be found in the
southern part of Peru. Those which Humboldt saw were in the
northern part of the country. The accounts the early writers have
left us of these works are unquestionably exaggerations. The highways were so much better than any they knew in Spain that they
magnified their excellencies. As the physical conformation of the
land has not changed through the ages, the routes of travel necessarily remain the same from year to year Great heaps of stones
indicate clearly the ancient and the modern lines of communication.
These great piles were formed by the contribution of a single stone
by each traveller as an offering to the spirit power that dominated
the mountains, and even to-day the passing Indian occasionally
adds his stone to those his fathers, travelling the same path centuries before, threw upon the heap. Between Jauja and Tarma
the writer was able, thirty years ago, to discern traces of the old
highway. The roadway was possibly twenty-five feet wide in the
more level portions. It was paved with large, flat stones, and was
raised somewhat in the middle. Lines of stones firmly bedded in
the ground marked the edges. The road ascended the mountains
by a succession of terraces thirty or forty feet in length, and was
sometimes hardly more than eight feet wide. Mr Squier sees no
reason for supposing that the highways suffered more in one part
of the country from time and the elements than another, and therefore concludes that they never existed in Southern Peru Hutchinson scouts at the idea of a highway in the level country between
the Andes and the ocean. He sought diligently for a thousand
miles, from Arica to San José, and found nothing that hinted at
its former existence. In the first place, he points out to us that
there is no such level country as Prescott mentioned, and, sec-
ondly, he insists that all the roads in the valleys near the coast
show unmistakable evidences of having been made by peoples who
dwelt in the land long before the Inca domination. Two Years
in Peru, p. 73 — M]

termed, made of the tough fibres of the maguey, or of the osier of the country, which has an extraordinary degree of tenacity and strength. These osiers were woven into cables of the thickness of a man's body. The huge ropes, then stretched across the water, were conducted through rings or holes cut in immense buttresses of stone raised on the opposite banks of the river and there secured to heavy pieces of timber. Several of these enormous cables, bound together, formed a bridge, which, covered with planks, well secured and defended by a railing of the same osier materials on the sides, affording a safe passage for the traveller. The length of this aërial bridge, sometimes exceeding two hundred feet, caused it, confined as it was only at the extremities, to dip with an alarming inclination towards the centre, while the motion given to it by the passenger occasioned an oscillation still more frightful, as his eye wandered over the dark abyss of waters that foamed and tumbled many a fathom beneath. Yet these light and fragile fabrics were crossed without fear by the Peruvians,* and are still retained by the Spaniards over those streams which, from the depth or im-

* [The suspension-bridges must still be crossed in many parts of the country. The osier ropes have, as a rule, been replaced by chain cables, or wire ropes, but the structures are not as well cared for as in the days of the Incas, and the traveller runs more risk than in that ancient time. Almost always one side of the bridge is higher than the other. Side ropes are usually lacking, and the flooring is very rarely in proper condition. Not often do travellers *ride* across them. The riding-mules and the pack-animals are sent upon the bridges one by one. The riders and the arrieros then force them across by throwing stones at them. It is a case where the training received in the "American National Game" shows to the greatest advantage.—M]

petuosity of the current, would seem impracticable for the usual modes of conveyances. The wider and more tranquil waters were crossed on *balsas* * —a kind of raft still much used by the natives— to which sails were attached, furnishing the only instance of this higher kind of navigation among the American Indians.[43]

The other great road of the Incas lay through the level country between the Andes and the ocean. It was constructed in a different manner, as demanded by the nature of the ground, which was for the most part low, and much of it sandy. The

[43] Garcilasso, Com. Real, Parte 1, lib. 3, cap. 7—A particular account of these bridges, as they are still to be seen in different parts of Peru, may be found in Humboldt. (Vues des Cordillères, p 230, et seq.) The *balsas* are described with equal minuteness by Stevenson. Residence in America, vol. ii. p. 222, et seq.

* [The *balsa* is still used in many places, especially along the northern coasts. Balsa-wood is almost as light as cork when it is first put into the water, but in course of time it becomes water-soaked and loses its buoyancy. When not in use, therefore, the rafts are taken apart and the logs are rolled high up upon the shore. The *balsa* is made of trunks of the balsa-tree lashed together with wires or ropes. Cross-pieces are used to strengthen the craft, and a rude mast with a square sail (the square sail is inevitable on the South American coast) furnishes the motive-power. Platforms are built upon the raft, varying according to the cargo to be carried. When once the *balsa* has been forced through the line of breakers, its course is tranquil. The trouble is to get it through At Eten, in 1873, the writer saw many loads of sugar that had been placed in sacks upon *balsas* completely spoiled in the attempt to launch the clumsy contrivances through the surf. In going up the Guayas River to the city of Guayaquil, in Ecuador, one may see the *balsa* in its glory as a house-boat. There may be several huts upon the raft. And upon them also one may see men, women, and children, the former partly, the latter entirely, naked, dwelling together in joyful amity with pigs and fowls, monkeys and other household pets. Four steersmen, with broad-bladed steering oars thrust through the spaces between the logs near the four corners, seemingly control the course of the craft without much difficulty.—M.]

causeway was raised on a high embankment of
earth, and defended on either side by a parapet or
wall of clay; and trees and odoriferous shrubs
were planted along the margin, regaling the sense
of the traveller with their perfumes, and refreshing him by their shades, so grateful under the burning sky of the tropics. In the strips of sandy waste
which occasionally intervened, where the light and
volatile soil was incapable of sustaining a road,
huge piles, many of them to be seen at this day,
were driven into the ground to indicate the route
to the traveller.[44]

All along these highways, caravansaries, or *tambos*,* as they were called, were erected, at the distance of ten or twelve miles from each other, for
the accommodation, more particularly, of the Inca
and his suite and those who journeyed on the public business. There were few other travellers in
Peru. Some of these buildings were on an extensive scale, consisting of a fortress, barracks, and
other military works, surrounded by a parapet of
stone and covering a large tract of ground. These
were evidently destined for the accommodation of

[44] Cieza de Leon, Cronica, cap. 60—Relacion del primer Descubrimiento de la Costa y Mar del Sur, MS—This anonymous document of one of the early Conquerors contains a minute and probably
trustworthy account of both the high-roads, which the writer saw in
their glory, and which he ranks among the greatest wonders of the
world.

* [A *tambo* to-day in the remote regions, and even in villages not
a hundred miles from Lima, is frequently only an adobe hut with a
bed of adobe bricks (on which the traveller is expected to spread
his own blankets, or, if he is addicted to luxury, the mattress which
he carries in an almofres upon a pack-mule) built up in one corner.
A table is usually found in the structure, but the chairs, or stools,
are almost always brought in from neighboring huts —M]

the imperial armies when on their march across the country. The care of the great roads was committed to the districts through which they passed, and under the Incas a large number of hands was constantly employed to keep them in repair. This was the more easily done in a country where the mode of travelling was altogether on foot; though the roads are said to have been so nicely constructed that a carriage might have rolled over them as securely as on any of the great roads of Europe.[45] Still, in a region where the elements of fire and water are both actively at work in the business of destruction, they must, without constant supervision, have gradually gone to decay. Such has been their fate under the Spanish conquerors, who took no care to enforce the admirable system for their preservation adopted by the Incas. Yet the broken portions that still survive here and there, like the fragments of the great Roman roads scattered over Europe, bear evidence to their primitive grandeur, and have drawn forth the eulogium from a discriminating traveller, usually not too profuse in his panegyric, that " the roads of the Incas were among the most useful and stupendous works ever executed by man." [46]

The system of communication through their do-

[45] Relacion del primer Descub, MS.—Cieza de Leon, Cronica, cap 37.—Zarate, Conq. del Peru, lib. 1, cap 11.—Garcilasso, Com. Real, Parte 1, lib. 9, cap. 13.

[46] " Cette chaussée, bordée de grandes pierres de taille, peut être comparée aux plus belles routes des Romains que j'aie vues en Italie, en France et en Espagne . . . Le grand chemin de l'Inca, un des ouvrages les plus utiles et en même temps des plus gigantesques que les hommes aient exécuté." Humboldt, Vues des Cordillères, p 294.

minions was still further improved by the Peruvian sovereigns by the introduction of posts, in the same manner as was done by the Aztecs. The Peruvian posts, however, established on all the great routes that conducted to the capital, were on a much more extended plan than those in Mexico. All along these routes, small buildings were erected, at the distance of less than five miles asunder,[47] in each of which a number of runners, or *chasquis*, as they were called, were stationed to carry forward the despatches of government.[48] These despatches were either verbal, or conveyed by means of *quipus*, and sometimes accompanied by a thread of the crimson fringe worn round the temples of the Inca, which was regarded with the same implicit deference as the signet-ring of an Oriental despot.[49]

The *chasquis* were dressed in a peculiar livery, intimating their profession. They were all trained to the employment, and selected for their speed and fidelity. As the distance each courier had to perform was small, and as he had ample time to refresh himself at the stations, they ran over the

[47] The distance between the post-houses is variously stated; most writers not estimating it at more than three-fourths of a league I have preferred the authority of Ondegardo, who usually writes with more conscientiousness and knowledge of his ground than most of his contemporaries.

[48] The term *chasqui*, according to Montesinos, signifies "one that receives a thing" (Mem. antiguas, MS, cap 7) But Garcilasso, a better authority for his own tongue, says it meant "one who makes an exchange." Com. Real., Parte 1, lib. 6, cap 8.

[49] "Con vn hilo de esta Borla, entregado á uno de aquellos Orejones, governaban la Tierra, i proveian lo que querian con maior obediencia, que en ninguna Provincia del Mundo se ha visto tener á las Provissiones de su Rei." Zarate, Conq del Peru, lib. 1, cap 9.

ground with great swiftness, and messages were carried through the whole extent of the long routes, at the rate of a hundred and fifty miles a day. The office of the *chasquis* was not limited to carrying despatches. They frequently brought various articles for the use of the court; and in this way fish from the distant ocean, fruits, game, and different commodities from the hot regions on the coast, were taken to the capital in good condition and served fresh at the royal table.[50] It is remarkable that this important institution should have been known to both the Mexicans and the Peruvians without any correspondence with one another, and that it should have been found among two barbarian nations of the New World long before it was introduced among the civilized nations of Europe.[51]

By these wise contrivances of the Incas, the most distant parts of the long-extended empire of Peru were brought into intimate relations with

[50] Sarmiento, Relacion, MS., cap. 18.—Dec. de la Aud. Real., MS. —If we may trust Montesinos, the royal table was served with fish, taken a hundred leagues from the capital, in twenty-four hours after it was drawn from the ocean! (Mem. antiguas, MS., lib. 2, cap. 7.) This is rather too expeditious for anything but railways.

[51] The institution of the Peruvian posts seems to have made a great impression on the minds of the Spaniards who first visited the country; and ample notices of it may be found in Sarmiento, Relacion, MS., cap. 15,—Dec. de la Aud. Real., MS.,—Fernandez, Hist. del Peru, Parte 2, lib. 3, cap. 5,—Conq i Pob. del Piru, MS., et auct. plurimis.—The establishment of posts is of old date among the Chinese, and probably still older among the Persians. (See Herodotus, Hist., Urania, sec. 98.) It is singular that an invention designed for the uses of a despotic government should have received its full application only under a free one. For in it we have the germ of that beautiful system of intercommunication which binds all the nations of Christendom together as one vast commonwealth.

each other. And while the capitals of Christendom, but a few hundred miles apart, remained as far asunder as if seas had rolled between them, the great capitals Cuzco and Quito were placed by the high-roads of the Incas in immediate correspondence. Intelligence from the numerous provinces was transmitted on the wings of the wind to the Peruvian metropolis, the great focus to which all the lines of communication converged. Not an insurrectionary movement could occur, not an invasion on the remotest frontier, before the tidings were conveyed to the capital and the imperial armies were on their march across the magnificent roads of the country to suppress it. So admirable was the machinery contrived by the American despots for maintaining tranquillity throughout their dominions! It may remind us of the similar institutions of ancient Rome, when, under the Cæsars, she was mistress of half the world.

A principal design of the great roads was to serve the purposes of military communication. It formed an important item of their military policy, which is quite as well worth studying as their municipal.

Notwithstanding the pacific professions of the Incas, and the pacific tendency, indeed, of their domestic institutions, they were constantly at war. It was by war that their paltry territory had been gradually enlarged to a powerful empire. When this was achieved, the capital, safe in its central position, was no longer shaken by these military movements, and the country enjoyed, in a great degree, the blessings of tranquillity and order.

But, however tranquil at heart, there is not a reign upon record in which the nation was not engaged in war against the barbarous nations on the frontier. Religion furnished a plausible pretext for incessant aggression, and disguised the lust of conquest in the Incas, probably from their own eyes, as well as from those of their subjects. Like the followers of Mahomet, bearing the sword in one hand and the Koran in the other, the Incas of Peru offered no alternative but the worship of the Sun or war.*

It is true, their fanaticism—or their policy—showed itself in a milder form than was found in the descendants of the Prophet. Like the great luminary which they adored, they operated by gentleness, more potent than violence.[52] They sought to soften the hearts of the rude tribes around them, and melt them by acts of condescension and kindness. Far from provoking hostilities, they allowed time for the salutary example of their own institutions to work its effect, trusting that their less civilized neighbors would submit to their sceptre, from a conviction of the blessings it would secure to them. When this course failed, they employed other measures, but still of a pacific character, and endeavored by negotiation, by conciliatory treatment, and by presents to the leading men, to win them over to their dominion. In short, they practised all the arts familiar to the

[52] " Mas se hicieron Señores al principio por maña, que por fuerza." Ondegardo, Rel. Prim , MS.

*[The followers of Mahomet offered still another choice,—namely, tribute. Strange that this fact should be so steadily forgotten!—M.]

most subtle politician of a civilized land to secure the acquisition of empire. When all these expedients failed, they prepared for war.

Their levies were drawn from all the different provinces; though from some, where the character of the people was particularly hardy, more than from others.[53] It seems probable that every Peruvian who had reached a certain age had been called to bear arms. But the rotation of military service, and the regular drills, which took place twice or thrice in a month, of the inhabitants of every village, raised the soldiers generally above the rank of a raw militia. The Peruvian army, at first inconsiderable, came with the increase of population, in the latter days of the empire, to be very large, so that their monarchs could bring into the field, as contemporaries assure us, a force amounting to two hundred thousand men. They showed the same skill and respect for order in their military organization as in other things. The troops were divided into bodies corresponding with our battalions and companies, led by officers, that rose, in regular gradation, from the lowest subaltern to the Inca noble who was intrusted with the general command.[54]

Their arms consisted of the usual weapons employed by nations, whether civilized or uncivilized, before the invention of powder,—bows and arrows, lances, darts, a short kind of sword, a battle-axe or partisan, and slings with which they were very expert. Their spears and arrows were

[53] Idem, Rel Prim, MS.—Dec de la Aud Real, MS
[54] Gomara, Cronica, cap. 195.—Conq. i Pob. del Piru, MS.

tipped with copper, or, more commonly, with bone, and the weapons of the Inca lords were frequently mounted with gold or silver. Their heads were protected by casques made either of wood or of the skins of wild animals, and sometimes richly decorated with metal and with precious stones, surmounted by the brilliant plumage of the tropical birds. These, of course, were the ornaments only of the higher orders. The great mass of the soldiery were dressed in the peculiar costume of their provinces, and their heads were wreathed with a sort of turban or roll of different-colored cloths, that produced a gay and animating effect. Their defensive armor consisted of a shield or buckler, and a close tunic of quilted cotton, in the same manner as with the Mexicans. Each company had its particular banner, and the imperial standard, high above all, displayed the glittering device of the rainbow,—the armorial ensign of the Incas, intimating their claims as children of the skies.[55]

By means of the thorough system of communication established in the country, a short time sufficed to draw the levies together from the most distant quarters. The army was put under the direction of some experienced chief, of the blood royal, or, more frequently, headed by the Inca in person. The march was rapidly performed, and with little fatigue to the soldier; for, all along

[55] Gomara, Cronica, ubi supra—Sarmiento, Relacion, MS., cap. 20.—Velasco, Hist. de Quito, tom. i pp 176–179.—This last writer gives a minute catalogue of the ancient Peruvian arms, comprehending nearly every thing familiar to the European soldier, except fire-arms. It was judicious in him to omit these.

the great routes, quarters were provided for him, at regular distances, where he could find ample accommodations. The country is still covered with the remains of military works, constructed of porphyry or granite, which tradition assures us were designed to lodge the Inca and his army.[56]

At regular intervals, also, magazines were established, filled with grain, weapons, and the different munitions of war, with which the army was supplied on its march. It was the especial care of the government to see that these magazines, which were furnished from the stores of the Incas, were always well filled. When the Spaniards invaded the country, they supported their own armies for a long time on the provisions found in them.[57] The Peruvian soldier was forbidden to commit any trespass on the property of the inhabitants whose territory lay in the line of march. Any violation of this order was punished with

---

[56] Zarate, Conq. del Peru, lib. 1, cap. 11.—Sarmiento, Relacion, MS., cap. 60.—Condamine speaks of the great number of these fortified places, scattered over the country between Quito and Lima, which he saw in his visit to South America in 1737; some of which he has described with great minuteness. Mémoire sur quelques anciens Monumens du Pérou, du Tems des Incas, ap. Histoire de l'Académie Royal des Sciences et de Belles-Lettres (Berlin, 1748), tom. ii p 438

[57] "E ansi cuando," says Ondegardo, speaking from his own personal knowledge, "el Señor Presidente Gasca passó con la gente de castigo de Gonzalo Pizarro por el valle de Jauja, estuvo alli siete semanas á lo que me acuerdo, se hallaron en deposito maiz de cuatro y de tres de dos años mas de 15 9 hanegas junto al camino, é alli comió la gente, y se entendió que si fuera menester muchas mas nó faltaran en el valle en aquellos depositos, conforme á la orden antigua, porque á mi cargo estubo el repartirlas y hacer la cuenta para pagarlas." Rel Seg, MS.

death.[58] The soldier was clothed and fed by the industry of the people, and the Incas rightly resolved that he should not repay this by violence. Far from being a tax on the labors of the husbandman, or even a burden on his hospitality, the imperial armies traversed the country, from one extremity to the other, with as little inconvenience to the inhabitants as would be created by a procession of peaceful burghers or a muster of holiday soldiers for a review.

From the moment war was proclaimed, the Peruvian monarch used all possible expedition in assembling his forces, that he might anticipate the movements of his enemies and prevent a combination with their allies. It was, however, from the neglect of such a principle of combination that the several nations of the country, who might have prevailed by confederated strength, fell one after another under the imperial yoke. Yet, once in the field, the Inca did not usually show any disposition to push his advantages to the utmost and urge his foe to extremity. In every stage of the war, he was open to propositions for peace; and, although he sought to reduce his enemies by carrying off their harvests and distressing them by famine, he allowed his troops to commit no unnecessary outrage on person or property. " We must spare our enemies," one of the Peruvian princes is quoted as saying, " or it will be our loss, since they and all that belongs to them must soon be ours." [59]

[58] Pedro Pizarro, Descub. y Conq , MS.—Cieza de Leon, Cronica, cap. 44 —Sarmiento, Relacion, MS., cap. 14.

[59] " Mandabase que en los mantenimientos y casas de los enemigos se hiciese poco daño, diciendoles el Señor, presto seràn estos nuestros

It was a wise maxim, and, like most other wise
maxims, founded equally on benevolence and prudence. The Incas adopted the policy claimed for
the Romans by their countryman, who tells us that
they gained more by clemency to the vanquished
than by their victories.[60]

In the same considerate spirit, they were most
careful to provide for the security and comfort of
their own troops; and when a war was long protracted, or the climate proved unhealthy, they took
care to relieve their men by frequent reinforcements, allowing the earlier recruits to return to
their homes.[61] But while thus economical of life,
both in their own followers and in the enemy, they
did not shrink from sterner measures when provoked by the ferocious or obstinate character of
the resistance; and the Peruvian annals contain
more than one of those sanguinary pages which
cannot be pondered at the present day without a
shudder. It should be added that the beneficent
policy which I have been delineating as characteristic of the Incas did not belong to all, and that
there was more than one of the royal line who
displayed a full measure of the bold and unscrupulous spirit of the vulgar conqueror.

The first step of the government after the reduction of a country was to introduce there the
worship of the Sun. Temples were erected, and

como los que ya lo son; como esto tenian conocido, procuraban que
la guerra fuese la mas liviana que ser pudiese." Sarmiento, Relacion, MS., cap. 14.

[60] " Plus pene parcendo victis, quàm vincendo imperium auxisse."
Livy, lib. 30, cap. 42.

[61] Garcilasso, Com. Real., Parte 1, lib. 6, cap. 18.

placed under the care of a numerous priesthood,
who expounded to the conquered people the mysteries of their new faith and dazzled them by the
display of its rich and stately ceremonial.[62]   Yet
the religion of the conquered was not treated with
dishonor.*   The Sun was to be worshipped above
all; but the images of their gods were removed to
Cuzco and established in one of the temples, to
hold their rank among the inferior deities of the
Peruvian Pantheon.   Here they remained as hostages, in some sort, for the conquered nation, which
would be the less inclined to forsake allegiance
when by doing so it must leave its own gods in
the hands of its enemies.[63]

The Incas provided for the settlement of their
new conquests, by ordering a census to be taken
of the population and a careful survey to be made
of the country, ascertaining its products and the
character and capacity of its soil.[64]   A division of
the territory was then made on the same principle
with that adopted throughout their own kingdom,
and their respective portions were assigned to the
Sun, the sovereign, and the people.   The amount
of the last was regulated by the amount of the
population, but the share of each individual was
uniformly the same.   It may seem strange that

[62] Sarmiento, Relacion, MS., cap. 14.
[63] Acosta, lib. 5, cap. 12.—Garcilasso, Com Real, Parte 1, lib 5,
cap. 12.
[64] Garcilasso, Com. Real., Parte 1, lib 5, cap. 13, 14.—Sarmiento,
Relacion, MS , cap 15

* [In this the Inca policy was not unlike that pursued by Pagan
Rome.—M.]

any people should patiently have acquiesced in
an arrangement which involved such a total sur-
render of property. But it was a conquered nation
that did so, held in awe, on the least suspicion of
meditated resistance, by armed garrisons, who
were established at various commanding points
throughout the country.[65] It is probable, too, that
the Incas made no greater changes than was essential to the new arrangement, and that they
assigned estates, as far as possible, to their former
proprietors. The curacas, in particular, were confirmed in their ancient authority; or, when it was
found expedient to depose the existing curaca, his
rightful heir was allowed to succeed him.[66] Every
respect was shown to the ancient usages and laws
of the land, as far as was compatible with the
fundamental institutions of the Incas. It must
also be remembered that the conquered tribes were,
many of them, too little advanced in civilization to
possess that attachment to the soil which belongs
to a cultivated nation.[67] But, to whatever it be referred, it seems probable that the extraordinary

[65] Sarmiento, Relacion, MS., cap. 19

[66] Fernandez, Hist. del Peru, Parte 2, lib. 3, cap. 11.

[67] Sarmiento has given a very full and interesting account of the
singularly humane policy observed by the Incas in their conquests,
forming a striking contrast with the usual course of those scourges
of mankind, whom mankind is wise enough to requite with higher
admiration, even, than it bestows on its benefactors. As Sarmiento,
who was President of the Royal Council of the Indies, and came
into the country soon after the Conquest, is a high authority, and
as his work,* lodged in the dark recesses of the Escorial, is almost
unknown, I have transferred the whole chapter to Appendix No 3.

* [Sarmiento never visited America, and, as already mentioned,
was not the author of the work here referred to.—K.]

institutions of the Incas were established with little opposition in the conquered territories.[68]

Yet the Peruvian sovereigns did not trust altogether to this show of obedience in their new vassals; and, to secure it more effectually, they adopted some expedients too remarkable to be passed over in silence. Immediately after a recent conquest, the curacas and their families were removed for a time to Cuzco. Here they learned the language of the capital, became familiar with the manners and usages of the court, as well as with the general policy of the government, and experienced such marks of favor from the sovereigns as would be most grateful to their feelings and might attach them most warmly to his person. Under the influence of these sentiments, they were again sent to rule over their vassals, but still leaving their eldest sons in the capital, to remain there as a guarantee for their own fidelity, as well as to grace the court of the Inca.[69] *

Another expedient was of a bolder and more original character. This was nothing less than to revolutionize the language of the country. South

[68] According to Velasco, even the powerful state of Quito, sufficiently advanced in civilization to have the law of property well recognized by its people, admitted the institutions of the Incas "not only without repugnance, but with joy." (Hist. de Quito, tom. ii. p. 183) But Velasco, a modern authority, believed easily,—or reckoned on his readers' doing so.

[69] Garcilasso, Com. Real., Parte 1, lib. 5, cap. 12; lib. 7, cap. 2.

* [So in imperial Rome were the sons of the Goths and the Vandals, the Lombards and the Franks, educated as hostages at the imperial court —M.]

America, like North America, had a great variety
of dialects, or rather languages, having little
affinity with one another. This circumstance occasioned great embarrassment to the government
in the administration of the different provinces
with whose idioms they were unacquainted. It
was determined, therefore, to substitute one universal language, the *Quichua*,—the language of
the court, the capital, and the surrounding country,—the richest and most comprehensive of the
South American dialects. Teachers were provided
in the towns and villages throughout the land, who
were to give instruction to all, even the humblest
classes; and it was intimated at the same time that
no one should be raised to any office of dignity or
profit who was unacquainted with this tongue.
The curacas and other chiefs who attended at the
capital became familiar with this dialect in their
intercourse with the court, and, on their return
home, set the example of conversing in it among
themselves. This example was imitated by their
followers, and the Quichua gradually became the
language of elegance and fashion, in the same
manner as the Norman French was affected by all
those who aspired to any consideration in England
after the Conquest. By this means, while each
province retained its peculiar tongue, a beautiful
medium of communication was introduced, which
enabled the inhabitants of one part of the country
to hold intercourse with every other, and the Inca
and his deputies to communicate with all. This
was the state of things on the arrival of the Spaniards. It must be admitted that history furnishes

few examples of more absolute authority than such a revolution in the language of an empire at the bidding of a master.[70]

Yet little less remarkable was another device of the Incas for securing the loyalty of their subjects. When any portion of the recent conquests showed a pertinacious spirit of disaffection, it was not uncommon to cause a part of the population, amounting, it might be, to ten thousand inhabitants or more, to remove to a distant quarter of the kingdom, occupied by ancient vassals of undoubted fidelity to the crown. A like number of these last was transplanted to the territory left vacant by the emigrants. By this exchange the population was composed of two distinct races, who regarded each other with an eye of jealousy, that served as an effectual check on any mutinous proceeding. In time, the influence of the well-affected prevailed, supported as they were by royal authority and by the silent working of the national institutions, to which the strange races became gradually accustomed. A spirit of loyalty sprang up by degrees in their bosoms, and before a generation had passed away the different tribes mingled in harmony together as members

[70] Garcilasso, Com. Real., Parte 1, lib 6, cap. 35; lib. 7, cap. 1, 2. —Ondegardo, Rel. Seg, MS —Sarmiento, Relacion, MS., cap. 55 — " Aun la Criatura no hubiese dejado el Pecho de su Madre quando le comenzasen á mostrar la Lengua que havia de saber; y aunque al principio fué dificultoso, é muchos se pusieron en no querer deprender mas lenguas de las suyas propias, los Reyes pudieron tanto que salieron con su intencion y ellos tubieron por bien de cumplir su mandado y tan de veras se entendió en ello que en tiempo de pocos años se savia y usaba una lengua en mas de mil y doscientas leguas." Ibid., cap. 21.

of the same community.[71] Yet the different races
continued to be distinguished by differences of
dress; since, by the law of the land, every citizen
was required to wear the costume of his native
province.[72] Neither could the colonist who had
been thus unceremoniously transplanted return to
his native district. For, by another law, it was forbidden to any one to change his residence without
license.[73] He was settled for life. The Peruvian
government prescrbed to every man his local habi-
tation, his sphere of action, nay, the very nature
and quality of that action. He ceased to be a free
agent; it might be almost said that it relieved him
of personal responsibility.

In following out this singular arrangement, the
Incas showed as much regard for the comfort and
convenience of the colonist as was compatible with
the execution of their design. They were careful
that the *mitimaes*, as these emigrants were styled,
should be removed to climates most congenial with
their own. The inhabitants of the cold countries
were not transplanted to the warm, nor the inhabitants of the warm countries to the cold.[74]
Even their habitual occupations were consulted,

[71] Ondegardo, Rel. Prim., MS.—Fernandez, Hist. del Peru, Parte
2, lib. 3, cap. 11

[72] "This regulation," says Father Acosta, "the Incas held to be
of great importance to the order and right government of the
realm" Lib. 6, cap 16

[73] Conq. i Pob. del Piru, MS.

[74] "Trasmutaban de las tales Provincias la cantidad de gente de
que de ella parecia convenir que saliese, á los cuales mandaban pasar
á poblar otra tierra del temple y manera de donde salian, si fria
fria, si caliente caliente, en donde les daban tierras, y campos, y
casas, tanto, y mas como dejaron." Sarmiento, Relacion, MS,
cap. 19.

and the fisherman was settled in the neighborhood
of the ocean or the great lakes, while such lands
were assigned to the husbandman as were best
adapted to the culture with which he was most
familiar.[75] And, as migration by many, perhaps
by most, would be regarded as a calamity, the government was careful to show particular marks of
favor to the *mitimaes*, and, by various privileges
and immunities, to ameliorate their condition, and
thus to reconcile them, if possible, to their lot.[76]

The Peruvian institutions, though they may
have been modified and matured under successive
sovereigns, all bear the stamp of the same original,
—were all cast in the same mould.   The empire,
strengthening and enlarging at every successive
epoch of its history, was in its latter days but the
development, on a great scale, of what it was in
miniature at its commencement, as the infant germ
is said to contain within itself all the ramifications
of the future monarch of the forest.   Each succeeding Inca seemed desirous only to tread in the
path and carry out the plans of his predecessor.
Great enterprises, commenced under one, were
continued by another, and completed by a third.
Thus, while all acted on a regular plan, without
any of the eccentric or retrograde movements
which betray the agency of different individuals,
the state seemed to be under the direction of a
single hand, and steadily pursued, as if through

---

[75] Ondegardo, Rel. Prim., MS.

[76] The descendants of these *mitimaes* are still to be found in
Quito, or were so at the close of the last century, according to
Velasco, distinguished by this name from the rest of the popula-
tion. Hist. de Quito, tom. I. p. 175.

one long reign, its great career of civilization and
of conquest.

The ultimate aim of its institutions was domestic
quiet. But it seemed as if this were to be obtained
only by foreign war. Tranquillity in the heart of
the monarchy, and war on its borders, was the condition of Peru. By this war it gave occupation
to a part of its people, and, by the reduction and
civilization of its barbarous neighbors, gave security to all. Every Inca sovereign, however mild
and benevolent in his domestic rule, was a warrior,
and led his armies in person. Each successive reign
extended still wider the boundaries of the empire.
Year after year saw the victorious monarch return
laden with spoils and followed by a throng of
tributary chieftains to his capital. His reception
there was a Roman triumph. The whole of its
numerous population poured out to welcome him,
dressed in the gay and picturesque costumes of the
different provinces, with banners waving above
their heads, and strewing branches and flowers
along the path of the conqueror. The Inca, borne
aloft in his golden chair on the shoulders of his
nobles, moved in solemn procession, under the tri-
umphal arches that were thrown across the way,
to the great temple of the Sun. There, without
attendants,—for all but the monarch were excluded from the hallowed precincts,—the victorious prince, stripped of his royal insignia, bare-
footed, and with all humility, approached the
awful shrine and offered up sacrifice and thanks-
giving to the glorious Deity who presided over
the fortunes of the Incas. This ceremony con-

cluded, the whole population gave itself up to festivity; music, revelry, and dancing were heard in every quarter of the capital, and illuminations and bonfires commemorated the victorious campaign of the Inca and the accession of a new territory to his empire.[77]

In this celebration we see much of the character of a religious festival. Indeed, the character of religion was impressed on all the Peruvian wars. The life of an Inca was one long crusade against the infidel, to spread wide the worship of the Sun, to reclaim the benighted nations from their brutish superstitions and impart to them the blessings of a well-regulated government. This, in the favorite phrase of our day, was the " mission " of the Inca. It was also the mission of the Christian conqueror who invaded the empire of this same Indian potentate. Which of the two executed his mission most faithfully, history must decide.

Yet the Peruvian monarchs did not show a childish impatience in the acquisition of empire. They paused after a campaign, and allowed time for the settlement of one conquest before they undertook another, and in this interval occupied themselves with the quiet administration of their kingdom, and with the long progresses which brought them into nearer intercourse with their people. During this interval, also, their new vassals had begun to accommodate themselves to the strange institutions of their masters. They learned to appreciate the value of a government

[77] Sarmiento, Relacion, MS., cap. 55 —Garcilasso, Com. Real., Parte 1, lib. 3, cap 11, 17; lib 6, cap. 16.

which raised them above the physical evils of a
state of barbarism, secured them protection of
person and a full participation in all the privileges
enjoyed by their conquerors; and, as they became
more familiar with the peculiar institutions of
the country, habit, that second nature, attached
them the more strongly to these institutions from
their very peculiarity.   Thus, by degrees, and
without violence, arose the great fabric of the
Peruvian empire, composed of numerous independent and even hostile tribes, yet, under the
influence of a common religion, common language, and common government, knit together
as one nation, animated by a spirit of love for its
institutions and devoted loyalty to its sovereign.
What a contrast to the condition of the Aztec
monarchy, on the neighboring continent, which,
composed of the like heterogeneous materials,
without any internal principle of cohesion, was
only held together by the stern pressure, from
without, of physical force!   Why the Peruvian
monarchy should have fared no better than its
rival in its conflict with European civilization will
appear in the following pages.

CHAPTER III

IT is a remarkable fact that many, if not most, of the rude tribes inhabiting the vast American continent, however disfigured their creeds may have been in other respects by a childish superstition, had attained to the sublime conception of one Great Spirit, the Creator of the Universe, who, immaterial in his own nature, was not to be dishonored by an attempt at visible representation, and who, pervading all space, was not to be circumscribed within the walls of a temple.* Yet

---

* [This statement represents what is still, probably, the common belief—based on the representations of the early missionaries and of many subsequent explorers—in regard to the religious ideas of the aboriginal races. The subject has, however, undergone of late a more critical investigation, in connection with the general inquiry as to the development of religious conceptions, and of monotheism, considered either as an original intuition or as the latest outcome of more primitive beliefs. Dr. Brinton, who considers that the intuition of an unseen power—"the sum of those intelligent activities which the individual, reasoning from the analogy of his own actions, imagines to be behind and to bring about natural phenomena"—is common to the species, traces this conception in the American mythologies, especially those in which the air, the breath of life, appears as the symbol of an animating or creative Spirit. Yet he adds, "Let none of these expressions, however, be construed to prove the distinct recognition of One Supreme Being. Of monotheism, either as displayed in the one personal definite God of the Semitic races, or in the dim pantheistic sense of the Brahmins, there was not a single instance on the American continent. . . . The phrases Good Spirit, Great Spirit, and similar ones, have occasioned endless discrepancies in the minds of travellers. In most instances they are entirely of modern origin, coined at the sug-

these elevated ideas, so far beyond the ordinary range of an untutored intellect, do not seem to have led to the practical consequences that might have been expected; and few of the American nations have shown much solicitude for the maintenance of a religious worship, or found in their faith a powerful spring of action.

But with progress in civilization ideas more akin to those of civilized communities were gradually unfolded; a liberal provision was made, and a separate order instituted, for the services of religion, which were conducted with a minute and magnificent ceremonial, that challenged comparison, in some respects, with that of the most polished nations of Christendom. This was the case with the nations inhabiting the table-land of North America, and with the natives of Bogotá, Quito, Peru, and the other elevated regions on the great Southern continent. It was, above all, the case with the Peruvians, who claimed a divine orginal for the founders of their empire, whose laws all rested on a divine sanction, and whose domestic institutions and foreign wars were alike directed to preserve and propagate their faith. Religion was the basis of their polity, the very

gestion of missionaries, applied to the white man's God." (Myths of the New World, p 52) Mr. Tylor finds among various races of North and South America, of Africa and of Polynesia, the " acknowledgment of a Supreme Creator." yet always in connection with a system of polytheism, of which this belief is the culmination. (Primitive Culture, 2d ed., vol. ii. p 332.) It may be doubted, however, whether it is possible to arrive at any certainty in regard to conceptions so vague in themselves and so liable to be moulded into definite shapes by the mediums through which they are communicated.—K]

condition, as it were, of their social existence. The government of the Incas, in its essential principles, was a theocracy.

Yet, though religion entered so largely into the fabric and conduct of the political institutions of the people, their mythology, that is, the traditionary legends by which they affected to unfold the mysteries of the universe, was exceedingly mean and puerile. Scarce one of their traditions—except the beautiful ones respecting the founders of their royal dynasty—is worthy of note, or throws much light on their own antiquities or the primitive history of man. Among the traditions of importance is one of the deluge, which they held in common with so many of the nations in all parts of the globe, and which they related with some particulars that bear resemblance to a Mexican legend.[1]

Their ideas in respect to a future state of being deserve more attention. They admitted the existence of the soul hereafter, and connected with this a belief in the resurrection of the body. They

[1] They related that, after the deluge, seven persons issued from a cave where they had saved themselves, and by them the earth was repeopled One of the traditions of the Mexicans deduced their descent, and that of the kindred tribes, in like manner, from seven persons who came from as many caves in Aztlan.* (Conf. Acosta, lib. 6, cap. 19; lib. 7, cap 2—Ondegardo, Rel. Prim., MS) The story of the deluge is told by different writers with many variations, in some of which it is not difficult to detect the plastic hand of the Christian convert

* [A similar tradition is found in some Sanscrit legends "This coincidence," remarks Dr. Brinton, "arises from the mystic powers attached to the number seven, derived from its frequent occurrence in astrology." (Myths of the New World, p. 203.) Yet the evidence he adduces will hardly apply to the American myths.—K]

assigned two distinct places for the residence of the good and of the wicked, the latter of which they fixed in the centre of the earth. The good, they supposed, were to pass a luxurious life of tranquillity and ease, which comprehended their highest notions of happiness. The wicked were to expiate their crimes by ages of wearisome labor. They associated with these ideas a belief in an evil principle or spirit, bearing the name of Çupay, whom they did not attempt to propitiate by sacrifices, and who seems to have been only a shadowy personification of sin,* that exercised little influence over their conduct.[2]

[2] Ondegardo, Rel Seg., MS.—Gomara, Hist de las Ind, cap. 123. —Garcilasso, Com. Real., Parte 1, lib. 2, cap. 2, 7.—One might suppose that the educated Peruvians—if I may so speak—imagined the common people had no souls, so little is said of their opinions as to the condition of these latter in a future life, while they are diffuse on the prospects of the higher orders, which they fondly believed were to keep pace with their condition here

* [Dr. Brinton, citing with approval the remark of Jacob Grimm, that "the idea of the Devil is foreign to all primitive religions," denies that such a conception had any existence in the American mythologies, and contends that "the Çupay of the Peruvians never was, as Prescott would have us believe, the shadowy embodiment of evil, but simply and solely their god of the dead, the Pluto of their pantheon, corresponding to the Mictla of the Mexicans." It is certain that many myths of the American Indians, in which a good and an evil power are opposed to each other, owed this idea to the later introduction of the Christian notions of Satan, or to the misconception of narrators influenced by the same belief. Yet Mr. Tylor, while admitting the skill with which many of these legends have been analyzed by Dr. Brinton, and the general force of his criticism, maintains that "rudimentary forms of Dualism, the antagonism of a Good and Evil Deity, are well known among the lower races of mankind," and, after reviewing the evidences of this conception in various stages of development, makes the pregnant remark that "the conception of the light-god as the good deity, in contrast to a rival god of evil, is one plainly suggested by nature." (Primitive Culture, i. 287–297.) It is therefore among the sun-

It was this belief in the resurrection of the body which led them to preserve the body with so much solicitude,—by a simple process, however, that, unlike the elaborate embalming of the Egyptians, consisted in exposing it to the action of the cold, exceedingly dry, and highly rarefied atmosphere of the mountains.[3] *   As they believed that the occupations in the future world would have great resemblance to those of the present, they buried with the deceased noble some of his apparel, his utensils, and, frequently, his treasures, and completed the gloomy ceremony by sacrificing his wives and favorite domestics, to bear him company and do him service in the happy regions beyond the clouds.[4] †   Vast mounds of an irregu-

[3] Such, indeed, seems to be the opinion of Garcilasso, though some writers speak of resinous and other applications for embalming the body. The appearance of the royal mummies found at Cuzco, as reported both by Ondegardo and Garcilasso, makes it probable that no foreign substance was employed for their preservation.

[4] Ondegardo, Rel. Seg., MS.—The Licentiate says that this usage continued even after the Conquest, and that he had saved the life of more than one favorite domestic who had fled to him for protection, as they were about to be sacrificed to the Manes of their deceased lords. Ibid., ubi supra.

---

worshippers that we might especially expect to find the instinctive conception of a power of darkness, as the representative not merely of death but of the evil principle   This dualism is, accordingly, the distinguishing feature of the Zoroastrian religion, and its existence in that of Peru cannot well be questioned on the sole ground of inherent improbability.—K.]

* [One may see to-day, in many a burial-place among the lofty table-lands, this natural process of embalming. No resinous substances are used: the flesh is left to dry up   Squier tells of thousands of desiccated bodies on the Tantana Marca (Steeps of Lamentation), near the fortress of Pisac (Peru, p. 531).—M.]

† [Markham will not admit that human sacrifices were made. "The statement that servants were sacrificed at the obsequies of

lar or, more frequently, oblong shape, penetrated by galleries running at right angles to each other, were raised over the dead, whose dried bodies or mummies have been found in considerable numbers, sometimes erect, but more often in the sitting posture common to the Indian tribes of both continents. Treasures of great value have also been occasionally drawn from these monumental deposits, and have stimulated speculators to repeated excavations with the hope of similar good fortune. It was a lottery like that of searching after mines, but where the chances have proved still more against the adventurers.[5]

The Peruvians, like so many other of the Indian races, acknowledged a Supreme Being, the Creator and Ruler of the Universe, whom they adored under the different names of Pachacamac * and

[5] Yet these sepulchral mines have sometimes proved worth the digging Sarmiento speaks of gold to the value of 100,000 *castellanos* as occasionally buried with the Indian lords (Relacion, MS, cap. 57); and Las Casas—not the best authority in numerical estimates—says that treasures worth more than half a million of ducats had been found within twenty years after the Conquest, in the tombs near Truxillo. (Œuvres, ed. Llorente (Paris, 1822), tom ii p 192) Baron Humboldt visited the sepulchre of a Peruvian prince, in the same quarter of the country, whence a Spaniard in 1576 drew forth a mass of gold worth a million of dollars! Vues des Cordillères, p. 29.

their masters is disproved by the fact, mentioned by the Anonymous Jesuit, that in none of the burial-places opened by the Spaniards in search of treasure were any human bones found except those of the buried lord himself" Winsor, Nar. and Crit Hist America, i. p 237 —M]

* [Whether Pachacamac was worshipped, at the place now bearing his name, before the days of the Incas or not, we may not know. What we do know is, that there was at Pachacamac a temple that had been for ages a great pilgrim resort long before the Incas conquered that part of the country. Squier, in his " Peru," devotes a

Viracocha.[6] No temple was raised to this invisible
Being, save one only in the valley which took its
name from the deity himself, not far from the
Spanish city of Lima. Even this temple had existed there before the country came under the
sway of the Incas, and was the great resort of
Indian pilgrims from remote parts of the land,
—a circumstance which suggests the idea that the
worship of this Great Spirit, though counte-

---

[6] *Pachacamac* signifies " He who sustains or gives life to the universe." The name of the great deity is sometimes expressed by
both Pachacamac and Viracocha combined. (See Balboa, Hist. du
Pérou, chap. 6 —Acosta, lib. 6, cap. 21.) An old Spaniard finds in
the popular meaning of *Viracocha*, " foam of the sea," an argument
for deriving the Peruvian civilization from some voyager from the
Old World. Conq i Pob. del Piru, MS.

---

chapter (iv.) to the ruins at Pachacamac His opinion is, that
the Incas built a vast Temple of the Sun and a House of Virgins of the Sun side by side with the shrine of the deity whose
worship they were too politic to suppress Adobe walls still mark
the site of that earliest temple El Castillo is to-day the name
given to those oldest ruins. Four vast terraces built around a
natural cave form a semi-lunar pyramid. At the southern corner
of the surface at the top, pilasters and other traces of the edifices
that once covered the spot may still be seen. " The only building
among the ruins having the Inca type is that called Mamacana,
which would seem to imply that it was a convent rather than a
temple" (p. 96) It is distant a mile and a half from El Castillo.
Built of the same material as the other structures, it differs in
style, and is unmistakably Inca in its doorways, niches, etc. Squier
found three strata of mummies—twelve desiccated bodies—at the
foot of the great temple when he visited the spot in 1865 or '66.
Other explorers, burrowing in the ruins since the twentieth century
began, have brought to light *five* strata, each stratum presenting in
the ornaments, pottery, metals, textile fabrics, etc., buried with the
dead strongly marked and easily distinguished characteristics On
that rainless coast adobe endures like granite Judging from the
strata of corpses below the temple walls, the structure may date
back even to the days of Solomon's Temple —M.]

nanced, perhaps, by their accommodating policy, did not originate with the Peruvian princes.[7] *

[7] Pedro Pizarro, Descub. y Conq., MS —Sarmiento, Relacion, MS, cap. 27.—Ulloa notices the extensive ruins of brick, which mark the probable site of the temple of Pachacamac, attesting by their present appearance its ancient magnificence and strength. Mémoires philsophiques, historiques, physiques (Paris, 1787), trad. Fr., p 78.

* [Not only this inference, but the facts on which it rests, are strenuously disputed by Mr Markham, on the ground that Pachacamac "is an Ynca word, and is wholly foreign to, and unconnected with, the coast language." It was the name, he says, given by the Incas to the coast-city, when they conquered it, "for some reason that has not been preserved, possibly on account of its size and importance" "The natives worshipped a fish-god there under a name now lost, which became famous as an oracle and attracted pilgrims, and when the Yncas conquered the place they raised a temple to the Sun on the summit of the hill commanding the city." "But they never built any temple to Pachacamac, and there never was one to that deity, except at Cuzco." (Reports of the Discovery of Peru, Introduction, xiv.–xx) There seems to be here much more of assertion than of argument or proof. The statement that there was a temple to Pachacamac at Cuzco is a novel one, for which no authority is adduced, and it is in direct contradiction to the re-iterated assertions of Garcilasso, that the Peruvians worshipped Pachacamac only "inwardly, as an unknown God," to whom they built no temples and offered no sacrifices For the statement that the Incas "*erected* a temple of the Sun" at Pachacamac (p. xix.), we are referred to Cieza de Leon, who says that "they agreed with the native chiefs and with the ministers of this god or devil, that the temple of Pachacamac should *continue* with the authority and reverence it formerly possessed, and that the loftiest part should be *set aside* as a temple of the Sun" That the temple had existed long prior to the conquest of the place by the Incas is asserted by all authorities and attested by the great antiquity of its remains. Garcilasso asserts that its builders had borrowed the conception of Pachacamac from the Incas,—a less probable supposition than that of Prescott, and equally rejected by Mr Markham, though the statement of the same author that "the Yncas placed their idols in this temple, which were figures of fishes," seems to be the chief foundation for his own account of the worship practised by the people of the coast, respecting which he admits that little is known. What is known of it with any certainty comes to us from Garcilasso de la Vega and Cieza de Leon, and both these authorities represent the temple and worship of Pachacamac as having existed in the valley of that name previous to the conquest, or rather peaceful

The deity whose worship they especially inculcated, and which they never failed to establish wherever their banners were known to penetrate, was the Sun.   It was he who, in a particular manner, presided over the destinies of man; gave light and warmth to the nations, and life to the vegetable world; whom they reverenced as the father of their royal dynasty, the founder of their empire; and whose temples rose in every city and almost every village throughout the land, while his altars smoked with burnt-offerings,—a form of sacrifice peculiar to the Peruvians among the semi-civilized nations of the New World.[8]

Besides the Sun, the Incas acknowledged various objects of worship in some way or other connected with this principal deity.   Such was the Moon, his sister-wife; the Stars, revered as part of her heavenly train,—though the fairest of them, Venus, known to the Peruvians by the name of Chasca, or the " youth with the long and curling locks," was adored as the page of the Sun, whom he attends so closely in his rising and in his setting. They dedicated temples also to the Thunder and Lightning,[9] in whom they recognized the Sun's

[8] At least, so says Dr. McCulloh; and no better authority can be required on American antiquities. (Researches, p. 392.)   Might he not have added *barbarous* nations, also?

[9] Thunder, Lightning, and Thunderbolt could be all expressed by the Peruvians in one word, *Illapa*.   Hence some Spaniards have inferred a knowledge of the Trinity in the natives!   " The Devil stole all he could," exclaims Herrera, with righteous indignation. (Hist. general, dec. 5, lib. 4, cap. 5.)   These, and even rasher con-

subjugation, of the province by the Incas, and their sanction of this religion, in conjunction with that of the Sun, as the result of a compromise.—K.]

dread ministers, and to the Rainbow, whom they worshipped as a beautiful emanation of their glorious deity.[10]

In addition to these, the subjects of the Incas enrolled among their inferior deities many objects in nature, as the elements, the winds, the earth,

clusions (see Acosta, lib. 5, cap 28), are scouted by Garcilasso, as inventions of Indian converts, willing to please the imaginations of their Christian teachers. (Com. Real, Parte 1, lib. 2, cap 5, 6; lib. 3, cap 21.) Imposture on the one hand, and credulity on the other, have furnished a plentiful harvest of absurdities, which has been diligently gathered in by the pious antiquary of a later generation.

[10] Garcilasso's assertion that these heavenly bodies were objects of reverence as holy things, but not of worship (Com. Real, Parte 1, lib, 2, cap 1, 23), is contradicted by Ondegardo, Rel. Seg, MS,—Dec. de la Aud. Real, MS.,—Herrera, Hist. general, dec 5, lib. 4, cap. 4,—Gomara, Hist. de las Ind, cap. 121,—and, I might add, by almost every writer of authority whom I have consulted.* It is contradicted, in a manner, by the admission of Garcilasso himself, that these several objects were all personified by the Indians as living beings, and had temples dedicated to them as such, with their effigies delineated in the same manner as was that of the Sun in his dwelling. Indeed, the effort of the historian to reduce the worship of the Incas to that of the Sun alone is not very reconcilable with what he elsewhere says of the homage paid to Pachacamac, above all, and to Rimac, the great oracle of the common people. The Peruvian mythology was, probably, not unlike that of Hindostan, where, under two, or at most three, principal deities, were assembled a host of inferior ones, to whom the nation paid religious homage, as personifications of the different objects in nature.

* ["Mr. Prescott gives his high authority in support of the Spanish historians Ondegardo, Herrera, and Gomara, and against Garcilasso de la Vega, in this matter [the worship of lightning and thunder as deities] Yet surely, in a question relating to the religion of his ancestors, the testimony of the Ynca . . . is worth more than that of all the Spanish historians put together, Cieza de Leon alone excepted" (Markham, translation of Garcilasso (1869), vol i p. 103, note.) "The sun, moon, and *thunder* appear to have been the deities next in importance to Pachayachachic; sacrifices were made to them at all the periodical festivities, and several of the prayers given by Molina are addressed to them" Markham, Rites and Laws of the Yncas (1873), Introduction, p. xi.—K.]

the air, great mountains and rivers, which impressed them with ideas of sublimity and power, or were supposed in some way or other to exercise a mysterious influence over the destinies of man.[11] They adopted also a notion, not unlike that professed by some of the schools of ancient philosophy, that every thing on earth had its archetype or idea, its *mother*, as they emphatically styled it, which they held sacred, as, in some sort, its spiritual essence.[12] But their system, far from being limited even to these multiplied objects of devotion, embraced within its ample folds the numerous deities of the conquered nations, whose images were transported to the capital, where the burdensome charges of their worship were defrayed by their respective provinces. It was a rare stroke of policy in the Incas, who could thus accommodate their religion to their interests.[13]

[11] Ondegardo, Rel. Seg., MS—These consecrated objects were termed *huacas*,—a word of most prolific import; since it signified a temple, a tomb, any natural object remarkable for its size or shape, in short, a cloud of meanings, which by their contradictory sense have thrown incalculable confusion over the writings of historians and travellers.

[12] "La orden por donde fundavan sus huacas que ellos llamavan á las Idolatrias hera porque decian que todas criava el sol i que les dava madre por madre que mostravan á la tierra, porque decian que tenia madre, i tenian lé echo su vulto i sus adoratorios, i al fuego decian que tambien tenia madre i al mais i á las otras sementeras i á las ovejas iganado decian que tenian madre, i á la chocha ques el brevaje que ellos usan decian que el vinagre della hera la madre i lo reverenciavan i llamavan mama agua madre del vinagre, i á cada cosa adoravan destas de su manera." Conq i Pob. del Piru, MS

[13] Pedro Pizarro, Descub y Conq, MS.—So it seems to have been regarded by the Licientiate Ondegardo: " E los Idolos estaban en aq¹ *galpon* grande de la casa del Sol, y cada Idolo destos tenia su servicio y gastos y mugeres, y en la casa del Sol le iban á hacer reverencia los que venian de su provincial para lo qual é sacrificios

But the worship of the Sun constituted the peculiar care of the Incas, and was the object of their lavish expenditure. The most ancient of the many temples dedicated to this divinity was in the island of Titicaca, whence the royal founders of the Peruvian line were said to have proceeded. From this circumstance, this sanctuary was held in peculiar veneration. Every thing which belonged to it, even the broad fields of maize which surrounded the temple and formed part of its domain, imbibed a portion of its sanctity. The yearly produce was distributed among the different public magazines, in small quantities to each, as something that would sanctify the remainder of the store. Happy was the man who could secure even an ear of the blessed harvest for his own granary![14]

But the most renowned of the Peruvian temples, the pride of the capital, and the wonder of the empire, was at Cuzco, where, under the munificence of successive sovereigns, it had become so enriched that it received the name of *Coricancha*, or "the Place of Gold." It consisted of a principal building and several chapels and inferior edifices, covering a large extent of ground in the heart of the city, and completely encompassed by a wall, which, with the edifices, was all constructed of stone. The work

que se hacian proveian de su misma tierra ordinaria é muy abundantemente por la misma orden que lo hacian quando estaba en la misma provincia, que daba gran autoridad á mi parecer é aun fuerza á estos Ingas que cierto me causó gran admiracion" Rel. Seg, MS

[14] Garcilasso, Com. Real., Parte 1, lib. 3, cap. 25.

was of the kind already described in the other public buildings of the country, and was so finely executed that a Spaniard who saw it in its glory assures us he could call to mind only two edifices in Spain which, for their workmanship, were at all to be compared with it.[15] Yet this substantial and, in some respects, magnificent structure was thatched with straw!

The interior of the temple was the most worthy of admiration. It was literally a mine of gold. On the western wall was emblazoned a representation of the deity, consisting of a human countenance looking forth from amidst innumerable rays of light, which emanated from it in every direction, in the same manner as the sun is often personified with us. The figure was engraved on a massive plate of gold of enormous dimensions, thickly powdered with emeralds and precious stones.[16] It was so situated in front of the great eastern portal that the rays of the morning sun fell directly upon it at its rising, lighting up the

[15] " Tenia este Templo en circuito mas de quatro cientos pasos, todo cercado de una muralla fuerte, labrado todo el edificio de cantera muy excelente de fina piedra, muy bien puesta y asentada, v algunas piedras eran muy grandes v soberbias, no tenian mezcla de tierra ni cal, sino con el betun que ellos suelen hacer sus edificios, y estan tan bien labradas estas piedras que no se les parece mezcla ni juntura ninguna   En toda España no he visto cosa que pueda comparar á estas paredes y postura de piedra, sino, á la torre que llaman la Calahorra que está junto con la puente de Cordoba, v á una obra que vi en Toledo, cuando fui á presentar la primera parte de mi Cronica al Principe Dⁿ Felipe." Sarmiento, Relacion, MS., cap. 24.

[16] Conq. i Pob. del Piru, MS —Cieza de Leon, Cronica, cap. 44, 92. —" La figura del Sol, muy grande, hecha de oro obrada muy primamente engastonada en muchas piedras ricas." Sarmiento, Relacion, MS., cap 24.

whole apartment with an effulgence that seemed
more than natural, and which was reflected back
from the golden ornaments with which the walls
and ceiling were everywhere incrusted. Gold, in
the figurative language of the people, was "the
tears wept by the sun,"[17] and every part of the
interior of the temple glowed with burnished
plates and studs of the precious metal. The
cornices which surrounded the walls of the sanctuary were of the same costly material; and a
broad belt or frieze of gold, let into the stone-
work, encompassed the whole exterior of the
edifice.[18]

Adjoining the principal structures were several chapels of smaller dimensions. One of them
was consecrated to the Moon, the deity held next
in reverence, as the mother of the Incas. Her
effigy was delineated in the same manner as that
of the Sun, on a vast plate that nearly covered one
side of the apartment. But this plate, as well as
all the decorations of the building, was of silver,
as suited to the pale, silvery light of the beautiful
planet. There were three other chapels, one of
which was dedicated to the host of Stars, who
formed the bright court of the Sister of the Sun;
another was consecrated to his dread ministers of
vengeance, the Thunder and the Lightning; and

[17] " I al oro asimismo decian que era lagrimas que el Sol llorava."
Conq. i Pob. del Piru, MS.

[18] Sarmiento, Relacion, MS, cap 24.—Antig y Monumentos del
Peru, MS.—"Cercada junto á la techumbre de una plancha de oro
de palmo i medio de ancho i lo mismo tenian por de dentro en cada
bohio ó casa i aposento." (Conq. i Pob del Piru, MS.) "Tenia
una cinta de planchas de oro de anchor de mas de un palmo enlaza-
das en las piedras." Pedro Pizarro, Descub. y Conq, MS.

a third, to the Rainbow, whose many-colored arch spanned the walls of the edifice with hues almost as radiant as its own.   There were, besides, several other buildings, or insulated apartments, for the accommodation of the numerous priests who officiated in the services of the temple.[19]

All the plate, the ornaments, the utensils of every description, appropriated to the uses of religion, were of gold or silver.   Twelve immense vases of the latter metal stood on the floor of the great saloon, filled with grain of the Indian corn;[20] the censers for the perfumes, the ewers which held the water for sacrifice, the pipes which conducted it through subterraneous channels into the buildings, the reservoirs that received it, even the agricultural implements used in the gardens of the temple, were all of the same rich materials. The gardens, like those described belonging to the royal palaces, sparkled with flowers of gold and silver, and various imitations of the vegetable kingdom.   Animals, also, were to be found there, —among which the llama, with its golden fleece, was most conspicuous—executed in the same style,

[19] Sarmiento, Relacion, MS., cap. 24.—Garcilasso, Com. Real, Parte 1, lib 3, cap 21.—Pedro Pizarro, Descub. y Conq, MS.

[20] " El bulto del Sol tenian mui grande de oro, i todo el servicio desta casa era de plata i oro, i tenian doze horones de plata blanca que dos hombres no abrazarian cada uno quadrados, i eran mas altos que una buena pica donde hechavan el maiz que havian de dar al Sol, segun ellos decian que comiese." Conq. i Pob. del Piru, MS.— The original, as the Spanish reader perceives, says each of these silver vases or bins was as high as a good lance, and so large that two men with outspread arms could barely encompass them!   As this might perhaps embarrass even the most accommodating faith, I have preferred not to become responsible for any particular dimensions.

and with a degree of skill which, in this instance, probably, did not surpass the excellence of the material.[21]

If the reader sees in this fairy picture only the romantic coloring of some fabulous *El Dorado,* he must recall what has been said before in reference to the palaces of the Incas, and consider that these " Houses of the Sun," as they were styled, were the common reservoir into which flowed all the streams of public and private benefaction throughout the empire. Some of the statements, through credulity, and others, in the desire of exciting admiration, may be greatly exaggerated; but in the coincidence of contemporary testimony it is not easy to determine the exact line which should mark the measure of our skepticism. Certain it is that the glowing picture I have given is warranted by those who saw these buildings in their pride, or shortly after they had been despoiled by the cupidity of their countrymen. Many of the costly articles were buried by the natives, or thrown into the waters of the rivers and the lakes; but enough remained to attest the

[21] Levinus Apollonius, fol. 38 Garcilasso, Com. Real , Parte 1, lib. 3, cap 24.—Pedro Pizarro, Descub. y Conq , MS —" Tenian un Jardin que los Terrones eran pedazos de oro fino y estaban artificiosamente sembrado de maizales los quales eran oro asi las Cañas de ello como las ojas y mazorcas, y estaban tan bien plantados que aunque hiciesen recios bientos no se arrancaban. Sin todo esto tenian hechas mas de veinte obejas de oro con sus Corderos y los Pastores con sus ondas y cayados que las guardaban hecho de este metal; havia mucha cantidad de Tinajas de oro y de Plata y esmeraldas, vasos, ollas y todo genero de vasijas todo de oro fino; por otras Paredes tenian esculpidas y pintadas otras mayores cosas, en fin era uno de los ricos Templos que hubo en el mundo." Sarmiento, Relacion, MS , cap. 24.

unprecedented opulence of these religious establishments. Such things as were in their nature portable were speedily removed, to gratify the craving of the Conquerors, who even tore away the solid cornices and frieze of gold from the great temple, filling the vacant places with the cheaper, but—since it affords no temptation to avarice—more durable, material of plaster. Yet even thus shorn of their splendor the venerable edifices still presented an attraction to the spoiler, who found in their dilapidated walls an inexhaustible quarry for the erection of other buildings. On the very ground once crowned by the gorgeous Coricancha rose the stately church of St. Dominic, one of the most magnificent structures of the New World. Fields of maize and lucerne now bloom on the spot which glowed with the golden gardens of the temple; and the friar chants his orisons within the consecrated precincts once occupied by the Children of the Sun.[22]

Besides the great temple of the Sun, there was a large number of inferior temples and religious houses in the Peruvian capital and its environs, amounting, as is stated, to three or four hundred.[23] For Cuzco was a sanctified spot, venerated not only as the abode of the Incas, but of all those deities who presided over the motley nations of the empire. It was the city beloved of the Sun; where his worship was maintained in its splendor;

[22] Miller's Memoirs, vol ii. pp. 223, 224
[23] Herrera, Hist. general, dec. 5, lib. 4, cap. 8.—"Havia en aquella ciudad y legua y media de la redonda quatrocientos y tantos lugares, donde se hacian sacrificios, y se gastava mucha suma de hacienda en ellos." Ondegardo, Rel. Prim., MS.

" where every fountain, pathway, and wall," says an ancient chronicler, "was regarded as a holy mystery." [24] And unfortunate was the Indian noble who, at some period or other of his life, had not made his pilgrimage to the Peruvian Mecca.

Other temples and religious dwellings were scattered over the provinces, and some of them constructed on a scale of magnificence that almost rivalled that of the metropolis. The attendants on these composed an army of themselves. The whole number of functionaries, including those of the sacerdotal order, who officiated at the Coricancha alone, was no less than four thousand.[25]

At the head of all, both here and throughout the land, stood the great High Priest, or Villac Vmu, as he was called. He was second only to the Inca in dignity, and was usually chosen from his brothers or nearest kindred. He was appointed by the monarch, and held his office for life; and he, in turn, appointed to all the subordinate stations of his own order. This order was very numerous. Those members of it who officiated in the House of the Sun, in Cuzco, were taken exclusively from the sacred race of the Incas. The ministers in the provincial temples were drawn from the families of the curacas; but the office

[24] " Que aquella ciudad del Cuzco era casa y morada de Dioses, é ansi nó habia en toda ella fuente ni paso ni pared que nó dixesen que tenia misterio." Ondegardo, Rel Seg, MS.

[25] Conq. i Pob del Piru, MS—An army, indeed, if, as Cieza de Leon states, the number of priests and menials employed in the famous temple of Bilcas, on the route to Chili, amounted to 40,000! (Cronica, cap 89.) Every thing relating to these Houses of the Sun appears to have been on a grand scale. But we may easily believe this a clerical error for 4000.

of high-priest in each district was reserved for one of the blood royal. It was designed by this regulation to preserve the faith in its purity, and to guard against any departure from the stately ceremonial which it punctiliously prescribed.[26]

The sacerdotal order, though numerous, was not distinguished by any peculiar badge or costume from the rest of the nation. Neither was it the sole depository of the scanty science of the country, nor was it charged with the business of instruction, nor with those parochial duties, if they may so be called, which bring the priest in contact with the great body of the people,—as was the case in Mexico. The cause of this peculiarity may probably be traced to the existence of a superior order, like that of the Inca nobles, whose sanctity of birth so far transcended all human appointments that they in a manner engrossed whatever there was of religious veneration in the people. They were, in fact, the holy order of the state. Doubtless, any of them might, as very many of them did, take on themselves the sacerdotal functions; and their own insignia and peculiar privileges were too well understood to require any further badge to separate them from the people.

The duties of the priest were confined to ministration in the temple. Even here his attendance

[26] Sarmiento, Relacion, MS., cap. 27 —Conq i Pob del Piru, MS. —It was only while the priests were engaged in the service of the temples that they were maintained, according to Garcilasso, from the estates of the Sun. At other times they were to get their support from their own lands, which, if he is correct, were assigned to them in the same manner as to the other orders of the nation Com. Real., Parte 1, lib. 5, cap. 8.

was not constant, as he was relieved after a stated interval by other brethren of his order, who succeeded one another in regular rotation. His science was limited to an acquaintance with the fasts and festivals of his religion, and the appropriate ceremonies which distinguished them. This, however frivolous might be its character, was no easy acquisition; for the ritual of the Incas involved a routine of observances as complex and elaborate as ever distinguished that of any nation, whether pagan or Christian. Each month had its appropriate festival, or rather festivals. The four principal had reference to the Sun, and commemorated the great periods of his annual progress, the solstices and equinoxes. Perhaps the most magnificent of all the national solemnities was the feast of Raymi, held at the period of the summer solstice, when the Sun, having touched the southern extremity of his course, retraced his path, as if to gladden the hearts of his chosen people by his presence. On this occasion the Indian nobles from the different quarters of the country thronged to the capital to take part in the great religious celebration.

For three days previous, there was a general fast, and no fire was allowed to be lighted in the dwellings. When the appointed day arrived, the Inca and his court, followed by the whole population of the city, assembled at early dawn in the great square to greet the rising of the Sun. They were dressed in their gayest apparel, and the Indian lords vied with each other in the display of costly ornaments and jewels on their persons, while canopies of gaudy feather-work and richly-tinted stuffs, borne by the attendants over their heads, gave to the great square, and the streets that emptied into it, the appearance of being spread over with one vast and magnificent awning. Eagerly they watched the coming of their deity, and no sooner did his first yellow rays strike the turrets and loftiest buildings of the capital than a shout of gratulation broke forth from the assembled multitude, accompanied by songs of triumph and the wild melody of barbaric instruments, that swelled louder and louder as his bright orb, rising above the mountain-range towards the east, shone in full splendor on his votaries. After the usual ceremonies of adoration, a libation was offered to the great deity by the Inca, from a huge golden vase, filled with the fermented liquor of maize or of maguey, which, after the monarch had tasted it himself, he dispensed among his royal kindred. These ceremonies completed, the vast assembly was arranged in order of procession and took its way towards the Coricancha.[27]

As they entered the street of the sacred edifice, all divested themselves of their sandals, except the Inca and his family, who did the same on passing through the portals of the temple, where none but these august personages were admitted.[28]   After

[27] Dec. de la Aud. Real., MS.—Sarmiento, Relacion, MS., cap. 27. —The reader will find a brilliant, and not very extravagant, account of the Peruvian festivals in Marmontel's romance of *Les Incas* The French author saw in their gorgeous ceremonial a fitting introduction to his own literary pageant. Tom. i. chap. 1–4.

[28] " Ningun Indio comun osaba pasar por la calle del Sol calzado; ni ninguno, aunque fuese mui grand Señor, entrava en las casas del Sol con zapatos." Conq. 1 Pob. del Piru, MS.

a decent time spent in devotion, the sovereign, attended by his courtly train, again appeared, and preparations were made to commence the sacrifice. This, with the Peruvians, consisted of animals, grain, flowers, and sweet-scented gums,—sometimes of human beings, on which occasions a child or beautiful maiden was usually selected as the victim. But such sacrifices were rare, being reserved to celebrate some great public event, as a coronation, the birth of a royal heir, or a great victory. They were never followed by those cannibal repasts familiar to the Mexicans and to many of the fierce tribes conquered by the Incas. Indeed, the conquests of these princes might well be deemed a blessing to the Indian nations, if it were only from their suppression of cannibalism, and the diminution, under their rule, of human sacrifices.[29]

[29] Garcilasso de la Vega flatly denies that the Incas were guilty of human sacrifices, and maintains, on the other hand, that they uniformly abolished them in every country they subdued, where they had previously existed. (Com. Real, Parte 1, lib 2, cap. 9, et alibi.) But in this material fact he is unequivocally contradicted by Sarmiento, Relacion, MS, cap. 22,—Dec. de la Aud. Real, MS.,—Montesinos, Mem antiguas, MS, lib 2, cap 8,—Balboa, Hist. du Pérou, chap. 5, 8,—Cieza de Leon, Cronica, cap. 72,—Ondegardo, Rel. Seg, MS.,—Acosta, lib. 5, cap. 19,—and I might add, I suspect, were I to pursue the inquiry, by nearly every ancient writer of authority; some of whom, having come into the country soon after the Conquest, while its primitive institutions were in vigor, are entitled to more deference in a matter of this kind than Garcilasso himself. It was natural that the descendant of the Incas should desire to relieve his race from so odious an imputation; and we must have charity for him if he does show himself on some occasions, where the honor of his country is at stake, "high gravel blind." It should be added, in justice to the Peruvian government, that the best authorities concur in the admission that the sacrifices were few,

At the feast of Raymi, the sacrifice usually
offered was that of the llama; and the priest,

both in number and in magnitude, being reserved for such extraordinary occasions as those mentioned in the text.*

* [Markham asserts that "the Incas did not offer up human sacrifices." He argues the question at length in a note appended to
his translation of Garcilasso de la Vega. Royal Commentaries,
Second Book (vol. i. pp. 139–142, of the Royal Commentaries of the
Inca, as published by the Hakluyt Society). The mistake of the
writers, quoted by Prescott, who asserted that the Incas did offer
human sacrifices, was due, Mr. Markham says, to their ignorance of
the Quichua language. Human sacrifices were offered up by many
of the tribes the Incas conquered, but never by the Incas themselves. As the matter must still be regarded as undecided, I give
the condensation of his argument, which Mr. Markham published
in the Narrative and Critical History of America, vol. i. pp.
237, 238, notes. "The sacrifices were called *runa, yuyac,* and
huahua. The Spaniards thought that runa and yuyac signified men,
and huahua, children. This was not the case when speaking of sac-
rificial victims. Runa was applied to a male sacrifice, huahua to the
lambs, and yuyac signified an adult, or full-grown animal. The sacri-
ficial animals were also called after the names of those who offered
them, which was another cause of erroneous assumptions by Spanish
writers. There was a law strictly prohibiting human sacrifices
among the conquered tribes; and the statement that servants were
sacrificed at the obsequies of their masters is disproved by the fact,
mentioned by the Anonymous Jesuit, that in none of the burial-
places opened by the Spaniards in search of treasure were any
human bones found except those of the buried lord himself.

"Prescott accepted the statement that human sacrifices were offered by the Incas because six authorities—Sarmiento, Cieza de
Leon, Montesinos, Balboa, Ondegardo, and Acosta—outnumbered
the single authority on the other side, Garcilasso de la Vega, who,
moreover, was believed to be prejudiced, owing to his relationship
to the Incas. Sarmiento and Cieza de Leon are one and the same
so that the number of authorities for human sacrifices is reduced to
five. Cieza de Leon, Montesinos, and Balboa adopted the belief that
human sacrifices were offered up, through a misunderstanding of
the words yuyac and huahua. Acosta had little or no acquaintance
with the language, as is proved by the numerous linguistic blunders
in his work. Ondegardo wrote at a time when he scarcely knew
the language and had no interpreters; for it was in 1554, when he
was judge at Cuzco. At that time all the annalists and old men
had fled into the forests, because of the insurrection of Francisco
Hernandez Giron." "The authorities who deny the practice are

after opening the body of his victim, sought in
the appearances which it exhibited to read the

numerous and important. These are Francisco de Chaves, one of
the best and most able of the original conquerors; Juan de Oliva;
the Licentiate Alvarez; Fray Marcos Jofre; the Licentiate Falcon,
in his Apologia pro Indis; Melchior Hernandez, in his dictionary,
under the words horpay and huahua; the Anonymous Jesuit, in his
most valuable narrative; and Garcilasso de la Vega These eight
authorities outweigh the five quoted by Prescott, both as regards
number and importance. So that the evidence against human sacrifices is conclusive. The quipus, as the Anonymous Jesuit tells us,
also prove that there was a law prohibiting human sacrifices

"The assertion that two hundred children and one thousand men
were sacrificed at the coronation of Huayna Ccapac was made; but
these huahuas were not children of men, but young lambs, which
are called children; and the yuyac and runa were not men, but
adult llamas."

Singularly enough, Mr. Markham says nothing of the account
Christoval de Molina gives of human sacrifices, although he had himself translated that account for the Hakluyt Society (Rites and
Laws of the Incas) It could not be because he believed Molina to
be as ignorant concerning the meaning of yuyac and huahua as
even Cieza de Leon; Montesinos, and Balboa. Of Molina he writes
(Winsor, Nar. and Crit. Hist. of America, p. 262, vol. 1.): "Next to
Blas Valera, the most important authority on Inca civilization
among the Spanish priests who were in Peru during the sixteenth
century, is undoubtedly Christoval de Molina. . . . His *mastery of
the Quichua language*, his intimacy with the native chiefs and
learned men, and his long residence at Cuzco give Molina a very
high place as an authority on Inca civilization."

Molina writes, "The Ccapac-cocha was instituted by Pachacutec
Inca Yupanqui (circa 1400), and was as follows: The provinces
. . brought to this city from each lineage or tribe one or two male
and female children, aged about ten years. They also brought
cloth and flocks . . . The children and the other sacrifices walked
around the statues of the Creator. . . . So the children were strangled and buried with the silver figures of sheep. . . They began to
make sacrifices in Cuzco in the following order: . . . After this
prayer they strangled the children, first giving them to eat and
drink, that they might not enter the presence of the Creator dis-
contented and hungry. From others they took out the hearts while
yet alive, . . . and finally they interred the bodies with the other
sacrifices .   *The children that could walk went on foot, and
others were carried in their mothers' arms.*   . They also had a
custom . . . of selecting some of the handsomest of the conquered

lesson of the mysterious future. If the auguries were unpropitious, a second victim was slaughtered, in the hope of receiving some more comfortable assurance. The Peruvian augur might have learned a good lesson of the Romans,—to consider every omen as favorable which served the interests of his country.[30]

[30] "Augurque cum esset, dicere ausus est, optimis auspiciis ea geri, quæ pro reipublicæ salute gererentur." (Cicero, De Senectute)—This inspection of the entrails of animals for the purpose of divination is worthy of note, as a most rare, if not a solitary, instance of the kind among the nations of the New World, though so familiar in the ceremonial of sacrifice among the pagan nations of the Old.

---

people and sending them to Cuzco, where they were sacrificed to the Sun," etc, etc. Markham's translation of Molina's Fables and Rites of the Incas (Hakluyt Society), pp 54–59.

In the same volume, Narratives of the Rites and Laws of the Incas, is also published a translation by Mr. Markham of Salcamayhua's Account of the Antiquities of Peru. Salcamayhua was an Indian author, but not of Inca lineage. "His narrative of events and record of customs and ceremonies are valuable so long as they are given their due place" . . . He "was intimately acquainted with the language, which was his own, and he received the traditions from his own people." (Markham, Introduction, p. xvi.) Salcamayhua, writing of Pachacutec's death, tells us that "many old captains were buried with him, together with all his pages, whom he would require for his service in the other life. They made them drunk before they were put to death" (p. 100) (Of course, these subordinates were not buried in his *grave*, for Pachacutec was placed in the house of the dead bodies of the other Incas) When Tupac Yupanqui died and Huayna Ccapac came to the throne (circa 1475), "they mourned for the Inca as they had done for Pachacutec, forming two armies, one of men, the other of women, and they buried many yanas (servants), pachac (officers in command of a hundred men), women, and servants who were beloved by the Inca" (p. 104).

These two writers are not in the list mentioned by Prescott, whose position is therefore strengthened by their testimony. Why they were not referred to by Markham in his discussion of the question in Winsor's History it is difficult to imagine. He had already translated their works, as he tells us on page 274, vol i., of that history.—M.]

A fire was then kindled by means of a concave mirror of polished metal, which, collecting the rays of the sun into a focus upon a quantity of dried cotton, speedily set it on fire. It was the expedient used on the like occasions in ancient Rome, at least under the reign of the pious Numa. When the sky was overcast, and the face of the good deity was hidden from his worshippers, which was esteemed a bad omen, fire was obtained by means of friction. The sacred flame was intrusted to the care of the Virgins of the Sun; and if, by any neglect, it was suffered to go out in the course of the year, the event was regarded as a calamity that boded some strange disaster to the monarchy.[31] A burnt-offering of the victims was then made on the altars of the deity. This sacrifice was but the prelude to the slaughter of a great number of llamas, part of the flocks of the Sun, which furnished a banquet not only for the Inca and his court, but for the people, who made amends at these festivals for the frugal fare to which they were usually condemned. A fine bread or cake, kneaded of maize flour by the fair hands of the Virgins of the Sun, was also placed on the royal board, where the Inca, presiding over the feast, pledged his great nobles in generous goblets of the fermented liquor of the country, and the long revelry of the day was closed at night by music

[31] "Vigilemque sacraverat ignem,
Excubias divûm æternas."

Plutarch, in his life of Numa, describes the reflectors used by the Romans for kindling the sacred fire, as concave instruments of brass, though not spherical like the Peruvian, but of a triangular form.

and dancing. Dancing and drinking were the
favorite pastimes of the Peruvians. These amuse-
ments continued for several days, though the sacrifices terminated on the first. Such was the great
festival of Raymi; and the recurrence of this and
similar festivities gave relief to the monotonous
routine of toil prescribed to the lower orders of
the community.[32]

In the distribution of bread and wine at this
high festival, the orthodox Spaniards who first
came into the country saw a striking resemblance
to the Christian communion;[33] as in the practice
of confession and penance, which, in a most irregular form indeed, seems to have been used by the
Peruvians, they discerned a coincidence with
another of the sacraments of the Church.[34] The
good fathers were fond of tracing such coincidences, which they considered as the contrivance
of Satan, who thus endeavored to delude his victims by counterfeiting the blessed rites of Christianity.[35] Others, in a different vein, imagined

[32] Acosta, lib. 5, cap 28, 29.—Garcilasso, Com. Real , Parte 1, lib.
6, cap. 23.

[33] " That which is most admirable in the hatred and presumption
of Sathan is, that he not onely counterfeited in idolatry and sacrifices, but also in certain ceremonies, our sacraments, which Jesus
Christ our Lord instituted, and the holy Church uses, having especially pretended to imitate, in some sort, the sacrament of the communion, which is the most high and divine of all others." Acosta,
lib. 5, cap 23.

[34] Herrera, Hist. general, dec. 5, lib. 4, cap 4.—Ondegardo, Rel.
Prim., MS.—"The father of lies would likewise counterfeit the
sacrament of Confession, and in his idolatries sought to be honored
with ceremonies very like to the manner of Christians." Acosta,
lib. 5, cap 25

[35] Cieza de Leon, not content with many marvellous accounts of
the influence and real apparition of Satan in the Indian ceremonies,

that they saw in such analogies the evidence that some of the primitive teachers of the gospel, perhaps an apostle himself, had paid a visit to these distant regions and scattered over them the seeds of religious truth.[36] But it seems hardly necessary to invoke the Prince of Darkness, or the intervention of the blessed saints, to account for coincidences which have existed in countries far removed from the light of Christianity, and in ages, indeed, when its light had not yet risen on the world. It is much more reasonable to refer such casual points of resemblance to the general constitution of man and the necessities of his moral nature.[37]

Another singular analogy with Roman Catholic institutions is presented by the Virgins of the Sun, the " elect," as they were called,[38] to whom I have

has garnished his volume with numerous wood-cuts representing the Prince of Evil in bodily presence, with the usual accompaniments of tail, claws, etc., as if to re-enforce the homilies in his text! The Peruvian saw in his idol a god His Christian conqueror saw in it the Devil One may be puzzled to decide which of the two might lay claim to the grossest superstition

[36] Piedrahita, the historian of the Muyscas, is satisfied that this apostle must have been St. Bartholomew, whose travels were known to have been extensive (Conq de Granada, Parte 1, lib. 1, cap. 3) The Mexican antiquaries consider St. Thomas as having had charge of the mission to the people of Anahuac. These two apostles, then, would seem to have divided the New World, at least the civilized portions of it, between them. How they came, whether by Behring's Straits, or directly across the Atlantic, we are not informed. Velasco—a writer of the eighteenth century!—has little doubt that they did really come. Hist de Quito, tom. 1 pp. 89, 90.

[37] The subject is illustrated by some examples in the " History of the Conquest of Mexico," vol. iv., Appendix, since the same usages in that country led to precisely the same rash conclusions among the Conquerors.

[38] " Llamavase Casa de Escogidas; porque las escogian, ó por Linage, ó por Hermosura " Garcilasso, Com. Real., Parte 1, lib. 4, cap. 1.

already had occasion to refer. These were young maidens, dedicated to the service of the deity, who, at a tender age, were taken from their homes and introduced into convents, where they were placed under the care of certain elderly matrons, *mamaconas,* who had grown gray within their walls.[39] Under these venerable guides the holy virgins were instructed in the nature of their religious duties. They were employed in spinning and embroidery, and, with the fine hair of the vicuña, wove the hangings for the temples, and the apparel for the Inca and his household.[40] It was their duty, above all, to watch over the sacred fire obtained at the festival of Raymi. From the moment they entered the establishment, they were cut off from all connection with the world, even with their own family and friends. No one but the Inca, and the Coya or queen, might enter the consecrated precincts. The greatest attention was paid to their morals, and visitors were sent every year to inspect the institutions and to report on the state of their discipline.[41] Woe to the unhappy maiden who was detected in an intrigue! By the stern law of the Incas, she was to be buried alive, her lover was to be strangled, and the town or village to which he belonged was to be razed to the ground, and "sowed with stones," as if to efface every me-

[39] Ondegardo, Rel Prim , MS.—The word *mamacona* signified "matron;" *mama,* the first half of this compound word, as already noticed, meaning "mother." See Garcilasso, Com. Real , Parte 1, lib. 4, cap. 1.

[40] Pedro Pizarro, Descub. y Conq., MS.

[41] Dec. de la Aud. Real , MS.

morial of his existence.[42]   One is astonished to find
so close a resemblance between the institutions of
the American Indian, the ancient Roman, and the
modern Catholic! Chastity and purity of life are
virtues in woman that would seem to be of equal
estimation with the barbarian and with the civilized.—Yet the ultimate destination of the inmates
of these religious houses was materially different.

The great establishment at Cuzco consisted
wholly of maidens of the royal blood, who
amounted, it is said, to no less than fifteen hundred.   The provincial convents were supplied
from the daughters of the curacas and inferior
nobles, and occasionally, where a girl was recommended by great personal attractions, from the
lower classes of the people.[43]   The " Houses of
the Virgins of the Sun " consisted of low ranges
of stone buildings, covering a large extent of
ground, surrounded by high walls, which excluded
those within entirely from observation.   They

[42] Balboa, Hist. du Pérou, chap. 9 —Fernandez, Hist. del Peru,
Parte 2, lib. 3, cap. 11.—Garcilasso, Com. Real., Parte 1, lib. 4, cap.
3.—According to the historian of the Incas, the terrible penalty
was never incurred by a single lapse on the part of the fair sister-
hood; though, if it had been, the sovereign, he assures us, would
have "exacted it to the letter, with as little compunction as he
would have drowned a puppy" (Com. Real, Parte 1, lib. 4, cap
3)   Other writers contend, on the contrary, that these Virgins had
very little claim to the reputation of Vestals   (See Pedro Pizarro,
Descub. y Conq, MS.—Gomara, Hist. de las Ind, cap. 121)   Such
imputations are common enough on the inhabitants of religious
houses, whether pagan or Christian.   They are contradicted in the
present instance by the concurrent testimony of most of those who
had the best opportunity of arriving at truth, and are made particularly improbable by the superstitious reverence entertained for
the Incas.

[43] Pedro Pizarro, Descub. y Conq, MS.—Garcilasso, Com Real.,
Parte 1, lib. 4, cap. 1.

were provided with every accommodation for the fair inmates, and were embellished in the same sumptuous and costly manner as the palaces of the Incas, and the temples; for they received the particular care of the government, as an important part of the religious establishment.[44]

Yet the career of all the inhabitants of these cloisters was not confined within their narrow walls. Though Virgins of the Sun, they were brides of the Inca, and at a marriageable age the most beautiful among them were selected for the honors of his bed and transferred to the royal seraglio. The full complement of this amounted in time not only to hundreds, but thousands, who all found accommodations in his different palaces throughout the country. When the monarch was disposed to lessen the number of his establishment, the concubine with whose society he was willing to dispense returned, not to her former monastic residence, but to her own home; where, however humble might be her original condition, she was maintained in great state, and, far from being dishonored by the situation she had filled, was held in universal reverence as the Inca's bride.[45]

The great nobles of Peru were allowed, like their sovereign, a plurality of wives. The people, generally, whether by law, or by necessity stronger than law, were more happily limited to one. Marriage was conducted in a manner that gave it quite as original a character as belonged to the other

[44] Ibid, Parte 1, lib. 4, cap. 5—Cieza de Leon, Cronica, cap. 44.
[45] Dec de la Aud Real, MS—Garcilasso, Com. Real, Parte 1, lib 4, cap 4—Montesinos, Mem. antiguas, MS, lib. 2, cap. 19.

institutions of the country. On an appointed day of the year, all those of a marriageable age— which, having reference to their ability to take charge of a family, in the males was fixed at not less than twenty-four years, and in the women at eighteen or twenty—were called together in the great squares of their respective towns and villages, throughout the empire. The Inca presided in person over the assembly of his own kindred, and, taking the hands of the different couples who were to be united, he placed them within each other, declaring the parties man and wife. The same was done by the curacas towards all persons of their own or inferior degree in their several districts. This was the simple form of marriage in Peru. No one was allowed to select a wife beyond the community to which he belonged, which generally comprehended all his own kindred; [46] nor was any but the sovereign authorized to dispense with the law of nature—or, at least, the usual law of nations—so far as to marry his own sister. [47] No marriage was esteemed valid without the consent of the parents; and the preference of the parties, it is said, was also to be consulted; though, considering the barriers imposed

[46] By the strict letter of the law, according to Garcilasso, no one was to marry out of his own lineage. But this narrow rule had a most liberal interpretation, since all of the same town, and even province, he assures us, were reckoned of kin to one another Com Real, Parte 1, lib. 4, cap 8

[47] Fernandez, Hist del Peru, Parte 2, lib. 3, cap 9—This practice, so revolting to our feelings that it might well be deemed to violate the law of nature, must not, however, he regarded as altogether peculiar to the Incas, since it was countenanced by some of the most polished nations of antiquity.

by the prescribed age of the candidates, this must have been within rather narrow and whimsical limits. A dwelling was got ready for the new-married pair at the charge of the district, and the prescribed portion of land assigned for their maintenance. The law of Peru provided for the future, as well as for the present. It left nothing to chance. The simple ceremony of marriage was followed by general festivities among the friends of the parties, which lasted several days; and as every wedding took place on the same day, and as there were few families who had not some one of their members or their kindred personally interested, there was one universal bridal jubilee throughout the empire.[48]

The extraordinary regulations respecting marriage under the Incas are eminently characteristic of the genius of the government; which, far from limiting itself to matters of public concern, penetrated into the most private recesses of domestic life, allowing no man, however humble, to act for himself, even in those personal matters in which none but himself, or his family at most, might be supposed to be interested. No Peruvian was too low for the fostering vigilance of government. None was so high that he was not made to feel his dependence upon it in every act of his life. His very existence as an individual was absorbed in that of the community. His hopes and his fears, his joys and his sorrows, the tenderest

[48] Ondegardo, Rel. Seg., MS.—Garcilasso, Com Real, Parte 1, lib 6, cap. 36 —Dec. de la Aud. Real., MS —Montesinos, Mem. antiguas, MS , lib. 2, cap. 6.

sympathies of his nature, which would most naturally shrink from observation, were all to be regulated by law. He was not allowed even to be happy in his own way. The government of the Incas was the mildest, but the most searching, of despotisms.

[The precise nature of the Peruvian religion does not seem to have been much elucidated by the discussions it has undergone in recent years. The chief source of perplexity lies in the recognition of a Creator, or World-Deity, side by side with the adoration of the Sun as the presiding divinity and direct object of worship Mr. Tylor speaks of this as a "rivalry full of interest in the history of barbaric religion," and he takes the view that the Sun, originally "a subordinate God," "the divine ancestor of the Inca family," "by virtue of his nearer intercourse and power," gradually "usurped the place of the Supreme Deity." (Conf. Primitive Culture, 1st edition, vol ii p 307, and 2d edition, vol ii p. 338) But the facts cited in support of this theory are too slight or too questionable to form a sufficient basis for it The reported speech of one of the later Incas, in which the doctrine that the Sun is "the maker of all things," or himself "a living thing," is condemned, and he is compared to "a beast who makes a daily round under the eye of a master," "an arrow which must go whither it is sent, not whither it wishes," may be regarded as, what Mr Tylor indeed calls it, "a philosophic protest," and as nothing more The forms of prayer collected by Molina from the lips of certain aged Indians, addressed conjointly to the Creator, the Sun, and the Thunder, prove, if any thing, that the supremacy of the first-mentioned person in this singular trinity was an article of that "state church" which, according to Mr. Tylor, organized the worship of the Sun and raised it to predominance As to the statement, on Mr Markham's authority, that the great temple at Cuzco was originally dedicated to Pachacamac, this seems to rest merely on a tradition related by Molina, which attributes the enlargement of the temple and the erection of a golden statue to the Creator to the same Inca who is represented as having denied the divinity of the Sun In fact, the whole of this evidence better accords with the view taken by M. Desjardins, who considers the Inca referred to—Yupanqui according to most authorities—as having introduced the worship of Pachacamac at Cuzco, where before the Sun had been worshipped as the Supreme God (Le Pérou avant la Conquête espagnole, p 94) "But these notions," he remarks, "of an immaterial, infinite, and eternal God could not easily penetrate the minds of the multitude, who adhered

to their ancient superstitions." (Ibid., p. 103.) That the complex
character of the Peruvian mythology proceeded chiefly from the
union under one government of several different races, and the tol-
erance, and to some extent the adoption, by the conquerors of
various local or tribal religions, is a point on which all who have
given the subject any close investigation concur. (See Brinton,
Myths of the New World, p. 176, et al.) Hence the variety and
conflicting character of the traditions, which cannot be constructed
into a system, since they represent diverse and perhaps fluctuating
conceptions.—K.]

CHAPTER IV

EDUCATION — QUIPUS — ASTRONOMY — AGRICUL-
TURE — AQUEDUCTS — GUANO — IMPORTANT
ESCULENTS

SCIENCE was not intended for the people; but
for those of generous blood. Persons of low
degree are only puffed up by it, and rendered vain
and arrogant. Neither should such meddle with
the affairs of government; for this would bring
high offices into disrepute, and cause detriment to
the state." [1] Such was the favorite maxim, often
repeated, of Tupac Inca Yupanqui, one of the
most renowed of the Peruvian sovereigns. It may
seem strange that such a maxim should ever have
been proclaimed in the New World, where popular
institutions have been established on a more extensive scale than was ever before witnessed;
where government rests wholly on the people, and
education—at least, in the great northern division
of the continent—is mainly directed to qualify the
people for the duties of government. Yet this
maxim was strictly conformable to the genius of
the Peruvian monarchy, and may serve as a key

---

[1] " No es lícito, que enseñen à los hijos de los Plebeios, las Cien-
cias, que pertenescen à los Generosos, y no mas; porque como Gente
baja, no se eleven, y ensobervezcan, y menoscaben, y apoquen la
Republica: bastales, que aprendan los Oficios de sus Padres; que
el Mandar, y Governar no es de Plebeios, que es hacer agravio al
Oficio, y à la Republica, encomendarsela à Gente comun." Garcilasso, Com. Real., Parte 1, lib. 8, cap. 8.

to its habitual policy; since, while it watched with unwearied solicitude over its subjects, provided for their physical necessities, was mindful of their morals, and showed, throughout, the affectionate concern of a parent for his children, it yet regarded them only as children, who were never to emerge from the state of pupilage, to act or to think for themselves, but whose whole duty was comprehended in the obligation of implicit obedience.

Such was the humiliating condition of the people under the Incas, while the numerous families of the blood royal enjoyed the benefit of all the light of education which the civilization of the country could afford, and long after the Conquest the spots continued to be pointed out where the seminaries had existed for their instruction. These were placed under the care of the *amautas*, or " wise men," who engrossed the scanty stock of science—if science it could be called—possessed by the Peruvians, and who were the sole teachers of youth. It was natural that the monarch should take a lively interest in the instruction of the young nobility, his own kindred. Several of the Peruvian princes are said to have built their palaces in the neighborhood of the schools, in order that they might the more easily visit them and listen to the lectures of the amautas, which they occasionally re-enforced by a homily of their own.[2] In these schools the royal pupils we instructed in all

[2] Garcilasso, Com. Real., Parte 1, lib. 7, cap. 10 —The descendant of the Incas notices the remains, visible in his day, of two of the palaces of his royal ancestors, which had been built in the vicinity of the schools, for more easy access to them.

the different kinds of knowledge in which their teachers were versed, with especial reference to the stations they were to occupy in after-life. They studied the laws, and the principles of administering the government, in which many of them were to take part. They were initiated in the peculiar rites of their religion most necessary to those who were to assume the sacerdotal functions. They learned also to emulate the achievements of their royal ancestors by listening to the chronicles compiled by the amautas. They were taught to speak their own dialect with purity and elegance; and they became acquainted with the mysterious science of the quipus, which supplied the Peruvians with the means of communicating their ideas to one another, and of transmitting them to future generations.[3]

The quipu was a cord about two feet long, composed of different-colored threads tightly twisted together, from which a quantity of smaller threads were suspended in the manner of fringe. The threads were of different colors, and were tied into knots. The word *quipu*, indeed, signifies *a knot*. The colors denoted sensible objects; as, for instance, *white* represented *silver*, and *yellow, gold*. They sometimes also stood for abstract ideas. Thus, *white* signified *peace*, and *red, war*. But the quipus were chiefly used for arithmetical purposes. The knots served instead of ciphers, and could be combined in such a manner as to represent numbers to any amount they required. By means of these they went through their calcula-

[3] Garcilasso, Com. Real, Parte 1, lib. 4, cap. 19

tions with great rapidity, and the Spaniards who first visited the country bear testimony to their accuracy.[4]

Officers were established in each of the districts, who, under the title of *quipucamayus,* or "keepers of the quipus," were required to furnish the government with information on various important matters. One had charge of the revenues, reported the quantity of raw material distributed among the laborers, the quality and quantity of the fabrics made from it, and the amount of stores, of various kinds, paid into the royal magazines. Another exhibited the register of births and deaths, the marriages, the number of those qualified to bear arms, and the like details in reference to the population of the kingdom. These returns were annually forwarded to the capital, where they were submitted to the inspection of officers acquainted with the art of deciphering these mystic records. The government was thus provided with a valuable mass of statistical information, and the skeins of many-colored threads, collected and carefully preserved, constituted what might be called the national archives.[5]

[4] Conquista i Poblacion del Piru, MS —Sarmiento, Relacion, MS., cap 9 —Acosta, lib 6, cap. 8.—Garcilasso, Com. Real., Parte 1, lib. 6, cap 8.

[5] Ondegardo expresses his astonishment at the variety of objects embraced by these simple records, "hardly credible by one who had not seen them." "En aquella ciudad se hallaron muchos viejos oficiales antiguos del Inga, asi de la religion, como del Govierno, y otra cosa que no pudiera creer sino la viera, que por hilos y nudos se hallan figuradas las leyes, y estatutos asi de lo uno como de lo otro, y las sucesiones de los Reyes y tiempo que governaron: y hallose lo que todo esto tenian a su cargo que no fue poco, y aun tube alguna claridad de los estatutos que en tiempo de cada uno se

But, although the quipus sufficed for all the purposes of arithmetical computation demanded by the Peruvians, they were incompetent to represent the manifold ideas and images which are expressed by writing. Even here, however, the invention was not without its use. For, independently of the direct representation of simple objects, and even of abstract ideas, to a very limited extent, as above noticed, it afforded great help to the memory by way of association. The peculiar knot or color, in this way, suggested what it could not venture to represent; in the same manner—to borrow the homely illustration of an old writer—as the number of the Commandment calls to mind the Commandment itself. The quipus, thus used, might be regarded as the Peruvian system of mnemonics.

Annalists were appointed in each of the prin-

havian puesto." (Rel. Prim, MS.) (See also Sarmiento, Relacion, MS, cap. 9.—Acosta, lib. 6, cap. 8.—Garcilasso, Parte 1, lib 6, cap. 8, 9.) A vestige of the quipus is still to be found in some parts of Peru, where the shepherds keep the tallies of their numerous flocks by means of this ancient arithmetic.*

* [The Swiss naturalist, Dr. Von Tschudi, who travelled in Peru during the years 1838–1842, writes: "This method of calculation is still practised by the shepherds of the Puna They explained it to me, and I could with very little trouble construe their quipus. On the first branch, or string, they usually placed the numbers of the bulls; on the second, that of the cows, the latter being classed into those which were milked and those which were not milked, on the next string were numbered the calves, according to their ages and sizes. Then came the sheep, in several subdivisions. Next followed the number of foxes killed, the quantity of salt consumed, and, finally, the cattle that had been slaughtered. Other quipus showed the produce of the herds in milk, cheese, wool, etc Each list was distinguished by a particular color, or by some peculiarity in the twisting of the string." Von Tschudi, Travels in Peru, pp. 492–493.—M]

cipal communities, whose business it was to record the most important events which occurred in them. Other functionaries of a higher character, usually the amautas, were intrusted with the history of the empire, and were selected to chronicle the great deeds of the reigning Inca, or of his ancestors.[6] The narrative, thus concocted, could be communicated only by oral tradition; but the quipus served the chronicler to arrange the incidents with method and to refresh his memory. The story, once treasured up in the mind, was indelibly impressed there by frequent repetition. It was repeated by the amauta to his pupils, and in this way history, conveyed partly by oral tradition and partly by arbitrary signs, was handed down from generation to generation, with sufficient discrepancy of details, but with a general conformity of outline to the truth.

The Peruvian quipus were, doubtless, a wretched substitute for that beautiful contrivance, the alphabet, which, employing a few simple characters as the representatives of sound instead of ideas, is able to convey the most delicate shades of thought that ever passed through the mind of man. The Peruvian invention, indeed, was far below that of the hieroglyphics, even below the rude picture-writing of the Aztecs; for the latter art, however incompetent to convey abstract ideas, could depict sensible objects with tolerable accuracy. It is an evidence of the total ignorance in which the two nations remained of each other, that the Peruvians should have bor-

[6] Garcilasso, ubi supra.

rowed nothing of the hieroglyphical system of the Mexicans,* and this, notwithstanding that the existence of the maguey-plant, *agave*, in South America might have furnished them with the very material used by the Aztecs for the construction of their maps.[7]

It is impossible to contemplate without interest the struggles made by different nations, as they emerge from barbarism, to supply themselves with some visible symbol of thought,—that mysterious agency by which the mind of the individual may be put in communication with the minds of a whole community. The want of such a symbol is itself the greatest impediment to the progress of civilization. For what is it but to imprison the thought, which has the elements of immortality, within the bosom of its author, or of the small circle who come in contact with him, instead of sending it abroad to give light to thousands and to generations yet unborn! Not only is such a symbol an essential element of civilization, but it may be assumed as the very criterion of civilization; for the intellectual advancement of a people will keep pace pretty nearly with its facilities for intellectual communication.

Yet we must be careful not to underrate the real

[7] Garcilasso, ubi supra —Dec de la Aud Real, MS.—Sarmiento, Relacion, MS, cap. 9 —Yet the quipus must be allowed to bear some resemblance to the belts of wampum—made of colored beads strung together—in familiar use among the North American tribes for commemorating treaties, and for other purposes.

* [The quipus were used in Mexico,—Boturini found some specimens at Tlascala According to him, their Mexican name was nepohualtzitin, a word derived from the verb to count. Boturini, Idea de una nueva Historia, p 85 —M.]

value of the Peruvian system, nor to suppose that the quipus were as awkward an instrument in the hand of a practised native as they would be in ours. We know the effect of habit in all mechanical operations, and the Spaniards bear constant testimony to the adroitness and accuracy of the Peruvians in this. Their skill is not more surprising than the facility with which habit enables us to master the contents of a printed page, comprehending thousands of separate characters, by a single glance, as it were, though each character must require a distinct recognition by the eye, and that, too, without breaking the chain of thought in the reader's mind. We must not hold the invention of the quipus too lightly, when we reflect that they supplied the means of calculation demanded for the affairs of a great nation, and that, however insufficient, they afforded no little help to what aspired to the credit of literary composition.

The office of recording the national annals was not wholly confined to the amautas. It was assumed in part by the *haravecs*, or poets, who selected the most brilliant incidents for their songs or ballads, which were chanted at the royal festivals and at the table of the Inca.[8] In this manner a body of traditional minstrelsy grew up, like the British and Spanish ballad poetry, by means of which the name of many a rude chieftain, that

---

[8] Dec. de la Aud Real, MS —Garcilasso, Com. Real., Parte 1, lib 2, cap 27 —The word *haravec* signified "inventor" or "finder," and in his title, as well as in his functions, the minstrel-poet may remind us of the Norman *trouvère* Garcilasso has translated one of the little lyrical pieces of his countrymen. It is light and lively; but one short specimen affords no basis for general criticism.

might have perished for want of a chronicler, has been borne down the tide of rustic melody to later generations.

Yet history may be thought not to gain much by this alliance with poetry; for the domain of the poet extends over an ideal realm peopled with the shadowy forms of fancy, that bear little resemblance to the rude realities of life. The Peruvian annals may be deemed to show somewhat of the effects of this union, since there is a tinge of the marvellous spread over them down to the very latest period, which, like a mist before the reader's eye, makes it difficult to distinguish between fact and fiction.

The poet found a convenient instrument for his purposes in the beautiful Quichua dialect. We have already seen the extraordinary measures taken by the Incas for propagating their language throughout their empire. Thus naturalized in the remotest provinces, it became enriched by a variety of exotic words and idioms, which, under the influence of the court and of poetic culture, if I may so express myself, was gradually blended, like some finished mosaic made up of coarse and disjointed materials, into one harmonious whole. The Quichua became the most comprehensive and various, as well as the most elegant, of the South American dialects.[9]

[9] Ondegardo, Rel Prim, MS.—Sarmiento justly laments that his countrymen should have suffered this dialect, which might have proved so serviceable in their intercourse with the motley tribes of the empire, to fall so much out of use as it has done: "Y con tanto digo que fué harto beneficio para los Españoles haver esta lengua, pues podian con ella andar por todas partes en algunas de las

Besides the compositions already noticed, the Peruvians, it is said, showed some talent for theatrical exhibitions; not those barren pantomimes which, addressed simply to the eye, have formed the amusement of more than one rude nation. The Peruvian pieces aspired to the rank of dramatic compositions, sustained by character and dialogue, founded sometimes on themes of tragic interest, and at others on such as, from their light and social character, belong to comedy.[10]   Of the execution of these pieces we have now no means of judging.*   It was prob-

quales ya se vá perdiendo." Relacion, MS , cap. 21.—According to Velasco, the Incas, on arriving with their conquering legions at Quito, were astonished to find a dialect of the Quichua spoken there, although it was unknown over much of the intermediate country; a singular fact, if true. (Hist. de Quito, tom i. p. 185.) The author, a native of that country, had access to some rare sources of information; and his curious volumes show an intimate analogy between the science and social institutions of the people of Quito and Peru. Yet his book betrays an obvious anxiety to set the pretensions of his own country in the most imposing point of view, and he frequently hazards assertions with a confidence that is not well calculated to secure that of his readers.

[10] Garcilasso, Com. Real, ubi supra.

* [According to Garcilasso de la Vega, Com. Real , Parte 1, lib. 2, cap 27, the kinsman of the Inca, and other noblemen, sons of Curacas, or Curacas themselves, were accustomed on high festivals to present comedies and tragedies before the Inca. The subject-matter of the tragedies referred to the victories and the grandeur of former rulers. The comedies dealt with familiar agricultural and household subjects "They did not allow improper or vile farces, but all the plays were on decorous and important subjects, the sentences being such as befitted the occasion." Presents were given to reward distinguished excellence in performers. Until the year 1780 it was the policy of the Spaniards to treat the native chiefs with consideration, and, as far as was deemed expedient, to allow them to retain usages and ceremonies that had been customary before the Conquest. Dramas, therefore, orally transmitted through the centuries by means of the quipus continued to be presented

ably rude enough, as befitted an unformed people.
But, whatever may have been the execution, the

before the Incas until the insurrection of Inca Tupac Amaru, in
1780–81. In 1781 Judge Areche set forth his decree prohibiting "the
representation of dramas, as well as other festivals which the Indians
celebrated in memory of their Incas."

Happily, one specimen of those ancient dramas has been preserved, "Ollanta; or, the Severity of a Father and the Generosity
of a King" This play, which was frequently performed in the
presence of Tupac Amaru, gives us a somewhat different idea respecting the absolutism of the Inca from that commonly held   It
was committed to writing by Dr. Don Antonio Valdez, priest of
Sicuani, in 1780 Dr Valdez, who lived until 1816, was a friend
of Tupac Amaru, and had frequently been present when the drama
was presented before the Inca. This copy by Valdez is perhaps the
best known, though it is by no means the oldest. There is one MS.
bearing the date 1730, and, according to the distinguished antiquarian Rivero, there are others dating from the previous century.

It was first described in the *Museo Erudito*, a periodical published at Cuzco in 1837. Rivero and Von Tschudi speak of it in
their "Antiguedades Peruanas," 1851, apparently knowing nothing
of the earlier mention The complete text in Quichua was published
by Von Tschudi in his work, "Die Kechua Sprache," in 1853   In
1871 Clements R Markham published the Quichua text and an
English translation in parallel columns. Mr Markham, who is,
perhaps, the foremost English-speaking scholar who has devoted
himself to the study of the Quichua language, is convinced that the
drama is a production dating from Inca days, and not a work of
Spanish origin, written in more modern times. With him all Quichua
scholars, almost without exception, agree   In 1875 Von Tschudi
sent forth the play in a new edition with a German translation:
"Ollanta: Ein altperuanisches Drama aus der Kechua Sprache,"
übersetzt und commentirt von J J J. von Tschudi, Wien, 1875.
This new edition differs somewhat from his first because he used
in its preparation another MS , which is dated La Paz, June 18,
1735. In 1878 Don Gavino Pacheco Zegarra, an accomplished Peruvian scholar, put forth another edition in the "Collection Linguis-
tique Americaine," tom. iv.: "Ollantaï, drama en vers Quechuas du
temps des Incas, traduit et commenté," Paris, 1878. His free translation and scholarly notes make his work the most valuable that has
yet appeared upon the subject. He has no doubt whatever concerning the antiquity of the play.

There is "not a single modern or Spanish word or phrase in the
whole work, nor is there the remotest allusion to Christianity or to
any thing Spanish." Some expressions are archaic. The only part

mere conception of such an amusement is a proof
of refinement that honorably distinguishes the

of the drama for which Dr. Valdez was responsible is the division
into scenes and the introduction of stage directions suggested to
him by the performances of the play which he had seen.

The play is cast in the reign of Pachacutec, in the latter part of
the fourteenth century. (According to the traditions, Pachacutec,
though of a somewhat strenuous life, yet lived to reach the age of
one hundred years.) Ollanta, one of the most famous generals of
the reign, who has extended his master's conquests among the Antis,
becomes enamoured of the Princess Cusi Coyllur (Joyful Star),
reigning beauty of the court and daughter of the Inca. Because
Ollanta was not of Inca blood, his love is sacrilegious. But, as is
always the case where real lovers are concerned, all attempts to
turn the stubborn chieftain from the object of his affections are in
vain. The high priest of the Sun uses a miracle (he squeezes water
from a dry flower) to enforce his admonitions, but his advice is no
more heeded than is that of Piqui Chaqui, Ollanta's trusty servant.
The latter, by his punning and his general buffoonery, furnishes
the comic element of the play. In the second scene the unhappy
princess laments the absence of Ollanta, and her father expresses
his warm love for his daughter. In the third scene Ollanta pro-
claims his love, demands the Joyful Star from her father, and is
indignantly condemned for his insolence, Piqui Chaqui throwing in
a little comedy to lighten the otherwise excessive gloom

The second act depicts the successful rebellion of Ollanta. His
warriors have hailed him as Inca, and he has defeated Rumi-ñaui
(the Stone-eyed), the Inca general who had been sent against him.
But meantime Cusi Coyllur has borne a child to Ollanta, Yma Sumac (How beautiful!), and has been immured by her angry father
in the dungeons of the Convent of the Virgins of the Sun. In this
horrible place she is confined for ten years or more, her daughter
being brought up in ignorance of her mother's existence. The long
speech in which the child describes her feelings when, wandering
in the garden, she hears her mother groaning in her unknown dungeon is one of the finest parts of the play. After a while the old
Inca dies and Yupanqui, his son, comes to the throne. He places
Rumi-ñaui once more in command of an army and sends him against
the rebels. Taught by bitter experience, the Stone-Eyed does not
attempt to vanquish Ollanta in open battle, but has recourse to
strategy. With face disfigured and covered with blood, he presents
himself before Ollanta. He pretends that he has been cruelly
treated by the Inca, and so has come to take service under his
enemies Ollanta, entirely deceived, takes the Stone-Eyed one into
his favor. Rumi-ñaui, the perfidious, straightway encourages the

Peruvian from the other American races, whose pastime was war, or the ferocious sports that reflect the image of it.

The intellectual character of the Peruvians, indeed, seems to have been marked rather by a tendency to refinement than by those hardier qualities which insure success in the severer walks of science. In these they were behind several of the semi-civilized nations of the New World. They had some acquaintance with geography, so far as related to their own empire, which was indeed extensive; and they constructed maps with lines

rebels to a grand orgy at the celebration of the festival of the Sun, and when all the rebel army are too drunk to offer any resistance, he admits his own men into the citadel and makes its defenders his captives.

The third act, in an affecting passage, introduces the child of Cusi to her mother in the dungeon In the second scene the stratagem of Rumi-ñaui is told to the Inca, and the prisoners are brought into his presence. The Inca, miracle of generosity, not only pardons Ollanta, but restores to him the honors he had once held With his own hands he places upon his head the fringe which marks him as one of his highest and most trusted officials. Yma Sumac now appeals to the Inca for the release of her mother Yupanqui, who had long believed his sister to be dead, willingly grants the petition, Ollanta finds in the released captive his own lost bride; Yupanqui places her in his arms, and the drama ends as happily as the most approved of modern plays.

It is doubtful whether the play has any basis of historic fact, even though the name Ollantaytambo survives in the great ruined fortress. Some scholars will have it that those ruins are older than those of Pachacamac On the other hand, the story of the mutilated face of Stone-Eyed is perpetuated in an ancient piece of Inca pottery. Some of the similes used in the play are striking and even startling. To say of the beautiful Cusi, when she has been confined for years in a dungeon, "Thy nose is like a cold potato," seems to us hardly poetical, even though the assertion may be eminently truthful But the play abounds in beautiful passages, and its moral, that Love at last comes out victorious over all obstacles, even those thrown in its way by an absolute Inca, is satisfactorily patent.—M.]

raised on them to denote the boundaries and localities, on a similar principle with those formerly used by the blind. In astronomy they appear to have made but moderate proficiency. They divided the year into twelve lunar months, each of which, having its own name, was distinguished by its appropriate festival.[11] They had, also, weeks, but of what length, whether of seven, nine, or ten days, is uncertain. As their lunar year would necessarily fall short of the true time, they rectified their calendar by solar observations made by means of a number of cylindrical columns raised on the high lands round Cuzco, which served them for taking azimuths; and by measuring their shadows they ascertained the exact times of the solstices. The period of the equinoxes they determined by the help of a solitary pillar, or gnomon, placed in the centre of a circle, which was described in the area of the great temple and traversed by a diameter that was drawn from east to west. When the shadows were scarcely visible under the noontide rays of the sun, they said that " the god sat with all his light upon the column." [12] Quito, which lay immediately under the equator, where the vertical rays of the sun threw no shadow at noon, was held in especial veneration as the favorite abode of the great deity. The period of

[11] Ondegardo, Rel. Prim., MS —Fernandez, who differs from most authorities in dating the commencement of the year from June, gives the names of the several months, with their appropriate occupations. Hist. del Peru, Parte 2, lib. 3, cap. 10.

[12] Garcilasso, Com. Real, Parte 1, lib. 2, cap. 22-26.—The Spanish conquerors threw down these pillars, as savoring of idolatry in the Indians. Which of the two were best entitled to the name of barbarians?

the equinoxes was celebrated by public rejoicings. The pillar was crowned by the golden chair of the Sun, and both then and at the solstices the columns were hung with garlands, and offerings of flowers and fruit were made, while high festival was kept throughout the empire. By these periods the Peruvians regulated their religious rites and ceremonial and prescribed the nature of their agricultural labors. The year itself took its departure from the date of the winter solstice.[13]

This meagre account embraces nearly all that has come down to us of Peruvian astronomy. It may seem strange that a nation which had proceeded thus far in its observations should have gone no farther, and that, notwithstanding its general advance in civilization, it should in this science have fallen so far short not only of the Mexicans, but of the Muyscas, inhabiting the same elevated regions of the great southern plateau with themselves. These latter regulated their calendar on the same general plan of cycles and periodical series as the Aztecs, approaching yet nearer to the system pursued by the people of Asia.[14]

[13] Betanzos, Nar. de los Ingas, MS., cap 16.—Sarmiento, Relacion, MS, cap. 23.—Acosta, lib. 6, cap. 3—The most celebrated gnomon in Europe, that raised on the dome of the metropolitan church of Florence, was erected by the famous Toscanelli—for the purpose of determining the solstices, and regulating the festivals of the Church—about the year 1468; perhaps at no very distant date from that of the similar astronomical contrivance of the American Indian. See Tiraboschi, Historia della Letteratura Italiana, tom vi. lib 2, cap 2, sec 38.

[14] A tolerably meagre account—yet as full, probably, as authorities could warrant—of this interesting people has been given by Piedrahita, Bishop of Panamá, in the first two Books of his Historia general de las Conquistas del neuvo Regno de Granada

It might have been expected that the Incas, the boasted children of the Sun, would have made a particular study of the phenomena of the heavens and have constructed a calendar on principles as scientific as that of their semi-civilized neighbors. One historian, indeed, assures us that they threw their years into cycles of ten, a hundred, and a thousand years, and that by these cycles they regulated their chronology.[15] But this assertion—not improbable in itself—rests on a writer but little gifted with the spirit of criticism, and is counterbalanced by the silence of every higher and earlier authority, as well as by the absence of any monument, like those found among other American nations, to attest the existence of such a calendar. The inferiority of the Peruvians may be, perhaps, in part explained by the fact of their priesthood being drawn exclusively from the body of the Incas, a privileged order of nobility, who had no need, by the assumption of superior learning, to fence themselves round from the approaches of the vulgar. The little true science possessed by the Aztec priest supplied him with a key to unlock the mysteries of the heavens, and the false

(Madrid, 1688).—M. de Humboldt was fortunate in obtaining a MS., composed by a Spanish ecclesiastic resident in Santa Fé de Bogotá, in relation to the Muysca calendar, of which the Prussian philosopher has given a large and luminous analysis. Vues des Cordillères, p 244

[15] Montesinos, Mem. antiguas, MS., lib. 2, cap. 7.—" Renovó la computacion de los tiempos, que se iba perdiendo, y se contaron en su Reynado los años por 365 dias y seis horas; á los años añadió decadas de diez años, á cada diez decadas una centuria de 100 años, y á cada diez centurias una capachoata ó Jutiphuacan, que son 1000 años, que quiere decir el grande año del Sol; asi contaban los siglos y los sucesos memorables de sus Reyes." Ibid., loc. cit.

system of astrology which he built upon it gave him credit as a being who had something of divinity in his own nature. But the Inca noble was divine by birth. The illusory study of astrology, so captivating to the unenlightened mind, engaged no share of his attention. The only persons in Peru who claimed the power of reading the mysterious future were the diviners, men who, combining with their pretensions some skill in the healing art, resembled the conjurers found among many of the Indian tribes. But the office was held in little repute, except among the lower classes, and was abandoned to those whose age and infirmity disqualified them for the real business of life.[16]

The Peruvians had knowledge of one or two constellations, and watched the motions of the planet Venus, to which, as we have seen, they dedicated altars. But their ignorance of the first principles of astronomical science is shown by their ideas of eclipses, which they supposed denoted some great derangement of the planet; and when the moon labored under one of these mysterious infirmities they sounded their instruments, and filled the air with shouts and lamentations, to rouse her from her lethargy. Such puerile conceits as these form a striking contrast with the

---

[16] " Ansi mismo les hicieron señalar gente para hechizeros que tambien es entre ellos, oficio publico y conoscido en todos, . . . los diputados para ello no lo tenian por travajo, por que ninguno podia tener semejante oficio como los dichos sino fuesen viejos é viejas, y personas inaviles para travajar, como mancos, cojos ó contrechos, y gente asi á quien faltava las fuerzas para ello." Ondegardo, Rel. Seg., MS

real knowledge of the Mexicans, as displayed in their hieroglyphical maps, in which the true cause of this phenomenon is plainly depicted.[17]

But, if less successful in exploring the heavens, the Incas must be admitted to have surpassed every other American race in their dominion over the earth. Husbandry was pursued by them on principles that may be truly called scientific. It was the basis of their political institutions. Having no foreign commerce, it was agriculture that furnished them with the means of their internal exchanges, their subsistence, and their revenues. We have seen their remarkable provisions for distributing the land in equal shares among the people, while they required every man, except the privileged orders, to assist in its cultivation. The Inca himself did not disdain to set the example. On one of the great annual festivals he proceeded to the environs of Cuzco, attended by his court, and, in the presence of all the people, turned up the earth with a golden plough,—or an instrument that served as such,—thus consecrating the occupation of the husbandman as one worthy to be followed by the Children of the Sun.[18]

[17] See Codex Tel.-Remensis, Part 4, Pl. 22, ap. Antiquities of Mexico, vol. i, London, 1829.

[18] Sarmiento, Relacion, MS., cap. 16.—The nobles, also, it seems, at this high festival, imitated the example of their master. " Pasadas todas las fiestas, en la ultima llevavan muchos arados de manos, los quales antiguamente heran de oro; i échos los oficios, tomava el Inga un arado i comenzava con el a romper la tierra, i lo mismo los demas señores, para que de alli adelante en todo su señorio hiciesen lo mismo, i sin que el Inga hiciese esto no avia Indio que osase romper la tierra, ni pensavan que produjese si el Inga no la rompia primero i esto vaste quanto á las fiestas " Conq. i Pob. del Piru, MS.

The patronage of the government did not stop with this cheap display of royal condescension, but was shown in the most efficient measures for facilitating the labors of the husbandman. Much of the country along the sea-coast suffered from want of water, as little or no rain fell there, and the few streams, in their short and hurried course from the mountains, exerted only a very limited influence on the wide extent of territory. The soil, it is true, was for the most part sandy and sterile; but many places were capable of being reclaimed, and, indeed, needed only to be properly irrigated to be susceptible of extraordinary production. To these spots water was conveyed by means of canals and subterraneous aqueducts executed on a noble scale. They consisted of large slabs of freestone nicely fitted together without cement, and discharged a volume of water sufficient, by means of latent ducts or sluices, to moisten the lands in the lower level, through which they passed. Some of these aqueducts were of great length. One that traversed the district of Condesuyu measured between four and five hundred miles. They were brought from some elevated lake or natural reservoir in the heart of the mountains, and were fed at intervals by other basins which lay in their route along the slopes of the sierra. In this descent a passage was sometimes to be opened through rocks,—and this without the aid of iron tools; impracticable mountains were to be turned, rivers and marshes to be crossed; in short, the same obstacles were to be encountered as in the construction of their mighty roads. But the Peruvians seemed to take pleasure in wrestling with the difficulties of nature. Near Caxamarca a tunnel is still visible which they excavated in the mountains to give an outlet to the waters of a lake when these rose to a height in the rainy seasons that threatened the country with inundation.[19]

Most of these beneficent works of the Incas were suffered to go to decay by their Spanish conquerors. In some spots the waters are still left to flow in their silent, subterraneous channels, whose windings and whose sources have been alike unexplored. Others, though partially dilapidated, and closed up with rubbish and the rank vegetation of the soil, still betray their course by occasional patches of fertility. Such are the remains in the valley of Nasca, a fruitful spot that lies between long tracts of desert; where the ancient water-courses of the Incas, measuring four or five feet in depth by three in width, and formed of large blocks of uncemented masonry, are conducted from an unknown distance.

The greatest care was taken that every occupant of the land through which these streams passed should enjoy the benefit of them. The

[19] Sarmiento, Relacion, MS., cap. 21.—Garcilasso, Com Real., Parte 1, lib. 5, cap. 24.—Stevenson, Narrative of a Twenty Years' Residence in South America (London, 1829), vol. 1 p. 412; ii. pp. 173, 174.—"Sacauan acequias en cabos y por partes que es cosa estraña afirmar lo: porque las echauan por lugares altos y baxos: y por laderas de los cabeços y haldas de sierras q̃ estan en los valles: y por ellos mismos atrauiessan muchas: unas por una parte, y otras por otra, que es gran delectaciō caminar por aquellos valles: porque parece que se anda entre huertas y florestas llenas de frescuras." Cieza de Leon, Cronica, cap. 66.

quantity of water allotted to each was prescribed by law; and royal overseers superintended the distribution and saw that it was faithfully applied to the irrigation of the ground.[20]

The Peruvians showed a similar spirit of enterprise in their schemes for introducing cultivation into the mountainous parts of their domain. Many of the hills, though covered with a strong soil, were too precipitous to be tilled. These they cut into terraces, faced with rough stone, diminishing in regular gradation towards the summit; so that, while the lower strip, or *anden*, as it was called by the Spaniards, that belted round the base of the mountain, might comprehend hundreds of acres, the uppermost was only large enough to accommodate a few rows of Indian corn.[21] Some of the eminences presented such a mass of solid rock that after being hewn into terraces they were obliged to be covered deep with earth before they could serve the purpose of the husbandman. With such patient toil did the Peruvians combat the formidable obstacles presented by the face of their country! Without the use of the tools or the machinery familiar to the European, each individual could have done little; but acting in

[20] Pedro Pizarro, Descub. y Conq., MS.—Memoirs of Gen. Miller, vol. ii p 220

[21] Miller supposes that it was from these *andenes* that the Spaniards gave the name of Andes to the South American Cordilleras. (Memoirs of Gen. Miller, vol ii. p 219) But the name is older than the Conquest, according to Garcilasso, who traces it to *Anti*, the name of a province that lay east of Cuzco. (Com. Real , Parte 1, lib. 2, cap. 11.) *Anta*, the word for copper, which was found abundant in certain quarters of the country, may have suggested the name of the province, if not immediately that of the mountains.

large masses, and under a common direction, they were enabled by indefatigable perseverance to achieve results to have attempted which might have filled even the European with dismay.[22]

In the same spirit of economical husbandry which redeemed the rocky sierra from the curse of sterility, they dug below the arid soil of the valleys and sought for a stratum where some natural moisture might be found. These excavations, called by the Spaniards *hoyas,* or " pits," were made on a great scale, comprehending frequently more than an acre, sunk to the depth of fifteen or twenty feet, and fenced round within by a wall of *adobes,* or bricks baked in the sun. The bottom of the excavation, well prepared by a rich manure of the sardines,—a small fish obtained in vast quantities along the coast,—was planted with some kind of grain or vegetable.[23]

The Peruvian farmers were well acquainted with the different kinds of manures, and made large use of them; a circumstance rare in the rich lands of the tropics, and probably not elsewhere practised by the rude tribes of America. They made great use of *guano,* the valuable deposit of sea-fowl, that has attracted so much attention of late from the agriculturists both of Europe and of our own country, and the stimulating and nutritious properties of which the Indians perfectly

[22] Memoirs of Gen Miller, ubi supra.—Garcilasso, Com. Real., Parte 1, lib 5, cap. 1.

[23] Cieza de Leon, Cronica, cap. 73 —The remains of these ancient excavations still excite the wonder of the modern traveller. See Stevenson, Residence in South America, vol. i. p. 359.—Also Mc-Culloh, Researches, p. 358.

appreciated. This was found in such immense quantities on many of the little islands along the coast as to have the appearance of lofty hills, which, covered with a white saline incrustation, led the Conquerors to give them the name of the *sierra nevada,* or " snowy mountains." *

The Incas took their usual precautions for securing the benefits of this important article to the husbandman. They assigned the small islands on the coast to the use of the respective districts which lay adjacent to them. When the island was large, it was distributed among several districts, and the boundaries for each were clearly defined. All encroachment on the rights of another was severely punished. And they secured the preservation of the fowl by penalties as stern as those by which the Norman tyrants of England protected their own game. No one was allowed to set foot on the island during the season for breeding, under pain of death; and to kill the birds at any time was punished in like manner.[24]

With this advancement in agricultural science, the Peruvians might be supposed to have had some knowledge of the plough, in such general use among the primitive nations of the Eastern conti-

[24] Acosta, lib. 4, cap 36.—Garcilasso, Com. Real, Parte 1, lib. 5, cap. 3.

* [The largest deposits were found on the Chincha, Guañape, and Macabi islands. From these islands it is estimated that 20,000,000 tons were taken between the years 1840 and 1900. As the guano sold at prices varying from forty-five to sixty-seven dollars per ton, it is evident that the wealth accumulated on those barren rocks was almost as startling as that obtained from the palaces of the Incas. The deposits are now almost entirely exhausted.—M.]

nent. But they had neither the iron ploughshare
of the Old World, nor had they animals for
draught, which, indeed, were nowhere found in
the New. The instrument which they used was a
strong, sharp-pointed stake, traversed by a horizontal piece, ten or twelve inches from the point,
on which the ploughman might set his foot and
force it into the ground. Six or eight strong men
were attached by ropes to the stake, and dragged
it forcibly along,—pulling together, and keeping
time as they moved by chanting their national
songs, in which they were accompanied by the
women who followed in the train, to break up the
sods with their rakes. The mellow soil offered
slight resistance; and the laborer, by long practice, acquired a dexterity which enabled him to
turn up the ground to the requisite depth with
astonishing facility. This substitute for the
plough was but a clumsy contrivance; yet it is
curious as the only specimen of the kind among
the American aborigines, and was perhaps not
much inferior to the wooden instrument introduced in its stead by the European conquerors.[25]

It was frequently the policy of the Incas, after
providing a deserted tract with the means for
irrigation and thus fitting it for the labors of the
husbandman, to transplant there a colony of
mitimaes, who brought it under cultivation by
raising the crops best suited to the soil. While
the peculiar character and capacity of the lands
were thus consulted, a means of exchange of the
different products was afforded to the neighbor-

[25] Garcilasso, Com. Real., Parte 1, lib. 5, cap. 2.

ing provinces, which, from the formation of the country, varied much more than usual within the same limits. To facilitate these agricultural exchanges, fairs were instituted, which took place three times a month in some of the most populous places, where, as money was unknown, a rude kind of commerce was kept up by the barter of their respective products. These fairs afforded so many holidays for the relaxation of the industrious laborer.[26]

Such were the expedients adopted by the Incas for the improvement of their territory; and, although imperfect, they must be allowed to show an acquaintance with the principles of agricultural science that gives them some claim to the rank of a civilized people. Under their patient and discriminating culture, every inch of good soil was tasked to its greatest power of production; while the most unpromising spots were compelled to contribute something to the subsistence of the people. Everywhere the land teemed with evidence of agricultural wealth, from the smiling valleys along the coast to the terraced steeps of the sierra, which, rising into pyramids of verdure, glowed with all the splendors of tropical vegetation.

The formation of the country was particularly favorable, as already remarked, to an infinite variety of products, not so much from its extent as from its various elevations, which, more remark-

---

[26] Sarmiento, Rel, MS, cap. 19.—Garcilasso, Com. Real, Parte 1, lib. 6, cap. 36; lib. 7, cap. 1.—Herrera, Hist. gen, dec. 5, lib. 4, cap. 3

able even than those in Mexico, comprehend every
degree of latitude from the equator to the polar
regions.   Yet, though the temperature changes
in this region with the degree of elevation, it remains nearly the same in the same spots throughout the year; and the inhabitant feels none of
those grateful vicissitudes of season which belong
to the temperate latitudes of the globe.   Thus,
while the summer lies in full power on the burning regions of the palm and the cocoa-tree that
fringe the borders of the ocean, the broad surface of the table-land blooms with the freshness
of perpetual spring, and the higher summits of
the Cordilleras are white with everlasting winter.

The Peruvians turned this fixed variety of climate, if I may so say, to the best account, by cultivating the productions appropriate to each; and
they particularly directed their attention to those
which afforded the most nutriment to man.   Thus,
in the lower level were to be found the cassava-
tree and the banana, that bountiful plant, which
seems to have relieved man from the primeval
curse—if it were not rather a blessing—of toil-
ing for his sustenance.[27]   As the banana faded
from the landscape, a good substitute was found
in the maize, the great agricultural staple of both
the northern and southern divisions of the Ameri-

[27] The prolific properties of the banana are shown by M. de Humboldt, who states that its productiveness, as compared with that of
wheat, is as 133 to 1, and with that of the potato, as 44 to 1. (Essai
politique sur le Royaume de la Nouvelle-Espagne (Paris, 1827),
tom. ii. p. 389.) It is a mistake to suppose that this plant was not
indigenous to South America. The banana-leaf has been frequently
found in ancient Peruvian tombs.

can continent, and which, after its exportation to
the Old World, spread so rapidly there as to suggest the idea of its being indigenous to it.[28]   The
Peruvians were well acquainted with the different
modes of preparing this useful vegetable, though
it seems they did not use it for bread, except at
festivals; and they extracted a sort of honey from
the stalk, and made an intoxicating liquor from
the fermented grain, to which, like the Aztecs,
they were immoderately addicted.[29]

The temperate climate of the table-land furnished them with the maguey, *agave Americana,*
many of the extraordinary qualities of which they
comprehended, though not its most important one
of affording a material for paper.   Tobacco, too,
was among the products of this elevated region.
Yet the Peruvians differed from every other
Indian nation to whom it was known, by using it
only for medicinal purposes, in the form of
snuff.[30]   They may have found a substitute for
its narcotic qualities in the coca (*Erythroxylum
Peruvianum*), or *cuca,* as called by the natives.

[28] The misnomer of *blé de Turquie* shows the popular error   Yet
the rapidity of its diffusion through Europe and Asia after the discovery of America is of itself sufficient to show that it could not
have been indigenous to the Old World and have so long remained
generally unknown there.

[29] Acosta, lib. 4, cap 16.—The saccharine matter contained in the
maize-stalk is much greater in tropical countries than in more
northern latitudes; so that the natives in the former may be seen
sometimes sucking it like the sugar-cane   One kind of the fermented liquors, *sora,* made from the corn, was of such strength that
the use of it was forbidden by the Incas, at least to the common
people.   Their injunctions do not seem to have been obeyed so im-
plicitly in this instance as usual.

[30] Garcilasso, Com Real, Parte 1, lib 2, cap 25.

This is a shrub which grows to the height of a man. The leaves when gathered are dried in the sun, and, being mixed with a little lime, form a preparation for chewing, much like the betel-leaf of the East.[31] With a small supply of this cuca in his pouch,* and a handful of roasted maize, the Peruvian Indian of our time performs his wearisome journeys, day after day, without fatigue, or, at least, without complaint. Even food the most invigorating is less grateful to him than his loved narcotic. Under the Incas, it is said to have been exclusively reserved for the noble orders. If so, the people gained one luxury by the Conquest; and after that period it was so extensively used by them that this article constituted a most important item of the colonial revenue of Spain.[32] Yet, with the soothing charms of an opiate, this

[31] The pungent leaf of the *betel* is in like manner mixed with lime when chewed. (Elphinstone, History of India (London, 1841), vol. i. p. 331.) The similarity of this social indulgence, in the remote East and West, is singular.

[32] Ondegardo, Rel. Seg., MS.—Acosta, lib. 4, cap. 22.—Stevenson, Residence in South America, vol. ii. p. 63.—Cieza de Leon, Cronica, cap. 96.

* [Besides a pouch full of cuca leaves, every Peruvian Indian, as he travels among the Andes to-day, carries a little, narrow bag filled with lime. To this bag is usually fastened a small, smooth stick, very like a " meat-peg." First the Indian takes from his pouch a few leaves of cuca. Next he moistens the meat-peg thoroughly by passing it between his lips. Then he thrusts the stick into the bag of lime. The lime upon the stick is then wiped off upon the leaves, the leaves are folded over it, and the quid is formed. The lime, of course, imparts great sharpness to the flavor. It does not seem to injure the gums of the Indians, but is at first excruciating in its effects upon more civilized mouths. Taken without the lime, the cuca is wonderfully stimulating and sustaining, even to the man who tries it for the first time. No evil consequences seem to follow from its use.—M.]

weed so much vaunted by the natives, when used
to excess, is said to be attended with all the mis-
chievous effects of habitual intoxication.[33]

Higher up on the slopes of the Cordilleras, beyond the limits of the maize and of the *quinoa*,—
a grain bearing some resemblance to rice, and
largely cultivated by the Indians,—was to be
found the potato,* the introduction of which into
Europe has made an era in the history of agriculture. Whether indigenous to Peru, or imported
from the neighboring country of Chili, it formed
the great staple of the more elevated plains, under
the Incas, and its culture was continued to a height
in the equatorial regions which reached many
thousand feet above the limits of perpetual snow
in the temperate latitudes of Europe.[34] Wild

[33] A traveller (Poeppig) noticed in the Foreign Quarterly Review
(No. 33) expatiates on the malignant effects of the habitual use of
the *cuca*, as very similar to those produced on the chewer of opium.
Strange that such baneful properties should not be the subject of
more frequent comment with other writers! I do not remember
to have seen them even adverted to

[34] Malte-Brun, book 86.—The potato, found by the early discoverers in Chili, Peru, New Granada, and all along the Cordilleras
of South America, was unknown in Mexico,—an additional proof
of the entire ignorance in which the respective nations of the two
continents remained of one another. M. de Humboldt, who has
bestowed much attention on the early history of this vegetable,

* [Cieza de Leon speaks of the potato as "a kind of earth-nut."
When found in its wild state, it is hardly larger than a nut. Markham says "there is a wild variety in Mexico, the size of a nut, and
attempts have been made during many years to increase its size
under cultivation, but without any result." (Narrative and Crit.
Hist. of America, p. 213) He rightly infers that this implies a long
period of time in the development of the vegetable to the size
found in Peru Von Tschudi thinks that the root is indigenous to
the high lands of Peru, and that the ancient Peruvians removed it
from the higher lands to cultivate it in more favorable soil. Travels
in Peru, p. 178 —M]

specimens of the vegetable might be seen still higher, springing up spontaneously amidst the stunted shrubs that clothed the lofty sides of the Cordilleras, till these gradually subsided into the mosses and the short yellow grass, *pajonal*, which, like a golden carpet, was unrolled around the base of the mighty cones, that rose far into the regions of eternal silence, covered with the snows of centuries.[35]

which has exerted so important an influence on European society, supposes that the cultivation of it in Virginia, where it was known to the early planters, must have been originally derived from the Southern Spanish colonies. Essai politique, tom. ii. p. 462.

[25] While Peru, under the Incas, could boast these indigenous products, and many others less familiar to the European, it was unacquainted with several, of great importance, which, since the Conquest, have thriven there as on their natural soil Such are the olive, the grape, the fig, the apple, the orange, the sugar-cane None of the cereal grains of the Old World were found there. The first wheat was introduced by a Spanish lady of Truxillo, who took great pains to disseminate it among the colonists, of which the government, to its credit, was not unmindful. Her name was Maria de Escobar History, which is so much occupied with celebrating the scourges of humanity, should take pleasure in commemorating one of its real benefactors.

CHAPTER V

A NATION which had made such progress in agriculture might be reasonably expected to have made also some proficiency in the mechanical arts,—especially when, as in the case of the Peruvians, their agricultural economy demanded in itself no inconsiderable degree of mechanical skill. Among most nations, progress in manufactures has been found to have an intimate connection with the progress of husbandry. Both arts are directed to the same great object of supplying the necessaries, the comforts, or, in a more refined condition of society, the luxuries, of life; and when the one is brought to a perfection that infers a certain advance in civilization, the other must naturally find a corresponding development under the increasing demands and capacities of such a state. The subjects of the Incas, in their patient and tranquil devotion to the more humble occupations of industry which bound them to their native soil, bore greater resemblance to the Oriental nations, as the Hindoos and Chinese, than they bore to the members of the great Anglo-Saxon family, whose hardy temper has driven them to seek their fortunes on the stormy ocean and to open a commerce with the most distant regions of the globe. The Peruvians, though lining a long extent of sea-coast, had no foreign commerce.

They had peculiar advantages for domestic manufacture in a material incomparably superior to any thing possessed by the other races of the Western continent. They found a good substitute for linen in a fabric which, like the Aztecs, they knew how to weave from the tough thread of the maguey. Cotton grew luxuriantly on the low, sultry level of the coast, and furnished them with a clothing suitable to the milder latitudes of the country. But from the llama and the kindred species of Peruvian sheep they obtained a fleece adapted to the colder climate of the table-land, "more estimable," to quote the language of a well-informed writer, "than the down of the Canadian beaver, the fleece of the *brebis des Calmoucks*, or of the Syrian goat." [1]

Of the four varieties of the Peruvian sheep, the llama, the one most familiarly known, is the least valuable on account of its wool. It is chiefly employed as a beast of burden, for which, although it is somewhat larger than any of the other varieties, its diminutive size and strength would seem to disqualify it. It carries a load of little more than a hundred pounds, and cannot travel above three or four leagues in a day.* But all this

[1] Walton, Historical and Descriptive Account of the Peruvian Sheep (London, 1811), p. 115 This writer's comparison is directed to the wool of the vicuña, the most esteemed of the genus for its fleece.

* [Because it does not graze during the night, but by day, as it is driven forward.—M.]

is compensated by the little care and cost required for its management and its maintenance. It picks up an easy subsistence from the moss and stunted herbage that grow scantily along the withered sides and the steeps of the Cordilleras. The structure of its stomach, like that of the camel, is such as to enable it to dispense with any supply of water for weeks, nay, months together. Its spongy hoof, armed with a claw or pointed talon to enable it to take secure hold on the ice, never requires to be shod; and the load laid upon its back rests securely in its bed of wool, without the aid of girth or saddle.* The llamas move in troops of five hundred or even a thousand, and thus, though each individual carries but little, the aggregate is considerable. The whole caravan travels on at its regular pace, passing the night in the open air without suffering from the coldest temperature, and marching in perfect order and in obedience to the voice of the driver. It is only when overloaded that the spirited little animal refuses to stir, and neither blows nor caresses can induce him to rise from the ground. He is as sturdy in asserting his rights on this occasion as he is usually docile and unresisting.[2]

The employment of domestic animals distinguished the Peruvians from the other races of the

[2] Walton, Hist. and Descrip. Account of the Peruvian Sheep, p. 23, et seq —Garcilasso, Com. Real., Parte 1, lib. 8, cap. 16.—Acosta, lib. 4, cap. 41.—*Llama*, according to Garcilasso de la Vega, is a Peruvian word signifying "flock." (Ibid., ubi supra.) The natives got no milk from their domesticated animals; nor was milk used, I believe, by any tribe on the American continent.

* [This is an error. The load must be tied on —M.]

New World. This economy of human labor by the substitution of the brute is an important element of civilization, inferior only to what is gained by the substitution of machinery for both. Yet the ancient Peruvians seem to have made much less account of it than their Spanish conquerors, and to have valued the llama, in common with the other animals of that genus, chiefly for its fleece. Immense herds of these "large cattle," as they were called, and of the "smaller cattle,"[3] or *alpacas*, were held by the government, as already noticed, and placed under the direction of shepherds, who conducted them from one quarter of the country to another, according to the changes of the season. These migrations were regulated with all the precision with which the code of the *mesta* determined the migrations of the vast merino flocks in Spain; and the Conquerors, when they landed in Peru, were amazed at finding a race of animals so similar to their own in properties and habits, and under the control of a system of legislation which might seem to have been imported from their native land.[4]

But the richest store of wool was obtained, not from these domesticated animals, but from the two other species, the *huanacos* and the *vicuñas*, which roamed in native freedom over the frozen ranges

[3] *Ganado maior, ganado menor.*

[4] The judicious Ondegardo emphatically recommends the adoption of many of these regulations by the Spanish government, as peculiarly suited to the exigencies of the natives: "En esto de los ganados paresció haber hecho muchas constituciones en diferentes tiempos é algunas tan utiles é provechosas para su conservacion que convendria que tambien guardasen agora." Rel. Seg., MS.

of the Cordilleras; where not unfrequently they
might be seen scaling the snow-covered peaks
which no living thing inhabits save the condor, the
huge bird of the Andes, whose broad pinions bear
him up in the atmosphere to the height of more
than twenty thousand feet above the level of the
sea.[5] In these rugged pastures, " the flock without a fold " finds sufficient sustenance in the *ychu*,
a species of grass which is found scattered all
along the great ridge of the Cordilleras, from the
equator to the southern limits of Patagonia. And
as these limits define the territory traversed by the
Peruvian sheep, which rarely, if ever, venture
north of the line, it seems not improbable that this
mysterious little plant is so important to their
existence that the absence of it is the principal
reason why they have not penetrated to the
northern latitudes of Quito and New Granada.[6]

But, although thus roaming without a master
over the boundless wastes of the Cordilleras, the
Peruvian peasant was never allowed to hunt these
wild animals, which were protected by laws as
severe as were the sleek herds that grazed on the
more cultivated slopes of the plateau. The wild
game of the forest and the mountain was as much
the property of the government as if it had been
enclosed within a park or penned within a fold.[7]
It was only on stated occasions, at the great hunts
which took place once a year, under the personal
superintendence of the Inca or his principal

[5] Malte-Brun, book 86.
[6] *Ychu*, called in the Flora Peruana *Jarava*, Class, Monandria
Digynia. See Walton, p. 17.
[7] Ondegardo, Rel. Prim., MS.

officers, that the game was allowed to be taken. These hunts were not repeated in the same quarter of the country oftener than once in four years, that time might be allowed for the waste occasioned by them to be replenished. At the appointed time, all those living in the district and its neighborhood, to the number, it might be, of fifty or sixty thousand men,[8] were distributed round, so as to form a cordon of immense extent, that should embrace the whole country which was to be hunted over. The men were armed with long poles and spears, with which they beat up game of every description lurking in the woods, the valleys, and the mountains, killing the beasts of prey without mercy, and driving the others, consisting chiefly of the deer of the country, and the huanacos and vicuñas, towards the centre of the wide-extended circle; until, as this gradually contracted, the timid inhabitants of the forests were concentrated on some spacious plain, where the eye of the hunter might range freely over his victims, who found no place for shelter or escape.

The male deer and some of the coarser kind of the Peruvian sheep were slaughtered; their skins were reserved for the various useful manufactures to which they are ordinarily applied, and their flesh, cut into thin slices, was distributed among the people, who converted it into *charqui*, the dried meat of the country, which constituted then

[8] Sometimes even a hundred thousand mustered, when the Inca hunted in person, if we may credit Sarmiento: "De donde haviendose ya juntado cinquenta ó sesenta mil Personas ó cien mil si mandado les era." Relacion, MS., cap. 13.

the sole, as it has since the principal, animal food of the lower classes of Peru.[9]

But nearly the whole of the sheep, amounting usually to thirty or forty thousand, or even a larger number, after being carefully sheared, were suffered to escape and regain their solitary haunts among the mountains. The wool thus collected was deposited in the royal magazines, whence, in due time, it was dealt out to the people. The coarser quality was worked up into garments for their own use, and the finer for the Inca; for none but an Inca noble could wear the fine fabric of the vicuña.[10]

The Peruvians showed great skill in the manufacture of different articles for the royal household from this delicate material, which, under the name of *vigonia* wool, is now familiar to the looms of Europe. It was wrought into shawls, robes. and other articles of dress for the monarch, and into carpets, coverlets, and hangings for the imperial palaces and the temples. The cloth was finished on both sides alike;[11] the delicacy of the texture was such as to give it the lustre of silk; and the brilliancy of the dyes excited the admiration and the envy of the European artisan.[12] The Peruvians produced also an article of great

[9] Ibid, ubi supra.—*Charqui;* hence, probably, says McCulloh, the term "jerked" applied to the dried beef of South America. Researches, p. 377

[10] Sarmiento, Relacion, MS, loc cit —Cieza de Leon, Cronica, cap. 81.—Garcilasso, Com. Real, Parte 1, lib. 6, cap. 6.

[11] Acosta, lib. 4, cap. 41.

[12] "Ropas finisimas para los Reyes, que lo eran tanto que parecian de sarga de seda y con colores tan perfectos quanto se puede afirmar." Sarmiento, Relacion, MS., cap. 13.

strength and durability by mixing the hair of animals with wool; and they were expert in the beautiful feather-work, which they held of less account than the Mexicans, from the superior quality of the materials for other fabrics which they had at their command.[13]

The natives showed a skill in other mechanical arts similar to that displayed by their manufacturers of cloth. Every man in Peru was expected to be acquainted with the various handicrafts essential to domestic comfort. No long apprenticeship was required for this, where the wants were so few as among the simple peasantry of the Incas. But, if this were all, it would imply but a very moderate advancement in the arts. There were certain individuals, however, carefully trained to those occupations which minister to the demands of the more opulent classes of society. These occupations, like every other calling and office in Peru, always descended from father to son.[14] The division of castes, in this particular, was as precise as that which existed in Egypt or Hindostan. If this arrangement be unfavorable to originality, or to the development of

[13] Pedro Pizarro, Descub. y Conq., MS.—"Ropa finissima para los señores Ingas de lana de las Vicunias. Y cierto fue tan prima esta ropa, como auran visto en España: por alguna que alla fue luego que se gano este reyno Los vestidos destos Ingas eran camisetas desta ropa: vnas pobladas de argenteria de oro, otras de esmeraldas y piedras preciosas: y algunas de plumas de aues: otras de solamente la manta. Para hazer estas ropas, tuuierō y tienen tan perfetas colores de carmesi, azul, amarillo, negro, y de otras suertes, que verdaderamente tienen ventaja á las de España" Cieza de Leon, Cronica, cap. 114.

[14] Ondegardo, Rel. Prim, et Seg., MSS.—Garcilasso, Com. Real., Parte 1, lib. 5, cap. 7, 9, 13.

the peculiar talent of the individual, it at least conduces to an easy and finished execution, by familiarizing the artist with the practice of his art from childhood.[15]

The royal magazines and the *huacas* or tombs of the Incas have been found to contain many specimens of curious and elaborate workmanship. Among these are vases of gold and silver, bracelets, collars, and other ornaments for the person; utensils of every description, some of fine clay, and many more of copper; mirrors of a hard, polished stone, or burnished silver, with a great variety of other articles made frequently on a whimsical pattern, evincing quite as much ingenuity as taste or inventive talent.[16] The character of the Peruvian mind led to imitation, in fact, rather than invention, to delicacy and minuteness of finish, rather than to boldness or beauty of design.

That they should have accomplished these difficult works with such tools as they possessed is truly wonderful. It was comparatively easy to cast and even to sculpture metallic substances, both of which they did with consummate skill.

[15] At least, such was the opinion of the Egyptians, who referred to this arrangement of castes as the source of their own peculiar dexterity in the arts See Diodorus Sic, lib. I, sec 74

[16] Ulloa, Not. Amer, ent. 21.—Pedro Pizarro, Descub. y Conq, MS.—Cieza de Leon, Cronica, cap. 114 —Condamine, Mém ap Hist. de l'Acad. Royale de Berlin, tom ii pp 451–456.—The last writer says that a large collection of massive gold ornaments of very rich workmanship was long preserved in the royal treasury of Quito But on his going there to examine them he learned that they had just been melted down into ingots to send to Carthagena, then besieged by the English! The art of war can flourish only at the expense of all the other arts

But that they should have shown the like facility in cutting the hardest substances, as emeralds and other precious stones, is not so easy to explain. Emeralds they obtained in considerable quantity from the barren district of Atacames, and this inflexible material seems to have been almost as ductile in the hands of the Peruvian artist as if it had been made of clay.[17]   Yet the natives were unacquainted with the use of iron, though the soil was largely impregnated with it.[18]   The tools used were of stone, or more frequently of copper. But the material on which they relied for the execution of their most difficult tasks was formed by combining a very small portion of tin with copper.[19] This composition gave a hardness to the metal which seems to have been little inferior to that of steel. With the aid of it, not only did the Peruvian artisan hew into shape porphyry and granite, but by his patient industry accomplished works which the European would not have ventured to undertake. Among the remains of the monuments of Cannar may be seen movable rings in the muzzles of animals, all nicely sculptured of one entire block of granite.[20]   It is worthy of

[17] They had turquoises, also, and might have had pearls, but for the tenderness of the Incas, who were unwilling to risk the lives of their people in this perilous fishery! At least, so we are assured by Garcilasso, Com. Real, Parte 1, lib. 8, cap. 23.

[18] "No tenian herramientas de hierro ni azero" Ondegardo, Rel. Seg., MS.—Herrera, Hist. general, dec. 5, lib 4, cap 4

[19] M. de Humboldt brought with him back to Europe one of these metallic tools, a chisel, found in a silver-mine opened by the Incas not far from Cuzco. On an analysis, it was found to contain 0.94 of copper and 0 06 of tin. See Vues des Cordilleres, p. 117.

[20] "Quoiqu'il en soit," says M. de la Condamine, " nous avons vu en quelques autres ruines des ornemens du même granit, qui repré-

remark that the Egyptians, the Mexicans, and the Peruvians, in their progress towards civilization, should never have detected the use of iron, which lay around them in abundance, and that they should each, without any knowledge of the other, have found a substitute for it in such a curious composition of metals as gave to their tools almost the temper of steel;[21] a secret that has been lost —or, to speak more correctly, has never been discovered—by the civilized European.

I have already spoken of the large quantity of gold and silver wrought into various articles of elegance and utility for the Incas; though the amount was inconsiderable, in comparison with what could have been afforded by the mineral riches of the land, and with what has since been obtained by the more sagacious and unscrupulous cupidity of the white man. Gold was gathered by the Incas from the deposits of the streams. They extracted the ore also in considerable quantities from the valley of Curimayo, northeast of Caxamarca, as well as from other places; and the silver-mines of Porco, in particular, yielded them considerable returns. Yet they did not attempt to penetrate into the bowels of the earth by sinking a shaft, but simply excavated a cavern in the steep sides of the mountain, or, at most, opened a horizontal vein of moderate depth. They were equally deficient in the knowledge of the best means of detaching the precious metal from the

sentoient des mufles d'animaux, dont les narines percées portoient des anneaux mobiles de la même pierre." Mém. ap. Hist. de l'Acad. Royale de Berlin, tom. ii. p. 452.

[21] See the History of the Conquest of Mexico, Book 1, chap. 5.

dross with which it was united, and had no idea
of the virtues of quicksilver—a mineral not rare
in Peru—as an amalgam to effect this decompo-
sition.[22] Their method of smelting the ore was by
means of furnaces built in elevated and exposed
situations, where they might be fanned by the
strong breezes of the mountains. The subjects
of the Incas, in short, with all their patient perseverance, did little more than penetrate below the
crust, the outer rind, as it were, formed over those
golden caverns which lie hidden in the dark depths
of the Andes. Yet what they gleaned from the
surface was more than adequate for all their demands. For they were not a commercial people,
and had no knowledge of money.[23] In this they
differed from the ancient Mexicans, who had an
established currency of a determinate value. In
one respect, however, they were superior to their
American rivals, since they made use of weights
to determine the quantity of their commodities, a
thing wholly unknown to the Aztecs. This fact
is ascertained by the discovery of silver balances,
adjusted with perfect accuracy, in some of the
tombs of the Incas.[24]

But the surest test of the civilization of a people
—at least, as sure as any—afforded by mechanical
art is to be found in their architecture, which pre-

[22] Garcilasso, Com. Real, Parte 1, lib. 8, cap. 25
[23] Garcilasso, Com. Real, Parte 1, lib. 5, cap. 7; lib. 6, cap. 8.—
Ondegardo, Rel. Seg, MS.—This, which Bonaparte thought so incredible of the little island of Loo Choo, was still more extraordinary in a great and flourishing empire like Peru,—the country,
too, which contained within its bowels the treasures that were one
day to furnish Europe with the basis of its vast metallic currency.
[24] Ulloa, Not Amer, ent. 21.

sents so noble a field for the display of the grand
and the beautiful, and which at the same time is
so intimately connected with the essential comforts of life. There is no object on which the
resources of the wealthy are more freely lavished,
or which calls out more effectually the inventive
talent of the artist. The painter and the sculptor
may display their individual genius in creations of
surpassing excellence, but it is the great monuments of architectural taste and magnificence that
are stamped in a peculiar manner by the genius of
the nation. The Greek, the Egyptian, the Sara-
cen, the Gothic,—what a key do their respective
styles afford to the character and condition of the
people! The monuments of China, of Hindostan,
and of Central America are all indicative of an
immature period, in which the imagination has not
been disciplined by study, and which, therefore, in
its best results, betrays only the ill-regulated aspi-
rations after the beautiful, that belong to a semi-
civilized people.

The Peruvian architecture, bearing also the
general characteristics of an imperfect state of
refinement, had still its peculiar character; and so
uniform was that character that the edifices
throughout the country seem to have been all
cast in the same mould.[25] They were usually
built of porphyry or granite; not unfrequently

[25] It is the observation of Humboldt. "Il est impossible d'exami-
ner attentivement un seul édifice du temps des Incas, sans recon-
noître le même type dans tous les autres qui couvrent le dos des
Andes, sur une longueur de plus de quatre cent cinquante lieues,
depuis mille jusqu'à quatre mille mètres d'élévation au-dessus du
niveau de l'Océan. On dirait qu'un seul architecte a construit ce
grand nombre de monumens" Vues des Cordillères, p. 197.

of brick. This, which was formed into blocks or squares of much larger dimensions than our brick, was made of a tenacious earth mixed up with reeds or tough grass, and acquired a degree of hardness with age that made it insensible alike to the storms and the more trying sun of the tropics.[26]   The walls were of great thickness, but low, seldom reaching to more than twelve or fourteen feet in height.*   It is rare to meet with accounts of a building that rose to a second story.[27]

The apartments had no communication with one another, but usually opened into a court; and, as they were unprovided with windows, or apertures that served for them, the only light from without must have been admitted by the doorways. These were made with the sides approaching each other towards the top, so that the lintel was considerably narrower than the threshold, a peculiarity, also, in Egyptian architecture. The roofs have, for the most part, disappeared with time.†   Some few sur-

---

[26] Ulloa, who carefully examined these bricks, suggests that there must have been some secret in their composition,—so superior in many respects to our own manufacture,—now lost. Not. Amer., ent. 20.

[27] Ibid., ubi supra.

* [This is an error. Squier says that walls remaining in Cuzco show that the buildings were from thirty-five to forty feet high, besides the spring of the roof. Those buildings were, perhaps, only one story high, but elsewhere there were edifices, public and private, of two and three stories, with windows such as were needed for lighting the interiors. Because of the coldness of the country, no more windows than were absolutely necessary were used by a people unacquainted with glass. Squier, Peru, p. 438. See, also Markham's Introduction to his translation of Cieza de Leon, p. xxix, and Rivero, Antiquities of Peru, p. 233.—M.]

† [One of the ancient roofs is still to be seen upon the Sondor-huasi, "one of the most remarkable monuments of antiquity in

vive in the less ambitious edifices, of a singular bell-shape, and made of a composition of earth and pebbles. They are supposed, however, to have been generally formed of more perishable materials, of wood or straw. It is certain that some of the most considerable stone buildings were thatched with straw. Many seem to have been constructed without the aid of cement; and writers have contended that the Peruvians were unacquainted with the use of mortar, or cement of any kind.[28] But a close, tenacious mould, mixed with lime, may be discovered, filling up the interstices of the granite in some buildings; and in others, where the well-fitted blocks leave no room for the coarser material, the eye of the antiquary has detected a fine bituminous glue, as hard as the rock itself.[29]

[28] Among others, see Acosta, lib. 6, cap. 15.—Robertson, History of America (London, 1796), vol iii. p. 213.

[29] Ondegardo, Rel Seg, MS—Ulloa, Not. Amer., ent. 21.—Humboldt, who analyzed the cement of the ancient structures at Cannar, says that it is a true mortar, formed of a mixture of pebbles and a clayey marl. (Vues des Cordillères, p 116.) Father Velasco is in raptures with an "almost imperceptible kind of cement" made of lime and a bituminous substance resembling glue, which incorporated with the stones so as to hold them firmly together like one

---

Peru, which retains its original thatched roof after a lapse of over three hundred years" (Squier, Peru, p. 393) The dome of this building is formed of bamboos, bent evenly to a central point over a series of hoops. Over this skeleton is a fine mat of the braided epidermis of the bamboo This is worked in panellings of different colors; and Squier compares it, in style and effect, to that of the cella of the temple of Venus, facing the Colosseum, in Rome. Then comes another coarser mat, in which was fastened a fleece of ichu. Over this was another transverse layer of coarser grass or weeds, then more ichu, and so on. The projecting ends of the various layers were cut off regularly, producing the effect of overlapping tiles.—M.]

The greatest simplicity is observed in the construction of the buildings, which are usually free from outward ornament; though in some the huge stones are shaped into a convex form with great regularity, and adjusted with such nice precision to one another that it would be impossible, but for the flutings, to determine the line of junction. In others the stone is rough, as it was taken from the quarry, in the most irregular forms, with the edges nicely wrought and fitted to each other. There is no appearance of columns or of arches; though there is some contradiction as to the latter point. But it is not to be doubted that, although they may have made some approach to this mode of construction by the greater or less inclination of the walls, the Peruvian architects were wholly unacquainted with the true principle of the circular arch reposing on its key-stone.[30]

The architecture of the Incas is characterized, says an eminent traveller, " by simplicity, symmetry, and solidity." [31] It may seem unphilosophical to condemn the peculiar fashion of a nation as indicating want of taste, because its standard of taste differs from our own. Yet there is an incongruity in the composition of the Peru-

solid mass, yet left nothing visible to the eye of the common observer. This glutinous composition, mixed with pebbles, made a sort of *macadamized* road much used by the Incas, as hard and almost as smooth as marble. Hist. de Quito, tom. i. pp. 126–128.

[30] Condamine, Mém. ap Hist de l'Acad. Royale de Berlin, tom. ii. p. 448.—Antig y Monumentos del Peru, MS.—Herrera, Hist. general, dec. 5, lib 4, cap. 4.—Acosta, lib 6, cap 14.—Ulloa, Voyage to South America, vol. i. p. 469 —Ondegardo, Rel. Seg., MS.

[31] " Simplicité, symétrie, et solidité, voilà les trois caractères par lesquels se distinguent avantageusement tous les édifices péruviens." Humboldt, Vues des Cordillères, p 115.

vian buildings which argues a very imperfect acquaintance with the first principles of architecture. While they put together their bulky masses of porphyry and granite with the nicest art, they were incapable of mortising their timbers, and, in their ignorance of iron, knew no better way of holding the beams together than tying them with thongs of maguey. In the same incongruous spirit, the building that was thatched with straw and unilluminated by a window was glowing with tapestries of gold and silver! These are the inconsistencies of a rude people, among whom the arts are but partially developed. It might not be difficult to find examples of like inconsistency in the architecture and domestic arrangements of our Anglo-Saxon and, at a still later period, of our Norman ancestors.

Yet the buildings of the Incas were accommodated to the character of the climate, and were well fitted to resist those terrible convulsions which belong to the land of volcanoes. The wisdom of their plan is attested by the number which still survive, while the more modern constructions of the Conquerors have been buried in ruins. The hand of the Conquerors, indeed, has fallen heavily on these venerable monuments, and, in their blind and superstitious search for hidden treasure, has caused infinitely more ruin than time or the earthquake.[32] Yet enough of these monuments still

[32] The anonymous author of the Antig. y Monumentos del Peru, MS, gives us, at second hand, one of those golden traditions which, in early times, fostered the spirit of adventure. The tradition, in this instance, he thinks well entitled to credit The reader will judge for himself·

remain to invite the researches of the antiquary. Those only in the most conspicuous situations have been hitherto examined. But, by the testimony of travellers, many more are to be found in the less frequented parts of the country; and we may hope they will one day call forth a kindred spirit of enterprise to that which has so successfully explored the mysterious recesses of Central America and Yucatan.*

" It is a well-authenticated report, and generally received, that there is a secret hall in the fortress of Cuzco, where an immense treasure is concealed, consisting of the statues of all the Incas, wrought in gold. A lady is still living, Doña Maria de Esquivel, the wife of the last Inca, who has visited this hall, and I have heard her relate the way in which she was carried to see it

"Don Carlos, the lady's husband, did not maintain a style of living becoming his high rank. Doña Maria sometimes reproached him, declaring that she had been deceived into marrying a poor Indian under the lofty title of Lord or Inca. She said this so frequently that Don Carlos one night exclaimed, 'Lady! do you wish to know whether I am rich or poor? You shall see that no lord nor king in the world has a larger treasure than I have.' Then, covering her eyes with a handkerchief, he made her turn round two or three times, and, taking her by the hand, led her a short distance before he removed the bandage On opening her eyes, what was her amazement! She had gone not more than two hundred paces, and descended a short flight of steps, and she now found herself in a large quadrangular hall, where, ranged on benches round the walls, she beheld the statues of the Incas, each of the size of a boy twelve years old, all of massive gold! She saw also many vessels of gold and silver. 'In fact,' she said, 'it was one of the most magnificent treasures in the whole world!'"

* [In the foregoing remarks the author has scarcely done justice to the artistic character of the Peruvian architecture, its great superiority to the Mexican, and the resemblances which it offers, in style and development, to the early stages of Greek and Egyptian art. The subject has been fully, and of course very ably, treated by Mr. Fergusson, in his Handbook of Architecture. The Peruvian pottery, which Prescott has passed over with a mere incidental mention, might also have claimed particular notice. Its characteristics are now more familiar, from numerous specimens in public and

I cannot close this analysis of the Peruvian institutions without a few reflections on their general character and tendency, which, if they involve some repetition of previous remarks, may, I trust, be excused, from my desire to leave a correct and consistent impression on the reader. In this survey we cannot but be struck with the total dissimilarity between these institutions and those of the Aztecs,—the other great nation who led in the march of civilization on this Western continent, and whose empire in the northern portion of it was as conspicuous as that of the Incas in the south. Both nations came on the plateau and commenced their career of conquest at dates, it may be, not far removed from each other.[33] And it is worthy of notice that, in America, the elevated region along the crests of the great mountain-ranges should have been the chosen seat of civilization in both hemispheres.

Very different was the policy pursued by the two races in their military career. The Aztecs, animated by the most ferocious spirit, carried on a war of extermination, signalizing their triumphs by the sacrifice of hecatombs of captives; while the Incas, although they pursued the game of conquest with equal pertinacity, preferred a milder policy, substituting negotiation and intrigue for violence, and dealt with their antagonists so that their future resources should not be crippled, and

[33] *Ante,* chap. 1.

private collections. For a description of these interesting relics, and a comparison with other remains of ancient ceramic art, see Wilson, Prehistoric Man, chap. 17.—K.]

that they should come as friends, not as foes, into the bosom of the empire.

Their policy towards the conquered forms a contrast no less striking to that pursued by the Aztecs. The Mexican vassals were ground by excessive imposts and military conscriptions. No regard was had to their welfare, and the only limit to oppression was the power of endurance. They were overawed by fortresses and armed garrisons, and were made to feel every hour that they were not part and parcel of the nation, but held only in subjugation as a conquered people. The Incas, on the other hand, admitted their new subjects at once to all the rights enjoyed by the rest of the community; and, though they made them conform to the established laws and usages of the empire, they watched over their personal security and comfort with a sort of parental solicitude. The motley population, thus bound together by common interest, was animated by a common feeling of loyalty, which gave greater strength and stability to the empire as it became more and more widely extended; while the various tribes who successively came under the Mexican sceptre, being held together only by the pressure of external force, were ready to fall asunder the moment that the force was withdrawn. The policy of the two nations displayed the principle of fear as contrasted with the principle of love.

The characteristic features of their religious systems had as little resemblance to each other. The whole Aztec pantheon partook more or less of the sanguinary spirit of the terrible war-god who presided over it, and the frivolous ceremonial almost always terminated with human sacrifice and cannibal orgies. But the rites of the Peruvians were of a more innocent cast, as they tended to a more spiritual worship. For the worship of the Creator is most nearly approached by that of the heavenly bodies, which, as they revolve in their bright orbits, seem to be the most glorious symbols of his beneficence and power.

In the minuter mechanical arts, both showed considerable skill; but in the construction of important public works, of roads, aqueducts, canals, and in agriculture in all its details, the Peruvians were much superior. Strange that they should have fallen so far below their rivals in their efforts after a higher intellectual culture, in astronomical science more especially, and in the art of communicating thought by visible symbols. When we consider the greater refinement of the Incas, their inferiority to the Aztecs in these particulars can be explained only by the fact that the latter in all probability were indebted for their science to the race who preceded them in the land,—that shadowy race whose origin and whose end are alike veiled from the eye of the inquirer, but who possibly may have sought a refuge from their ferocious invaders in those regions of Central America, the architectural remains of which now supply us with the most pleasing monuments of Indian civilization. It is with this more polished race, to whom the Peruvians seem to have borne some resemblance in their mental and moral organization, that they should be compared. Had the empire of the

Incas been permitted to extend itself with the
rapid strides with which it was advancing at the
period of the Spanish conquest, the two races
might have come into conflict, or perhaps into
alliance, with one another.

The Mexicans and Peruvians, so different in
the character of their peculiar civilization, were,
it seems probable, ignorant of each other's existence; and it may appear singular that, during the
simultaneous continuance of their empires, some
of the seeds of science and of art which pass so
imperceptibly from one people to another should
not have found their way across the interval which
separated the two nations. They furnish an interesting example of the opposite directions which
the human mind may take in its struggle to
emerge from darkness into the light of civilization.*

* [Professor Daniel Wilson, commenting on this passage, remarks
that, "whilst there seems little room for doubt that those two
nations were ignorant of each other at the period of the discovery
of America, there are many indications in some of their arts of an
earlier intercourse between the northern and southern continent."
(Prehistoric Man, 2d edition, p. 285.) This supposition is connected
with a theory put forward by the learned writer in regard to the
aboriginal population of America. Rejecting the common opinion
of its ethnical unity, he considers the indications as pointing to two,
or possibly three, great divisions of race, with as many distinct lines
of immigration. He conceives " the earliest current of population"
from "a supposed Asiatic cradle land" "to have spread through
the islands of the Pacific and to have reached the South American
continent long before an excess of Asiatic population had diffused
itself into its own inhospitable northern steppes. By an Atlantic
Ocean migration, another wave of population occupied the Canaries,
Madeira, and the Azores, and so passed to the Antilles, Central
America, and probably by the Cape Verdes, or, guided by the more
southern equatorial current, to Brazil Latest of all, Behring
Straits and the North Pacific Islands may have become the highway

A closer resemblance—as I have more than once taken occasion to notice—may be found between the Peruvian institutions and some of the despotic governments of Eastern Asia; those governments where despotism appears in its more mitigated form, and the whole people, under the patriarchal sway of the sovereign, seem to be gathered together like the members of one vast family. Such were the Chinese, for example, whom the Peruvians resembled in their implicit obedience to authority, their mild yet somewhat stubborn temper, their solicitude for forms, their reverence for ancient usage, their skill in the minuter manufactures, their imitative rather than inventive cast of mind, and their invincible patience, which serves instead of a more adventurous spirit for the execution of difficult undertakings.[34]

"Count Carli has amused himself with tracing out the different points of resemblance between the Chinese and the Peruvians. The

for a northern migration by which certain striking diversities of nations of the northern continent, including the conquerors of the Mexican plateau, are most easily accounted for." (Ibid., p. 604.) "The north and south tropics were the centres of two distinct and seemingly independent manifestations of native development," but with "clear indications of an overlapping of two or more distinct migratory trails leading from opposite points." (Ibid., p. 602.) It is to be remarked that the novelty of this theory consists, not in any new suggestion to account for the original settlement of America, but in the adoption and symmetrical blending of various conjectures, and the application of them to explain the differences of physical characteristics, customs, development, etc., between the savage and civilized or semi-civilized nations scattered over the continent. The evidence offered in its support does not admit of being summarized here. Elaborate as it is, it will scarcely be considered sufficient to establish the certainty of the general conclusions deduced by the author. On the other hand, his arguments in disproof of a supposed craniological uniformity of type among the American aborigines appear to be irresistible, and to justify the

A still closer analogy may be found with the natives of Hindostan in their division into castes, their worship of the heavenly bodies and the elements of nature, and their acquaintance with the scientific principles of husbandry. To the ancient Egyptians, also, they bore considerable resemblance in the same particulars, as well as in those ideas of a future existence which led them to attach so much importance to the permanent preservation of the body.

But we shall look in vain in the history of the East for a parallel to the absolute control exercised by the Incas over their subjects. In the East, this was founded on physical power,—on the external resources of the government. The authority of the Inca might be compared with that of the Pope in the day of his might, when Christendom trembled at the thunders of the Vatican, and the successor of St. Peter set his foot on the necks of princes. But the authority of the Pope was founded on opinion. His temporal power was nothing. The empire of the Incas rested on both. It was a theocracy more potent in its operations than that of the Jews; for, though the sanction of the law might be as great among the latter, the law was expounded by a

Emperor of China was styled the son of Heaven or of the Sun. He also held a plough once a year in presence of his people, to show his respect for agriculture. And the solstices and the equinoxes were noted, to determine the periods of their religious festivals. The coincidences are curious. Lettres Américaines, tom. ii. pp. 7, 8.

---

statement that "the form of the human skull is just as little constant among different tribes or races of the New World as of the Old." (Ibid., p. 483.)—K.]

human lawgiver, the servant and representative of Divinity. But the Inca was both the lawgiver and the law. He was not merely the representative of Divinity, or, like the Pope, its vicegerent, but he was Divinity itself. The violation of his ordinance was sacrilege. Never was there a scheme of government enforced by such terrible sanctions, or which bore so oppressively on the subjects of it. For it reached not only to the visible acts, but to the private conduct, the words, the very thoughts, of its vassals.

It added not a little to the efficacy of the government that below the sovereign there was an order of hereditary nobles of the same divine original with himself, who, placed far below himself, were still immeasurably above the rest of the community, not merely by descent, but, as it would seem, by their intellectual nature. These were the exclusive depositaries of power, and, as their long hereditary training made them familiar with their vocation and secured them implicit deference from the multitude, they became the prompt and well-practised agents for carrying out the executive measures of the administration. All that occurred throughout the wide extent of his empire—such was the perfect system of communication—passed in review, as it were, before the eyes of the monarch, and a thousand hands, armed with irresistible authority, stood ready in every quarter to do his bidding. Was it not, as we have said, the most oppressive, though the mildest, of despotisms?

It was the mildest, from the very circumstance

that the transcendent rank of the sovereign, and the humble, nay, superstitious, devotion to his will, made it superfluous to assert this will by acts of violence or rigor. The great mass of the people may have appeared to his eyes as but little removed above the condition of the brute, formed to minister to his pleasures. But from their very helplessness he regarded them with feelings of commiseration, like those which a kind master might feel for the poor animals committed to his charge, or—to do justice to the beneficent character attributed to many of the Incas—that a parent might feel for his young and impotent offspring. The laws were carefully directed to their preservation and personal comfort. The people were not allowed to be employed on works pernicious to their health, nor to pine—a sad contrast to their subsequent destiny—under the imposition of tasks too heavy for their powers. They were never made the victims of public or private extortion; and a benevolent forecast watched carefully over their necessities and provided for their relief in seasons of infirmity and for their sustenance in health. The government of the Incas, however arbitrary in form, was in its spirit truly patriarchal.

Yet in this there was nothing cheering to the dignity of human nature. What the people had was conceded as a boon, not as a right. When a nation was brought under the sceptre of the Incas, it resigned every personal right, even the rights dearest to humanity. Under this extraordinary polity, a people advanced in many of the social refinements, well skilled in manufactures and agriculture, were unacquainted, as we have seen, with money. They had nothing that deserved to be called property. They could follow no craft, could engage in no labor, no amusement, but such as was specially provided by law. They could not change their residence or their dress without a license from the government. They could not even exercise the freedom which is conceded to the most abject in other countries,—that of selecting their own wives. The imperative spirit of despotism would not allow them to be happy or miserable in any way but that established by law. The power of free agency—the inestimable and inborn right of every human being—was annihilated in Peru.

The astonishing mechanism of the Peruvian polity could have resulted only from the combined authority of opinion and positive power in the ruler to an extent unprecedented in the history of man. Yet that it should have so successfully gone into operation, and so long endured, in opposition to the taste, the prejudices, and the very principles of our nature, is a strong proof of a generally wise and temperate administration of the government.

The policy habitually pursued by the Incas for the *prevention* of evils that might have disturbed the order of things is well exemplified in their provisions against poverty and idleness. In these they rightly discerned the two great causes of disaffection in a populous community. The industry of the people was secured not only by their compulsory occupations at home, but by their employment on those great public works which covered every part of the country, and which still bear testimony in their decay to their primitive grandeur. Yet it may well astonish us to find that the natural difficulty of these undertakings, sufficiently great in itself, considering the imperfections of their tools and machinery, was inconcievably enhanced by the politic contrivance of the government. The royal edifices of Quito, we are assured by the Spanish conquerors, were constructed of huge masses of stone, many of which were carried all the way along the mountain-roads from Cuzco, a distance of several hundred leagues.[35] The great square of the capital was filled to a considerable depth with mould brought with incredible labor up the steep slopes of the Cordilleras from the distant shores of the Pacific Ocean.[36] Labor was regarded not only as a means, but as an end, by the Peruvian law.

[35] "Era muy principal intento que la gente no holgase, que dava causa a que despues que los Ingas estuvieron en paz hacer traer de Quito al Cuzco piedra que venia de provincia en provincia para hacer casas para si ó pª el Sol en gran cantidad, y del Cuzco llevalla a Quito pª el mismo efecto, . . . y asi destas cosas hacian los Ingas muchas de poco provecho y de escesivo travajo en que traian ocupadas las provincias ordinariamte, y en fin el travajo era causa de su conservacion." Ondegardo, Rel Prim., MS—Also Antig. y Monumentos del Peru, MS.

[36] This was literally gold dust; for Ondegardo states that, when governor of Cuzco, he caused great quantities of gold vessels and ornaments to be disinterred from the sand in which they had been secreted by the natives: "Que toda aquella plaza del Cuzco le sacaron la tierra propia, y se llevó á otras partes por cosa de gran estima, é la hincheron de arena de la costa de la mar, como hasta dos palmos y medio en algunas partes, mas sembraron por toda ella muchos vasos de oro é plata, y hovejuelas y hombrecillos pequeños de lo mismo, lo cual se ha sacado en mucha cantidad, que todo lo

With their manifold provisions against poverty the reader has already been made acquainted. They were so perfect that in their wide extent of territory—much of it smitten with the curse of barrenness—no man, however humble, suffered for the want of food and clothing. Famine, so common a scourge in every other American nation, so common at that period in every country of civilized Europe, was an evil unknown in the dominions of the Incas.

The most enlightened of the Spaniards who first visited Peru, struck with the general appearance of plenty and prosperity, and with the astonishing order with which every thing throughout the country was regulated, are loud in their expressions of admiration. No better government, in their opinion, could have been devised for the people. Contented with their condition, and free from vice, to borrow the language of an eminent authority of that early day, the mild and docile character of the Peruvians would have well fitted them to receive the teachings of Christianity, had the love of conversion, instead of gold, animated the breasts of the Conquerors.[37]   And a philoso-

hemos visto; desta arena estaba toda la plaza, quando yo fui á governar aquella Ciudad; é si fue verdad que aquella se trajo de ellos, afirman é tienen puestos en sus registros, paresceme que sea ansí, que toda la tierra junta tubo necesidad de entender en ello, por que la plaza es grande, y no tiene numero las cargas que en ella entraron; y la costa por lo mas cerca esta mas de nobenta leguas á lo que creo, y cierto yo me satisfice, porque todos dicen, que aquel genero de arena, no lo hay hasta la costa" Rel. Seg, MS.

[37] "Y si Dios permitiera que tubieran quien con celo de Cristiandad, y no con ramo de codicia, en lo pasado, les dieran entera noticia de nuestra sagrada Religion, era gente en que bien imprimiera, segun vemos por lo que ahora con la buena orden que hay se

pher of a later time, warmed by the contemplation
of the picture—which his own fancy had colored
—of public prosperity and private happiness
under the rule of the Incas, pronounces "the
moral man in Peru far superior to the Europeans." [38]

Yet such results are scarcely reconcilable with
the theory of the government I have attempted
to analyze. Where there is no free agency there
can be no morality. Where there is no temptation
there can be little claim to virtue. Where the
routine is rigorously prescribed by law, the law,
and not the man, must have the credit of the conduct. If that government is the best which is felt
the least, which encroaches on the natural liberty
of the subject only so far as is essential to civil
subordination, then of all governments devised by

obra." Sarmiento, Relacion, MS., cap. 22.—But the most emphatic
testimony to the merits of the people is that afforded by Mancio
Sierra Lejesema, the last survivor of the early Spanish Conquerors,
who settled in Peru. In the preamble to his testament, made, as he
states, to relieve his conscience, at the time of his death, he declares
that the whole population, under the Incas, was distinguished by
sobriety and industry; that such things as robbery and theft were
unknown; that, far from licentiousness, there was not even a pros-
titute in the country; and that every thing was conducted with the
greatest order, and entire submission to authority. The panegyric
is somewhat too unqualified for a whole nation, and may lead one
to suspect that the stings of remorse for his own treatment of the
natives goaded the dying veteran into a higher estimate of their
deserts than was strictly warranted by facts. Yet this testimony
by such a man at such a time is too remarkable, as well as too honorable to the Peruvians, to be passed over in silence by the historian;
and I have transferred the document in the original to Appendix
No. 4.

[38] " Sans doute l'homme moral du Pérou étoit infiniment plus per-
fectionné que l'Européen." Carli, Lettres Américaines, tom. i.
p. 215.

man the Peruvian has the least real claim to our admiration.

It is not easy to comprehend the genius and the full import of institutions so opposite to those of our own free republic, where every man, however humble his condition, may aspire to the highest honors of the state,—may select his own career and carve out his fortune in his own way; where the light of knowledge, instead of being concentrated on a chosen few, is shed abroad like the light of day, and suffered to fall equally on the poor and the rich; where the collision of man with man wakens a generous emulation that calls out latent talent and tasks the energies to the utmost; where consciousness of independence gives a feeling of self-reliance unknown to the timid subjects of a despotism; where, in short, the government is made for man,—not as in Peru, where man seemed to be made only for the government. The New World is the theatre on which these two political systems, so opposite in their character, have been carried into operation. The empire of the Incas has passed away and left no trace. The other great experiment is still going on,—the experiment which is to solve the problem, so long contested in the Old World, of the capacity of man for self-government. Alas for humanity, if it should fail!

The testimony of the Spanish conquerors is not uniform in respect to the favorable influence exerted by the Peruvian institutions on the character of the people. Drinking and dancing are said to have been the pleasures to which they were immoderately addicted. Like the slaves and serfs in other lands, whose position excluded them from more serious and ennobling occupations, they found a substitute in frivolous or sensual indulgence. Lazy, luxurious, and licentious, are. the epithets bestowed on them by one of those who saw them at the Conquest, but whose pen was not too friendly to the Indian.[39]   Yet the spirit of independence could hardly be strong in a people who had no interest in the soil, no personal rights to defend; and the facility with which they yielded to the Spanish invader—after every allowance for their comparative inferiority—argues a deplorable destitution of that patriotic feeling which holds life as little in comparison with freedom.

But we must not judge too hardly of the unfortunate native because he quailed before the civilization of the European. We must not be insensible to the really great results that were achieved by the government of the Incas. We must not forget that under their rule the meanest of the people enjoyed a far greater degree of personal comfort, at least a greater exemption

[39] "Heran muy dados á la lujuria y al bever, tenian acceso carnal con las hermanas y las mugeres de sus padres como no fuesen sus mismas madres, y aun algunos avia que con ellas mismas lo hacian y ansi mismo con sus hijas. Estando borrachos tocavan algunos en el pecado nefando, emborrachavanse muy á menudo, y estando borrachos todo lo que el demonio les traia á la voluntad hacian. Ileran estos orejones muy soberbios y presuntuosos. . . . Tenian otras muchas maldades que por ser muchas no las digo." Pedro Pizarro, Descub. y Conq., MS —These random aspersions of the hard conqueror show too gross an ignorance of the institutions of the people to merit much confidence as to what is said of their character.

from physical suffering, than was possessed by similar classes in other nations on the American continent,—greater, probably, than was possessed by these classes in most of the countries of feudal Europe. Under their sceptre the higher orders of the state had made advances in many of the arts that belong to a cultivated community. The foundations of a regular government were laid, which, in an age of rapine, secured to its subjects the inestimable blessings of tranquillity and safety. By the well-sustained policy of the Incas, the rude tribes of the forest were gradually drawn from their fastnesses and gathered within the folds of civilization; and of these materials was constructed a flourishing and populous empire, such as was to be found in no other quarter of the American continent. The defects of this government were those of over-refinement in legislation,—the last defects to have been looked for, certainly, in the American aborigines.

Note.—I have not thought it necessary to swell this Introduction by an inquiry into the origin of Peruvian civilization, like that appended to the history of the Mexican. The Peruvian history, doubtless suggests analogies with more than one nation in the East, some of which have been briefly adverted to in the preceding pages; although these analogies are adduced there not as evidence of a common origin, but as showing the coincidences which might naturally spring up among different nations under the same phase of civilization. Such coincidences are neither so numerous nor so striking as those afforded by the Aztec history The correspondence presented by the astronomical science of the Mexicans is alone of more importance than all the rest. Yet the light of analogy afforded by the institutions of the Incas seems to point, as far as it goes, towards the same direction; and as the investigation could present but little substantially to confirm, and still less to confute, the views taken in the former disquisition, I have not thought it best to fatigue the reader with it.

Two of the prominent authorities on whom I have relied in this Introductory portion of the work are Juan de Sarmiento and the Licentiate Ondegardo. Of the former I have been able to collect no information beyond what is afforded by his own writings In the title prefixed to his manuscript he is styled President of the Council of the Indies, a post of high authority, which infers a weight of character and means of information that entitle his opinions on colonial topics to great deference.

These means of information were much enlarged by Sarmiento's visit to the colonies during the administration of Gasca. Having conceived the design of compiling a history of the ancient Peruvian institutions, he visited Cuzco, as he tells us, in 1550, and there drew from the natives themselves the materials for his narrative His position gave him access to the most authentic sources of knowledge, and from the lips of the Inca nobles, the best-instructed of the conquered race, he gathered the traditions of their national history and institutions. The quipus formed, as we have seen, an imperfect system of mnemonics, requiring constant attention, and much inferior to the Mexican hieroglyphics. It was only by diligent instruction that they were made available to historical purposes; and this instruction was so far neglected after the Conquest that the ancient annals of the country would have perished with the generation which was the sole depositary of them, had it not been for the efforts of a few intelligent scholars, like Sarmiento, who saw the importance, at this critical period, of cultivating an intercourse with the natives and drawing from them their hidden stores of information.

To give still further authenticity to this work, Sarmiento travelled over the country, examined the principal objects of interest with his own eyes, and thus verified the accounts of the natives as far as possible by personal observation. The result of these labors was his work entitled " Relacion de la sucesion y govierno de las Yngas Señores naturales que fueron de las Provincias del Peru y otras cosas tocantes á aquel Reyno, para el Iltmo. Señor Dⁿ Juan Sarmiento, Presidente del Consejo Rˡ de Indias." *

* [It is singular that Prescott should have fallen into the error of supposing this language to indicate that the work was the composition of the person whose name appears on the title. Señor Gayangos, in a letter to Mr. Squier which that gentleman has kindly communicated to the editor, says, "It is evident to me that this Relation was written—perhaps by order of Don Juan Sarmiento, president of the Council of the Indies—*for* him, and not *by* him, as stated by Prescott;" and he points out the improbability of Sarmiento's ever having visited America, as well as of his having used the deferential tone in which the author of the manuscript addresses certain members of the Royal Audience, persons far

It is divided into chapters, and embraces about four hundred folio pages in manuscript. The introductory portion of the work is occupied with the traditionary tales of the origin and early period of the Incas; teeming, as usual in the antiquities of a barbarous people, with legendary fables of the most wild and monstrous character. Yet these puerile conceptions afford an inexhaustible mine for the labors of the antiquarian, who endeavors to unravel the allegorical web which a cunning priesthood had devised as symbolical of those mysteries of creation that it was beyond their power to comprehend. But Sarmiento happily confines himself to the mere statement of traditional fables, without the chimerical ambition to explain them.

From this region of romance Sarmiento passes to the institutions of the Peruvians, describes their ancient polity, their religion, their progress in the arts, especially agriculture, and presents, in short, an elaborate picture of the civilization which they reached under the Inca dynasty. This part of his work, resting, as it does, on the best authority, confirmed in many instances by his own observation, is of unquestionable value, and is written with an apparent respect for truth, that engages the confidence of the reader. The concluding portion of the manuscript is occupied with the civil history of the country The reigns of the early Incas, which lie beyond the sober province of history, he despatches with commendable brevity. But on the three last reigns—fortunately, those of the greatest princes who occupied the Peruvian throne—he is more diffuse. This was comparatively firm ground for the chronicler, for the events were too recent to be obscured by the vulgar legends that gather like moss round every incident of the older time. His account stops with the Spanish invasion; for this story, Sarmiento

---

inferior in rank to an ecclesiastic of high position holding one of the first offices in the kingdom The mistake was so far fortunate that the doubts suggested by it seem to have led to an investigation, with the result of determining the real authorship of this important Relation, and of clearing up, at the same time, another mooted and not less interesting point in regard to one of the chief authorities for early Peruvian history. Señor Gonzalez de la Rosa, a learned Peruvian, is able, according to a recent statement (London Athenæum, July 5, 1873), "to prove that the manuscript in question is really the second part of the 'Chronicle of Peru' by Cieza de Leon, hitherto supposed to be lost." The evidence promised has not yet been adduced. It consists, no doubt, chiefly of those internal proofs which are in fact sufficient to put the matter beyond question,*

* [The internal proofs are specified in Markham's introduction to his translation of the "Second Part of the Chronicle of Peru," published by the Hakluyt Society.—M.]

felt, might be safely left to his contemporaries who acted a part in it, but whose taste and education had qualified them but indifferently for exploring the antiquities and social institutions of the natives.

Sarmiento's work is composed in a simple, perspicuous style, without that ambition of rhetorical display too common with his countrymen. He writes with honest candor, and, while he does ample justice to the merits and capacities of the conquered races, he notices with indignation the atrocities of the Spaniards and the demoralizing tendency of the Conquest. It may be thought, indeed, that he forms too high an estimate of the attainments of the nation under the Incas. And it is not improbable that, astonished by the vestiges it afforded of an original civilization, he became enamored of his subject, and thus exhibited it in colors somewhat too glowing to the eye of the European. But this was an amiable failing, not too largely shared by the stern Conquerors, who subverted the institutions of the country, and saw little to admire in it save its gold. It must be further admitted that Sarmiento has no design to impose on his reader, and that he is careful to distinguish between what he reports on hearsay and what on personal experience The Father of History himself does not discriminate between these two things more carefully.

Neither is the Spanish historian to be altogether vindicated from the superstition which belongs to his time; and we often find him referring to the immediate interposition of Satan those effects which might quite as well be charged on the perverseness of man. But this was common to the age, and to the wisest men in it; and it is too much to demand of a man to be wiser than his generation. It is sufficient praise of Sarmiento, that, in an age when superstition was too often allied with fanaticism, he seems to have had no tincture of bigotry in his nature His heart opens with benevolent fulness to the unfortunate native; and his language, while it is not kindled into the religious glow of the missionary, is warmed by a generous ray of philanthropy that embraces the conquered, no less than the conquerors, as his brethren

Notwithstanding the great value of Sarmiento's work for the information it affords of Peru under the Incas, it is but little known, has been rarely consulted by historians, and still remains among the unpublished manuscripts which lie, like uncoined bullion, in the secret chambers of the Escorial.

The other authority to whom I have alluded, the Licentiate Polo de Ondegardo, was a highly respectable jurist, whose name appears frequently in the affairs of Peru. I find no account of the period

---

and which will find more appropriate mention in connection with Prescott's account of the life and writings of Cieza de Leon, *infra,* vol. ii. book iv, chap 9.—K.]

when he first came into the country. But he was there on the arrival of Gasca, and resided at Lima under the usurpation of Gonzalo Pizarro. When the artful Cepeda endeavored to secure the signatures of the inhabitants to the instrument proclaiming the sovereignty of his chief, we find Ondegardo taking the lead among those of his profession in resisting it. On Gasca's arrival he consented to take a commission in his army. At the close of the rebellion he was made corregidor of La Plata, and subsequently of Cuzco, in which honorable station he seems to have remained several years. In the exercise of his magisterial functions he was brought into familiar intercourse with the natives, and had ample opportunity for studying their laws and ancient customs He conducted himself with such prudence and moderation that he seems to have won the confidence not only of his countrymen but of the Indians; while the administration was careful to profit by his large experience in devising measures for the better government of the colony.

The *Relaciones*, so often cited in this History, were prepared at the suggestion of the viceroys, the first being addressed to the Marques de Cañete, in 1561, and the second, ten years later, to the Conde de Nieva.* The two cover about as much ground as Sarmiento's manuscript; and the second memorial, written so long after the first, may be thought to intimate the advancing age of the author, in the greater carelessness and diffuseness of the composition.

As these documents are in the nature of answers to the interrogatories propounded by the government, the range of topics might seem to be limited within narrower bounds than the modern historian would desire. These queries, indeed, had particular reference to the revenues, the tributes,—the financial administration, in short, —of the Incas; and on these obscure topics the communication of Ondegardo is particularly full But the enlightened curiosity of the government embraced a far wider range; and the answers necessarily implied an acquaintance with the domestic policy of the Incas, with their laws and social habits, their religion, science, and arts, in short, with all that make up the elements of civilization. Ondegardo's memoirs, therefore, cover the whole ground of inquiry for the philosophic historian.

In the management of these various subjects Ondegardo displays both acuteness and erudition. He never shrinks from the discussion, however difficult; and while he gives his conclusions with an air of modesty, it is evident that he feels conscious of having derived his information through the most authentic channels. He rejects the fabulous with disdain; decides on the probabilities of such facts as he relates, and candidly exposes the deficiency of evidence. Far from displaying the simple enthusiasm of the well-meaning but

* [The Conde de Nieva died in 1564.—M.]

credulous missionary, he proceeds with the cool and cautious step of a lawyer accustomed to the conflict of testimony and the uncertainty of oral tradition. This circumspect manner of proceeding, and the temperate character of his judgments, entitle Ondegardo to much higher consideration as an authority than most of his countrymen who have treated of Indian antiquities.

There runs through his writings a vein of humanity, shown particularly in his tenderness to the unfortunate natives, to whose ancient civilization he does entire, but not extravagant, justice; while, like Sarmiento, he fearlessly denounces the excesses of his own countrymen, and admits the dark reproach they had brought on the honor of the nation. But while this censure forms the strongest ground for condemnation of the Conquerors, since it comes from the lips of a Spaniard like themselves, it proves, also, that Spain in this age of violence could send forth from her bosom wise and good men who refused to make common cause with the licentious rabble around them. Indeed, proof enough is given in these very memorials of the unceasing°efforts of the colonial government, from the good viceroy Mendoza downwards, to secure protection and the benefit of a mild legislation to the unfortunate natives. But the iron Conquerors, and the colonist whose heart softened only to the touch of gold, presented a formidable barrier to improvement.

Ondegardo's writings are honorably distinguished by freedom from that superstition which is the debasing characteristic of the times,—a superstition shown in the easy credit given to the marvellous, and this equally whether in heathen or in Christian story; for in the former the eye of credulity could discern as readily the direct interposition of Satan, as in the latter the hand of the Almighty. It is this ready belief in a spiritual agency, whether for good or for evil, which forms one of the most prominent features in the writings of the sixteenth century. Nothing could be more repugnant to the true spirit of philosophical inquiry, or more irreconcilable with rational criticism. Far from betraying such weakness, Ondegardo writes in a direct and business-like manner, estimating things for what they are worth by the plain rule of common sense. He keeps the main object of his argument ever in view, without allowing himself, like the garrulous chroniclers of the period, to be led astray into a thousand rambling episodes that bewilder the reader and lead to nothing.

Ondegardo's memoirs deal not only with the antiquities of the nation, but with its actual condition, and with the best means for redressing the manifold evils to which it was subjected under the stern rule of its conquerors. His suggestions are replete with wisdom, and a merciful policy, that would reconcile the interests of government with the prosperity and happiness of its humblest vassal. Thus, while his contemporaries gathered light from his suggestions as to the present condition of affairs, the historian of later times is no less indebted to him for information in respect to the past. His manuscript was freely consulted by Herrera, and the reader, as he peruses the pages of the learned historian of the Indies, is unconsciously enjoying the benefit of the researches of Ondegardo. His valuable *Relaciones* thus had their uses for future generations, though they have never been admitted to the honors of the press The copy in my possession, like that of Sarmiento's manuscript, for which I am indebted to that industrious bibliographer Mr. Rich, formed part of the magnificent collection of Lord Kingsborough,—a name ever to be held in honor by the scholar for his indefatigable efforts to illustrate the antiquities of America.

Ondegardo's manuscripts, it should be remarked, do not bear his signature. But they contain allusions to several actions of the writer's life, which identify them, beyond any reasonable doubt, as his production In the archives of Simancas is a duplicate copy of the first memorial, *Relacion Primera,* though, like the one in the Escorial, without its author's name. Muñoz assigns it to the pen of Gabriel de Rojas, a distinguished cavalier of the Conquest This is clearly an error, for the author of the manuscript identifies himself with Ondegardo, by declaring, in his reply to the fifth interrogatory, that he was the person who discovered the mummies of the Incas in Cuzco,—an act expressly referred, both by Acosta and Garcilasso, to the Licentiate Polo de Ondegardo, when corregidor of that city Should the *savans* of Madrid hereafter embrace among the publication of valuable manuscripts these *Relaciones,* they should be careful not to be led into an error here by the authority of a critic like Muñoz, whose criticism is rarely at fault.

BOOK II

DISCOVERY OF PERU

CHAPTER I

WHATEVER difference of opinion may exist as to the comparative merit of the ancients and the moderns in the arts, in poetry, eloquence, and all that depends on imagination, there can be no doubt that in science the moderns have eminently the advantage. It could not be otherwise. In the early ages of the world, as in the early period of life, there was the freshness of a morning existence, when the gloss of novelty was on every thing that met the eye; when the senses, not blunted by familiarity, were more keenly alive to the beautiful, and the mind, under the influence of a healthy and natural taste, was not perverted by philosophical theory; when the simple was necessarily connected with the beautiful, and the epicurean intellect, sated by repetition, had not begun to seek for stimulants in the fantastic and capricious. The realms of fancy were all untravelled, and its fairest flowers had not been gathered, nor its beauties despoiled, by the rude touch of those who affected to cultivate them. The wing of genius was not bound to the earth by the cold and conventional rules of criti-

cism, but was permitted to take its flight far and
wide over the broad expanse of creation.

But with science it was otherwise. No genius
could suffice for the creation of facts,—hardly for
their detection. They were to be gathered in by
painful industry; to be collected from careful
observation and experiment. Genius, indeed,
might arrange and combine these facts into new
forms, and elicit from their combinations new
and important inferences, and in this process
might almost rival in originality the creations of
the poet and the artist. But if the processes of
science are necessarily slow, they are sure. There
is no retrograde movement in her domain. Arts
may fade, the Muse become dumb, a moral lethargy may lock up the faculties of a nation, the
nation itself may pass away and leave only the
memory of its existence, but the stores of science
it has garnered up will endure forever. As other
nations come upon the stage, and new forms of
civilization arise, the monuments of art and of
imagination, productions of an older time, will lie
as an obstacle in the path of improvement. They
cannot be built upon; they occupy the ground
which the new aspirant for immortality would
cover. The whole work is to be gone over again,
and other forms of beauty—whether higher or
lower in the scale of merit, unlike the past—must
arise to take a place by their side. But, in science, every stone that has been laid remains as the
foundation for another. The coming generation
takes up the work where the preceding left it.
There is no retrograde movement. The individual

nation may recede, but science still advances. Every step that has been gained makes the ascent easier for those who come after. Every step carries the patient inquirer after truth higher and higher towards heaven, and unfolds to him, as he rises, a wider horizon, and new and more magnificent views of the universe.

Geography partook of the embarrassments which belonged to every other department of science in the primitive ages of the world. The knowledge of the earth could come only from an extended commerce; and commerce is founded on artificial wants or an enlightened curiosity, hardly compatible with the earlier condition of society. In the infancy of nations, the different tribes, occupied with their domestic feuds, found few occasions to wander beyond the mountain chain or broad stream that formed the natural boundary of their domains. The Phœnicians, it is true, are said to have sailed beyond the Pillars of Hercules, and to have launched out on the great western ocean. But the adventures of these ancient voyagers belong to the mythic legends of antiquity, and ascend far beyond the domain of authentic record.

The Greeks, quick and adventurous, skilled in mechanical art, had many of the qualities of successful navigators, and within the limits of their little inland sea ranged fearlessly and freely. But the conquests of Alexander did more to extend the limits of geographical science, and opened an acquaintance with the remote countries of the East. Yet the march of the conqueror is slow in comparison with the movements of the unencumbered traveller. The Romans were still less enterprising than the Greeks, were less commercial in their character. The contributions to geographical knowledge grew with the slow acquisitions of empire. But their system was centralizing in its tendency; and, instead of taking an outward direction and looking abroad for discovery, every part of the vast imperial domain turned towards the capital as its head and central point of attraction. The Roman conqueror pursued his path by land, not by sea. But the water is the great highway between nations, the true element for the discoverer. The Romans were not a maritime people. At the close of their empire, geographical science could hardly be said to extend farther than to an acquaintance with Europe,—and this not its more northern division, —together with a portion of Asia and Africa; while they had no other conception of a world beyond the Western waters than was to be gathered from the fortunate prediction of the poet.[1]

Then followed the Middle Ages; the dark ages, as they are called, though in their darkness were matured those seeds of knowledge which, in ful-

---

[1] Seneca's well-known prediction, in his Medea, is perhaps the most remarkable random prophecy on record. For it is not a simple extension of the boundaries of the known parts of the globe that is so confidently announced, but the existence of a *New World* across the waters, to be revealed in coming ages:

"Quibus Oceanus
Vincula rerum laxet, et ingens
Pateat tellus, Typhisque Novos
Detegat Orbes "

It was the lucky hit of the philosopher rather than the poet.

ness of time, were to spring up into new and more glorious forms of civilization. The organization of society became more favorable to geographical science. Instead of one overgrown, lethargic empire, oppressing every thing by its colossal weight, Europe was broken up into various independent communities, many of which, adopting liberal forms of government, felt all the impulses natural to freemen; and the petty republics on the Mediterranean and the Baltic sent forth their swarms of seamen in a profitable commerce, that knit together the different countries scattered along the great European waters.

But the improvements which took place in the art of navigation, the more accurate measurement of time, and, above all, the discovery of the polarity of the magnet, greatly advanced the cause of geographical knowledge. Instead of creeping timidly along the coast, or limiting his expeditions to the narrow basins of inland waters, the voyager might now spread his sails boldly on the deep, secure of a guide to direct his bark unerringly across the illimitable waste. The consciousness of this power led thought to travel in a new direction; and the mariner began to look with earnestness for another path to the Indian Spice-islands than that by which the Eastern caravans had traversed the continent of Asia. The nations on whom the spirit of enterprise at this crisis naturally descended were Spain and Portugal, placed as they were on the outposts of the European continent, commanding the great theatre of future discovery.

Both countries felt the responsibility of their new position. The crown of Portugal was constant in its efforts, through the fifteenth century, to find a passage round the southern point of Africa into the Indian Ocean; though so timid was the navigation that every fresh headland became a formidable barrier, and it was not till the latter part of the century that the adventurous Diaz passed quite round the Stormy Cape, as he termed it, but which John the Second, with happier augury, called the Cape of Good Hope. But, before Vasco da Gama had availed himself of this discovery to spread his sails in the Indian seas, Spain entered on her glorious career and sent Columbus across the Western waters.

The object of the great navigator was still the discovery of a route to India, but by the west instead of the east. He had no expectation of meeting with a continent in his way, and, after repeated voyages, he remained in his original error, dying, as is well known, in the conviction that it was the eastern shore of Asia which he had reached. It was the same object which directed the nautical enterprises of those who followed in the Admiral's track; and the discovery of a strait into the Indian Ocean was the burden of every order from the government, and the design of many an expedition to different points of the new continent, which seemed to stretch its leviathan length along from one pole to the other. The discovery of an Indian passage is the true key to the maritime movements of the fifteenth and the first half of the sixteenth century. It was the great leading idea that gave its peculiar character to the enterprise of the age.

It is not easy at this time to comprehend the impulse given to Europe by the discovery of America. It was not the gradual acquisition of some border territory, a province or a kingdom that had been gained, but a new world that was now thrown open to the European. The races of animals, the mineral treasures, the vegetable forms, and the varied aspects of nature, man in the different phases of civilization, filled the mind with entirely new sets of ideas, that changed the habitual current of thought and stimulated it to indefinite conjecture. The eagerness to explore the wonderful secrets of the new hemisphere became so active that the principal cities of Spain were, in a manner, depopulated, as emigrants thronged one after another to take their chance upon the deep.[2] It was a world of romance that was thrown open; for, whatever might be the luck of the adventurer, his reports on his return were tinged with a coloring of romance that stimulated still higher the sensitive fancies of his countrymen and nourished the chimerical sentiments of an age of chivalry. They listened with attentive ears to tales of Amazons which seemed to realize the classic legends of antiquity, to stories of Patagonian giants, to flaming pictures of an *El*

---

[2] The Venetian ambassador Andrea Navagiero, who travelled through Spain in 1525, near the period of the commencement of our narrative, notices the general fever of emigration Seville, in particular, the great port of embarkation, was so stripped of its inhabitants, he says, "that the city was left almost to the women." Viaggio fatto in Spagna (Vinegia, 1563), fol. 15.

Dorado where the sands sparkled with gems and golden pebbles as large as birds' eggs were dragged in nets out of the rivers.

Yet that the adventurers were no impostors, but dupes, too easy dupes, of their own credulous fancies, is shown by the extravagant character of their enterprises; by expeditions in search of the magical Fountain of Health, of the golden Temple of Doboyba, of the golden sepulchres of Zenu; for gold was ever floating before their distempered vision, and the name of *Castilla del Oro*, Golden Castile, the most unhealthy and unprofitable region of the Isthmus, held out a bright promise to the unfortunate settler, who too frequently, instead of gold, found there only his grave.

In this realm of enchantment, all the accessories served to maintain the illusion. The simple natives, with their defenceless bodies and rude weapons, were no match for the European warrior armed to the teeth in mail. The odds were as great as those found in any legend of chivalry, where the lance of the good knight overturned hundreds at a touch. The perils that lay in the discoverer's path, and the sufferings he had to sustain, were scarcely inferior to those that beset the knight-errant. Hunger and thirst and fatigue, the deadly effluvia of the morass with its swarms of venomous insects, the cold of mountain snows, and the scorching sun of the tropics, these were the lot of every cavalier who came to seek his fortunes in the New World. It was the reality of romance. The life of the Spanish adventurer was one chapter more—and not the least remarkable—in the chronicles of knight-errantry.

The character of the warrior took on somewhat of the exaggerated coloring shed over his exploits. Proud and vainglorious, swelled with lofty anticipations of his destiny and an invincible confidence in his own resources, no danger could appall and no toil could tire him. The greater the danger, indeed, the higher the charm; for his soul revelled in excitement, and the enterprise without peril wanted that spur of romance which was necessary to rouse his energies into action. Yet in the motives of action meaner influences were strangely mingled with the loftier, the temporal with the spiritual. Gold was the incentive and the recompense, and in the pursuit of it his inflexible nature rarely hesitated as to the means. His courage was sullied with cruelty, the cruelty that flowed equally—strange as it may seem—from his avarice and his religion; religion as it was understood in that age,—the religion of the Crusader. It was the convenient cloak for a multitude of sins, which covered them even from himself. The Castilian, too proud for hypocrisy, committed more cruelties in the name of religion than were ever practised by the pagan idolater or the fanatical Moslem. The burning of the infidel was a sacrifice acceptable to Heaven, and the conversion of those who survived amply atoned for the foulest offences. It is a melancholy and mortifying consideration that the most uncompromising spirit of intolerance—the spirit of the Inquisitor at home, and of the Crusader abroad—should have emanated from a religion which preached peace upon earth and good will towards man!

What a contrast did these children of Southern Europe present to the Anglo-Saxon races who scattered themselves along the great northern division of the Western hemisphere! For the principle of action with these latter was not avarice, nor the more specious pretext of proselytism; but independence,—independence religious and political. To secure this, they were content to earn a bare subsistence by a life of frugality and toil. They asked nothing from the soil but the reasonable returns of their own labor. No golden visions threw a deceitful halo around their path and beckoned them onwards through seas of blood to the subversion of an unoffending dynasty. They were content with the slow but steady progress of their social polity. They patiently endured the privations of the wilderness, watering the tree of liberty with their tears and with the sweat of their brow, till it took deep root in the land and sent up its branches high towards the heavens; while the communities of the neighboring continent, shooting up into the sudden splendors of a tropical vegetation, exhibited, even in their prime, the sure symptoms of decay.

It would seem to have been especially ordered by Providence that the discovery of the two great divisions of the American hemisphere should fall to the two races best fitted to conquer and colonize them. Thus, the northern section was consigned to the Anglo-Saxon race, whose orderly, industrious habits found an ample field for development under its colder skies and on its more rugged soil; while the southern portion, with its rich tropical products and treasures of mineral wealth, held out the most attractive bait to invite the enterprise of the Spaniard. How different might have been the result if the bark of Columbus had taken a more northerly direction, as he at one time meditated, and landed its band of adventurers on the shores of what is now Protestant America!

Under the pressure of that spirit of nautical enterprise which filled the maritime communities of Europe in the sixteenth century, the whole extent of the mighty continent, from Labrador to Terra del Fuego, was explored in less than thirty years after its discovery; and in 1521 the Portuguese Maghellan, sailing under the Spanish flag, solved the problem of the strait, and found a westerly way to the long-sought Spice-islands of India,—greatly to the astonishment of the Portuguese, who, sailing from the opposite direction, there met their rivals, face to face, at the antipodes. But while the whole eastern coast of the American continent had been explored, and the central portion of it colonized,—even after the brilliant achievement of the Mexican conquest, —the veil was not yet raised that hung over the golden shores of the Pacific.

Floating rumors had reached the Spaniards, from time to time, of countries in the far west, teeming with the metal they so much coveted; but the first distinct notice of Peru was about the year 1511, when Vasco Nuñez de Balboa, the discoverer of the Southern Sea, was weighing some gold

which he had collected from the natives. A young
barbarian chieftain, who was present, struck the
scales with his fist, and, scattering the glittering
metal around the apartment, exclaimed, " If this
is what you prize so much that you are willing to
leave your distant homes and risk even life itself
for it, I can tell you of a land where they eat and
drink out of golden vessels, and gold is as cheap
as iron is with you." It was not long after this
startling intelligence that Balboa achieved the
formidable adventure of scaling the mountain-
rampart of the isthmus which divides the two
mighty oceans from each other; when, armed with
sword and buckler, he rushed into the waters of
the Pacific, and cried out, in the true chivalrous
vein, that " he claimed this unknown sea, with all
that it contained, for the King of Castile, and that
he would make good the claim against all, Christian or infidel, who dared to gainsay it"![3] All
the broad continent and sunny isles washed by the
waters of the Southern Ocean! Little did the bold
cavalier comprehend the full import of his magnificent vaunt.

On this spot he received more explicit tidings
of the Peruvian empire, heard proofs recounted
of its civilization, and was shown drawings of the
llama, which, to the European eye, seemed a
species of the Arabian camel. But, although he
steered his caravel for these golden realms, and
even pushed his discoveries some twenty leagues
south of the Gulf of St. Michael, the adventure

    [3] Herrera, Hist. general, dec. 1, lib. 10, cap. 2.—Quintana, Vidas
de Españoles célebres (Madrid, 1830), tom ii. p. 44.

was not reserved for him. The illustrious discoverer was doomed to fall a victim to that miserable jealousy with which a little spirit regards the achievements of a great one.

The Spanish colonial domain was broken up into a number of petty governments, which were dispensed sometimes to court favorites, though, as the duties of the post, at this early period, were of an arduous nature, they were more frequently reserved for men of some practical talent and enterprise. Columbus, by virtue of his original contract with the crown, had jurisdiction over the territories discovered by himself, embracing some of the principal islands, and a few places on the continent. This jurisdiction differed from that of other functionaries, inasmuch as it was hereditary; a privilege found in the end too considerable for a subject, and commuted, therefore, for a title and a pension. These colonial governments were multiplied with the increase of empire, and by the year 1524, the period at which our narrative properly commences, were scattered over the islands, along the Isthmus of Darien, the broad tract of Tierra Firma, and the recent conquests in Mexico. Some of these governments were of no great extent; others, like that of Mexico, were of the dimensions of a kingdom; and most had an indefinite range for discovery assigned to them in their immediate neighborhood, by which each of the petty potentates might enlarge his territorial sway and enrich his followers and himself. This politic arrangement best served the ends of the crown, by affording a perpetual incentive to the spirit of enterprise. Thus living on their own little domains at a long distance from the mother-country, these military rulers held a sort of vice-regal sway, and too frequently exercised it in the most oppressive and tyrannical manner,—oppressive to the native, and tyrannical towards their own followers. It was the natural consequence, when men originally low in station, and unprepared by education for office, were suddenly called to the possession of a brief, but in its nature irrespon-sible, authority. It was not till after some sad experience of these results that measures were taken to hold these petty tyrants in check by means of regular tribunals, or Royal Audiences, as they were termed, which, composed of men of character and learning, might interpose the arm of the law, or at least the voice of remonstrance, for the protection of both colonist and native.

Among the colonial governors who were in-debted for their situation to their rank at home was Don Pedro Arias de Avila, or Pedrarias, as usually called. He was married to a daughter of Doña Beatriz de Bobadilla, the celebrated March-ioness of Moya, best known as the friend of Isa-bella the Catholic. He was a man of some military experience and considerable energy of character. But, as it proved, he was of a malig-nant temper; and the base qualities which might have passed unnoticed in the obscurity of private life were made conspicuous, and perhaps created in some measure, by sudden elevation to power; as the sunshine, which operates kindly on a generous soil and stimulates it to production, calls forth from the unwholesome marsh only foul and pestilent vapors. This man was placed over the territory of *Castilla del Oro*, the ground selected by Nuñez de Balboa for the theatre of his discoveries. Success drew on this latter the jealousy of his superior, for it was crime enough in the eyes of Pedrarias to deserve too well. The tragical history of this cavalier belongs to a period somewhat earlier than that with which we are to be occupied. It has been traced by abler hands than mine, and, though brief, forms one of the most brilliant passages in the annals of the American conquerors.[4]

But, though Pedrarias was willing to cut short the glorious career of his rival, he was not insensible to the important consequences of his discoveries. He saw at once the unsuitableness of Darien for prosecuting expeditions on the Pacific, and, conformably to the original suggestion of Balboa, in 1519 he caused his rising capital to be transferred from the shores of the Atlantic to the ancient site of Panamá, some distance east of the present city of that name.[5] This most un-

[4] The memorable adventures of Vasco Nuñez de Balboa have been recorded by Quintana (Españoles célebres, tom ii.) and by Irving in his Companions of Columbus. It is rare that the life of an individual has formed the subject of two such elegant memorials, produced at nearly the same time, and in different languages, without any communication between the authors.

[5] The court gave positive instructions to Pedrarias to make a settlement in the Gulf of St. Michael, in obedience to the suggestion of Vasco Nuñez, that it would be the most eligible site for discovery and traffic in the South Sea: "El asiento que se oviere de hacer en el golfo de S. Miguel en la mar del sur debe ser en el puerto que mejor se hallare y mas convenible para la contratacion de aquel golfo, porque segund lo que Vasco Nuñez escribe, seria muy necesario que allí haya algunos navíos, así para descubrir las cosas del golfo, y de la comarca dél, como para la contratacion de

healthy spot, the cemetery of many an unfortunate colonist, was favorably situated for the great
object of maritime enterprise; and the port, from
its central position, afforded the best point of departure for expeditions, whether to the north or
south, along the wide range of undiscovered coast
that lined the Southern Ocean. Yet in this new
and more favorable position several years were
suffered to elapse before the course of discovery
took the direction of Peru. This was turned exclusively towards the north, or rather west, in
obedience to the orders of the government, which
had ever at heart the detection of a strait that, as
was supposed, must intersect some part or other
of the long-extended Isthmus. Armament after
armament was fitted out with this chimerical object; and Pedrarias saw his domain extending
every year farther and farther without deriving
any considerable advantage from his acquisitions.
Veragua, Costa Rica, Nicaragua, were successively occupied; and his brave cavaliers forced
a way across forest and mountain and warlike
tribes of savages, till, at Honduras, they came in
collision with the companions of Cortés, the Conquerors of Mexico, who had descended from the
great northern plateau on the regions of Central
America, and thus completed the survey of this
wild and mysterious land.

It was not till 1522 that a regular expedition

rescates de las otras cosas necesarias al buen proveimiento de
aquello; é para que estos navíos aprovechen es menester que se
hagan allá." Capítulo de Carta escrita por el Rey Católico á Pedrarias Dávila, ap. Navarrete, Coleccion de los Viages y Descubrimientos (Madrid, 1829), tom. iii. No. 3.

was despatched in the direction south of Panamá, under the conduct of Pascual de Andagoya, a cavalier of much distinction in the colony. But that officer penetrated only to the Puerto de Piñas, the limit of Balboa's discoveries, when the bad state of his health compelled him to re-embark and abandon his enterprise at its commencement.[6]

Yet the floating rumors of the wealth and civilization of a mighty nation at the south were continually reaching the ears and kindling the dreamy imaginations of the colonists; and it may seem astonishing that an expedition in that direction should have been so long deferred. But the exact position and distance of this fairy realm were matter of conjecture. The long tract of intervening country was occupied by rude and warlike races; and the little experience which the Spanish navigators had already had of the neighboring coast and its inhabitants, and, still more, the tempestuous character of the seas,—for their expeditions had taken place at the most unpropitious seasons of the year,—enhanced the apparent diffi-

---

[6] According to Montesinos, Andagoya received a severe injury by a fall from his horse, while showing off the high-mettled animal to the wondering eyes of the natives. (Annales del Peru, MS., año 1524.) But the Adelantado, in a memorial of his own discoveries, drawn up by himself, says nothing of this unlucky feat of horsemanship, but imputes his illness to his having fallen into the water, an accident by which he was near being drowned, so that it was some years before he recovered from the effects of it,—a mode of accounting for his premature return, more soothing to his vanity, probably, than the one usually received. This document, important as coming from the pen of one of the primitive discoverers, is preserved in the Indian Archives of Seville, and was published by Navarrete, Coleccion, tom. III. No. 7.

culties of the undertaking and made even their stout hearts shrink from it.

Such was the state of feeling in the little community of Panamá for several years after its foundation. Meanwhile, the dazzling conquest of Mexico gave a new impulse to the ardor of discovery, and in 1524 three men were found in the colony in whom the spirit of adventure triumphed over every consideration of difficulty and danger that obstructed the prosecution of the enterprise. One among them was selected as fitted by his character to conduct it to a successful issue. That man was Francisco Pizarro; and, as he held the same conspicuous post in the Conquest of Peru that was occupied by Cortés in that of Mexico, it will be necessary to take a brief review of his early history.

... as arming from r.

Such was the state of feeling in the little community of Panamá for several years after its foundation. Meanwhile, the dazzling conquest of Mexico gave a new impulse to the ardor of discovery, and individuals were found in Castile in whom the spirit of adventure triumphed over every consideration of difficulty and danger that obstructed the prosecution of the enterprise. One among them was selected, as fitted by his character to conduct it to a successful issue. This man was Francisco Pizarro; and, as he held a conspicuous post in the Conquest of Peru, next to that occupied by Cortés in that of Mexico, it seems proper to take a brief review

CHAPTER II

FRANCISCO PIZARRO—HIS EARLY HISTORY—FIRST EXPEDITION TO THE SOUTH—DISTRESSES OF THE VOYAGERS — SHARP ENCOUNTERS — RETURN TO PANAMÁ—ALMAGRO'S EXPEDITION

1524–1525

FRANCISCO PIZARRO was born at Truxillo, a city of Estremadura, in Spain. The period of his birth is uncertain; but probably it was not far from 1471.[1] He was an illegitimate child, and that his parents should not have taken pains to perpetuate the date of his birth is not surprising. Few care to make a particular record of their transgressions. His father, Gonzalo Pi-

[1] The few writers who venture to assign the date of Pizarro's birth do it in so vague and contradictory a manner as to inspire us with but little confidence in their accounts Herrera, it is true, says positively that he was sixty-three years old at the time of his death, in 1541 (Hist. general, dec. 6, lib. 10, cap. 6.) This would carry back the date of his birth only to 1478. But Garcilasso de la Vega affirms that he was more than fifty years old in 1525 (Com. Real, Parte 2, lib. 1, cap. 1.) This would place his birth before 1475. Pizarro y Orellana, who, as a kinsman of the Conqueror, may be supposed to have had better means of information, says he was fifty-four years of age at the same date of 1525 (Varones ilustres del Nuevo-Mundo (Madrid, 1639), p. 128) But at the period of his death he calls him nearly eighty years old! (p 185) Taking this latter as a round exaggeration for effect in the particular connection in which it is used, and admitting the accuracy of the former statement, the epoch of his birth will conform to that given in the text. This makes him somewhat late in life to set about the conquest of an empire. But Columbus, when he entered on his career, was still older.

zarro, was a colonel of infantry, and served with some distinction in the Italian campaigns under the Great Captain, and afterwards in the wars of Navarre. His mother, named Francisca Gonzales, was a person of humble condition in the town of Truxillo.[2]

But little is told of Francisco's early years, and that little not always deserving of credit. According to some, he was deserted by both his parents, and left as a foundling at the door of one of the principal churches of the city. It is even said that he would have perished, had he not been nursed by a sow.[3] This is a more discreditable fountain of supply than that assigned to the infant Romulus. The early history of men who have made their names famous by deeds in afterlife, like the early history of nations, affords a fruitful field for invention.

It seems certain that the young Pizarro received little care from either of his parents, and was suffered to grow up as nature dictated. He was neither taught to read nor write, and his principal occupation was that of a swineherd. But this torpid way of life did not suit the stirring spirit of Pizarro, as he grew older, and listened to the tales, widely circulated and so captivating to the youthful fancy, of the New World. He shared in the popular enthusiasm, and availed himself

[2] Xerez, Conquista del Peru, ap. Barcia, tom. iii. p. 179.—Zarate, Conq. del Peru, lib. 1, cap. 1.—Pizarro y Orellana, Varones ilustres, p. 128.

[3] "Nació en Truxillo, i echaronlo à la puerta de la Inglesia, mamò una Puerca ciertos Dias, no se hallando quien le quisiese dàr leche." Gomara, Hist. de las Ind, cap 144.

of a favorable moment to abandon his ignoble charge and escape to Seville, the port where the Spanish adventurers embarked to seek their fortunes in the West. Few of them could have turned their backs on their native land with less cause for regret than Pizarro.[4]

In what year this important change in his destiny took place we are not informed. The first we hear of him in the New World is at the island of Hispaniola, in 1510, where he took part in the expedition to Uraba in Terra Firma, under Alonzo de Ojeda, a cavalier whose character and achievements find no parallel but in the pages of Cervantes. Hernando Cortés, whose mother was a Pizarro, and related, it is said, to the father of Francis, was then in St. Domingo, and prepared to accompany Ojeda's expedition, but was prevented by a temporary lameness. Had he gone, the fall of the Aztec empire might have been postponed for some time longer, and the sceptre of Montezuma have descended in peace to his posterity. Pizarro shared in the disastrous fortunes of Ojeda's colony, and by his discretion obtained so far the confidence of his commander as to be left in charge of the settlement when the latter returned for supplies to the islands. The lieutenant continued at his perilous post for nearly two months, waiting deliberately until death

---

[4] According to the Comendador Pizarro y Orellana, Francis Pizarro served, while quite a stripling, with his father, in the Italian wars, and afterwards, under Columbus and other illustrious discoverers, in the New World, whose successes the author modestly attributes to his kinsman's valor as a principal cause! Varones ilustres, p. 187.

should have thinned off the colony sufficiently to allow the miserable remnant to be embarked in the single small vessel that remained to it.[5]

After this, we find him associated with Balboa, the discoverer of the Pacific, and co-operating with him in establishing the settlement at Darien. He had the glory of accompanying this gallant cavalier in his terrible march across the mountains, and of being among the first Europeans, therefore, whose eyes were greeted with the long-promised vision of the Southern Ocean.

After the untimely death of his commander, Pizarro attached himself to the fortunes of Pedrarias, and was employed by that governor in several military expeditions, which, if they afforded nothing else, gave him the requisite training for the perils and privations that lay in the path of the future Conqueror of Peru.

In 1515 he was selected, with another cavalier, named Morales, to cross the Isthmus and traffic with the natives on the shores of the Pacific. And there, while engaged in collecting his booty of gold and pearls from the neighboring islands, as his eye ranged along the shadowy line of coast till it faded in the distance, his imagination may have been first fired with the idea of, one day, attempting the conquest of the mysterious regions beyond the mountains. On the removal of the seat of government across the Isthmus to Panamá, Pizarro accompanied Pedrarias, and his name

[5] Pizarro y Orellana, Varones ilustres, pp. 121–128.—Herrera, Hist gen., dec. 1, lib. 7, cap. 14.—Montesinos, Annales, MS, año 1510.

became conspicuous among the cavaliers who extended the line of conquest to the north over the martial tribes of Veragua. But all these expeditions, whatever glory they may have brought him, were productive of very little gold, and at the age of fifty the captain Pizarro found himself in possession only of a tract of unhealthy land in the neighborhood of the capital, and of such *repartimientos* of the natives as were deemed suited to his military services.[6] The New World was a lottery, where the great prizes were so few that the odds were much against the player; yet in the game he was content to stake health, fortune, and, too often, his fair fame.

Such was Pizarro's situation when, in 1522, Andagoya returned from his unfinished enterprise to the south of Panamá, bringing back with him more copious accounts than any hitherto received of the opulence and grandeur of the countries that lay beyond.[7] It was at this time, too, that the splendid achievements of Cortés made their impression on the public mind and gave a new impulse to the spirit of adventure. The southern expeditions became a common topic of speculation among the colonists of Panamá. But the region

[6] "Teniendo su casa, i Hacienda, i Repartimiento de Indios como uno de los Principales de la Tierra; porque siempre lo fue" Xerez, Conq. del Peru, ap. Barcia, tom iii. p. 79.

[7] Andagoya says that he obtained, while at Birú, very minute accounts of the empire of the Incas, from certain itinerant traders who frequented that country: "En esta provincia supe y hube relacion, ansí de los señores como de mercaderes é intérpretes que ellos tenian, de toda la costa de todo lo que despues se ha visto hasta el Cuzco, particularmente de cada provincia la manera y gente della, porque estos alcanzaban, por via de mercaduria mucha tierra." Navarrete, Coleccion, tom. iii. No. 7.

of gold, as it lay behind the mighty curtain of the Cordilleras, was still veiled in obscurity. No idea could be formed of its actual distance; and the hardships and difficulties encountered by the few navigators who had sailed in that direction gave a gloomy character to the undertaking, which had hitherto deterred the most daring from embarking in it. There is no evidence that Pizarro showed any particular alacrity in the cause. Nor were his own funds such as to warrant any expectation of success without great assistance from others. He found this in two individuals of the colony, who took too important a part in the subsequent transactions not to be particularly noticed.

One of them, Diego de Almagro, was a soldier of fortune, somewhat older, it seems probable, than Pizarro; though little is known of his birth, and even the place of it is disputed. It is supposed to have been the town of Almagro in New Castile, whence his own name, for want of a better source, was derived; for, like Pizarro, he was a foundling.[8] Few particulars are known of him till the present period of our history; for he was one of those whom the working of turbulent times first throws upon the surface,—less fortunate, perhaps, than if left in their original obscurity. In his military career, Almagro had earned the

---

[8] "Decia el que hera de *Almagro*," says Pedro Pizarro, who knew him well. Relacion del Descubrimiento y Conquista de los Reynos del Peru, MS.—See also Zarate, Conq. del Peru, lib 1, cap 1.— Gomara, Hist. de las Ind , cap. 141 —Pizarro y Orellana, Varones ilustres, p. 211. The last writer admits that Almagro's parentage is unknown, but adds that the character of his early exploits infers an illustrious descent This would scarcely pass for evidence with the College of Heralds.

THE CONQUISTADORE:

reputation of a gallant soldier. He was frank and liberal in his disposition, somewhat hasty and ungovernable in his passions, but, like men of a sanguine temperament, after the first sallies had passed away, not difficult to be appeased. He had, in short, the good qualities and the defects incident to an honest nature not improved by the discipline of early education or self-control.

The other member of the confederacy was Hernando de Luque, a Spanish ecclesiastic, who exercised the functions of vicar at Panamá, and had formerly filled the office of schoolmaster in the Cathedral of Darien. He seems to have been a man of singular prudence and knowledge of the world, and by his respectable qualities had acquired considerable influence in the little community to which he belonged, as well as the control of funds, which made his co-operation essential to the success of the present enterprise.

It was arranged among the three associates that the two cavaliers should contribute their little stock towards defraying the expenses of the armament, but by far the greater part of the funds was to be furnished by Luque. Pizarro was to take command of the expedition, and the business of victualling and equipping the vessels was assigned to Almagro. The associates found no difficulty in obtaining the consent of the governor to their undertaking. After the return of Andagoya, he had projected another expedition, but the officer to whom it was to be intrusted died. Why he did not prosecute his original purpose, and commit the affair to an experienced captain like Pizarro, does not appear. He was probably not displeased that the burden of the enterprise should be borne by others, so long as a good share of the profits went into his own coffers. This he did not overlook in his stipulations.[9]

Thus fortified with the funds of Luque and the consent of the governor, Almagro was not slow to make preparations for the voyage. Two small vessels were purchased, the larger of which had been originally built by Balboa for himself, with a view to this same expedition. Since his death, it had lain dismantled in the harbor of Panamá. It was now refitted as well as circumstances would permit, and put in order for sea, while the stores and provisions were got on board with an alacrity which did more credit, as the event proved, to Almagro's zeal than to his forecast.

There was more difficulty in obtaining the necessary complement of hands; for a general feeling of distrust had gathered round expeditions in this direction, which could not readily be overcome. But there were many idle hangers-on in the

[9] " Asi que estos tres compañeros ya dichos acordaron de yr á conquistar esta provincia ya dicha. Pues consultandolo con Pedro Arias de Avila que á la sazon hera governador en tierra firme, vino en ello haziendo compañia con los dichos compañeros con condicion que Pedro Arias no havia de contribuir entonces con ningun dinero ni otra cosa sino de lo que se hallase en la tierra de lo que á el le cupiese por virtud de la compañia de allí se pagasen los gastos que á el le cupiesen. Los tres compañeros vinieron en ello por aver esta licencia porque de otra manera no la alcanzaran." (Pedro Pizarro, Descub. y Conq., MS.) Andagoya, however, affirms that the governor was interested equally with the other associates in the adventure, each taking a fourth part on himself. (Navarrete, Coleccion, tom. iii. No. 7.) But whatever was the original interest of Pedrarias, it mattered little, as it was surrendered before any profits were realized from the expedition.

colony, who had come out to mend their fortunes, and were willing to take their chance of doing so, however desperate. From such materials as these, Almagro assembled a body of somewhat more than a hundred men; [10] and, every thing being ready, Pizarro assumed the command, and, weighing anchor, took his departure from the little port of Panamá about the middle of November, 1524. Almagro was to follow in a second vessel of inferior size, as soon as it could be fitted out. [11]

The time of year was the most unsuitable that could have been selected for the voyage; for it was the rainy season, when the navigation to the south, impeded by contrary winds, is made doubly dangerous by the tempests that sweep over the coast. But this was not understood by the adventurers. After touching at the Isle of Pearls, the frequent resort of navigators, at a few leagues' distance from Panamá, Pizarro held his way across the Gulf of St. Michael, and steered almost due south for the Puerto de Piñas, a headland in

[10] Herrera, the most popular historian of these transactions, estimates the number of Pizarro's followers at only eighty But every other authority which I have consulted raises them to over a hundred Father Naharro, a contemporary, and resident at Lima, even allows a hundred and twenty-nine. Relacion sumaria de la Entrada de los Españoles en el Peru, MS.

[11] There is the usual discrepancy among authors about the date of this expedition. Most fix it at 1525. I have conformed to Xerez, Pizarro's secretary, whose narrative was published ten years after the voyage, and who could hardly have forgotten the date of so memorable an event in so short an interval of time (See his Conquista del Peru, ap. Barcia, tom. iii p 179)—The year seems to be settled by Pizarro's *Capitulacion* with the crown, which I had not examined till after the above was written This instrument, dated July, 1529, speaks of his first expedition as having taken place about five years previous. (See Appendix No. 7.)

the province of Biruquete, which marked the limit of Andagoya's voyage. Before his departure, Pizarro had obtained all the information which he could derive from that officer in respect to the country, and the route he was to follow. But the cavalier's own experience had been too limited to enable him to be of much assistance.

Doubling the Puerto de Piñas, the little vessel entered the river Birú, the misapplication of which name is supposed by some to have given rise to that of the empire of the Incas.[12] * After sailing up this stream for a couple of leagues, Pizarro came to anchor, and, disembarking his whole force except the sailors, proceeded at the head of it to explore the country. The land spread out into a vast swamp, where the heavy rains had settled in pools of stagnant water, and the muddy soil afforded no footing to the traveller. This dismal morass was fringed with woods, through whose thick and tangled undergrowth they found it difficult to penetrate; and, emerging from them, they came out on a hilly country, so rough and rocky in its character that their feet were cut to the bone, and the weary soldier, encumbered with his heavy mail or thick-padded doublet of

[12] Zarate, Conq. del Peru, lib. 1, cap. 1.—Herrera, Hist. general, dec 3, lib. 6, cap. 13.

* [There was a chief named Birú on the Pacific coast, whose lands were first visited by Spaniards in 1515. For ten years his were the most southern lands known, and consequently the general term Birú, or Peru, came to be applied to all the regions beyond According to Markham (Winsor, Nar. and Crit. Hist. of America, ii p 505), the land of the Incas came to be known by this name before it was discovered. Dr. Kohl finds the name for the first time upon a map, in one made by Ribero in 1529.—M.]

cotton, found it difficult to drag one foot after the other. The heat at times was oppressive; and, fainting with toil and famished for want of food, they sank down on the earth from mere exhaustion. Such was the ominous commencement of the expedition to Peru.

Pizarro, however, did not lose heart. He endeavored to revive the spirits of his men, and besought them not to be discouraged by difficulties which a brave heart would be sure to overcome, reminding them of the golden prize which awaited those who persevered. Yet it was obvious that nothing was to be gained by remaining longer in this desolate region. Returning to their vessel, therefore, it was suffered to drop down the river and proceed along its southern course on the great ocean.

After coasting a few leagues, Pizarro anchored off a place not very inviting in its appearance, where he took in a supply of wood and water. Then, stretching more towards the open sea, he held on in the same direction towards the south. But in this he was baffled by a succession of heavy tempests, accompanied with such tremendous peals of thunder and floods of rain as are found only in the terrible storms of the tropics. The sea was lashed into fury, and, swelling into mountain billows, threatened every moment to overwhelm the crazy little bark, which opened at every seam. For ten days the unfortunate voyagers were tossed about by the pitiless elements, and it was only by incessant exertions—the exertions of despair— that they preserved the ship from foundering. To add to their calamities, their provisions began to fail, and they were short of water, of which they had been furnished only with a small number of casks; for Almagro had counted on their recruiting their scanty supplies, from time to time, from the shore. Their meat was wholly consumed, and they were reduced to the wretched allowance of two ears of Indian corn a day for each man.

Thus harassed by hunger and the elements, the battered voyagers were too happy to retrace their course and regain the port where they had last taken in supplies of wood and water. Yet nothing could be more unpromising than the aspect of the country. It had the same character of low, swampy soil that distinguished the former landing-place; while thick-matted forests, of a depth which the eye could not penetrate, stretched along the coast to an interminable length. It was in vain that the wearied Spaniards endeavored to thread the mazes of this tangled thicket, where the creepers and flowering vines, that shoot up luxuriant in a hot and humid atmosphere, had twined themselves round the huge trunks of the forest-trees and made a net-work that could be opened only with the axe. The rain, in the mean time, rarely slackened, and the ground, strewed with leaves and saturated with moisture, seemed to slip away beneath their feet.

Nothing could be more dreary and disheartening than the aspect of these funereal forests, where the exhalations from the overcharged surface of the ground poisoned the air, and seemed to allow no life, except that, indeed, of myriads

of insects, whose enamelled wings glanced to and
fro, like sparks of fire, in every opening of the
woods. Even the brute creation appeared instinc-
tively to have shunned the fatal spot, and neither
beast nor bird of any description was seen by the
wanderers. Silence reigned unbroken in the heart
of these dismal solitudes; at least, the only sounds
that could be heard were the plashing of the rain-
drops on the leaves, and the tread of the forlorn
adventurers.[13]

Entirely discouraged by the aspect of the country, the Spaniards began to comprehend that they
had gained nothing by changing their quarters
from sea to shore, and they felt the most serious
apprehensions of perishing from famine in a
region which afforded nothing but such unwholesome berries as they could pick here and there in
the woods. They loudly complained of their hard
lot, accusing their commander as the author of all
their troubles, and as deluding them with promises
of a fairy-land, which seemed to recede in proportion as they advanced. It was of no use, they
said, to contend against fate, and it was better to
take their chance of regaining the port of Panamá
in time to save their lives, than to wait where they
were to die of hunger.

But Pizarro was prepared to encounter much
greater evils than these before returning to
Panamá, bankrupt in credit, an object of de-

---

[13] Xerez, Conq. del Peru, ap. Barcia, tom. iii. p. 180.—Relacion
del primer Descub., MS.—Montesinos, Annales, MS., año 1515.—
Zarate, Conq. del Peru, lib. 1, cap. 1.—Garcilasso, Com. Real., Parte
2, lib. 1, cap. 7.—Herrera, Hist. general, dec. 3, lib. 6, cap. 13.

rision as a vainglorious dreamer who had persuaded others to embark in an adventure which he had not the courage to carry through himself. The present was his only chance. To return would be ruin. He used every argument, therefore, that mortified pride or avarice could suggest to turn his followers from their purpose; represented to them that these were the troubles that necessarily lay in the path of the discovery, and called to mind the brilliant successes of their countrymen in other quarters, and the repeated reports which they had themselves received of the rich regions along this coast, of which it required only courage and constancy on their part to become the masters. Yet, as their present exigencies were pressing, he resolved to send back the vessel to the Isle of Pearls, to lay in a fresh stock of provisions for his company, which might enable them to go forward with renewed confidence. The distance was not great, and in a few days they would all be relieved from their perilous position. The officer detached on this service was named Montenegro; and, taking with him nearly half the company, after receiving Pizarro's directions, he instantly weighed anchor and steered for the Isle of Pearls.

On the departure of his vessel, the Spanish commander made an attempt to explore the country and see if some Indian settlement might not be found, where he could procure refreshments for his followers. But his efforts were vain, and no trace was visible of a human dwelling; though in the dense and impenetrable foliage of the equatorial regions the distance of a few rods might suffice to screen a city from observation. The only means of nourishment left to the unfortunate adventurers were such shell-fish as they occasionally picked up on the shore, or the bitter buds of the palm-tree, and such berries and unsavory herbs as grew wild in the woods. Some of these were so poisonous that the bodies of those who ate them swelled up and were tormented with racking pains. Others, preferring famine to this miserable diet, pined away from weakness and actually died of starvation. Yet their resolute leader strove to maintain his own cheerfulness and to keep up the drooping spirits of his men. He freely shared with them his scanty stock of provisions, was unwearied in his endeavors to procure them sustenance, tended the sick, and ordered barracks to be constructed for their accommodation, which might at least shelter them from the drenching storms of the season. By this ready sympathy with his followers in their sufferings he obtained an ascendency over their rough natures which the assertion of authority, at least in the present extremity, could never have secured to him.

Day after day, week after week, had now passed away, and no tidings were heard of the vessel that was to bring relief to the wanderers. In vain did they strain their eyes over the distant waters to catch a glimpse of their coming friends. Not a speck was to be seen in the blue distance, where the canoe of the savage dared not venture, and the sail of the white man was not yet spread.

Those who had borne up bravely at first now gave way to despondency, as they felt themselves abandoned by their countrymen on this desolate shore. They pined under that sad feeling which "maketh the heart sick." More than twenty of the little band had already died, and the survivors seemed to be rapidly following.[14]

At this crisis reports were brought to Pizarro of a light having been seen through a distant opening in the woods. He hailed the tidings with eagerness, as intimating the existence of some settlement in the neighborhood, and, putting himself at the head of a small party, went in the direction pointed out, to reconnoitre. He was not disappointed, and, after extricating himself from a dense wilderness of underbrush and foliage, he emerged into an open space, where a small Indian village was planted. The timid inhabitants, on the sudden apparition of the strangers, quitted their huts in dismay; and the famished Spaniards, rushing in, eagerly made themselves masters of their contents. These consisted of different articles of food, chiefly maize and cocoanuts. The supply, though small, was too seasonable not to fill them with rapture.

The astonished natives made no attempt at resistance. But, gathering more confidence as no violence was offered to their persons, they drew nearer the white men, and inquired, " Why they did not stay at home and till their own lands, instead of roaming about to rob others who had

[14] Herrera, Hist general, dec. 3, lib. 6, cap. 13 —Relacion del primer Descub., MS.—Xerez, Conq. del Peru, ubi supra.

never harmed them?"[15]   Whatever may have been their opinion as to the question of right, the Spaniards, no doubt, felt then that it would have been wiser to do so.   But the savages wore about their persons gold ornaments of some size, though of clumsy workmanship.   This furnished the best reply to their demand.   It was the golden bait which lured the Spanish adventurer to forsake his pleasant home for the trials of the wilderness. From the Indians Pizarro gathered a confirmation of the reports he had so often received of a rich country lying farther south; and at the distance of ten days' journey across the mountains, they told him, there dwelt a mighty monarch whose dominions had been invaded by another still more powerful, the Child of the Sun.[16]   It may have been the invasion of Quito that was meant, by the valiant Inca Huayna Capac, which took place some years previous to Pizarro's expedition.

At length, after the expiration of more than six weeks, the Spaniards beheld with delight the return of the wandering bark that had borne away

[15] "Porque decian à los Castellanos, que por què no sembraban, i cogian, sin andar tomando los Bastimentos agenos, pasando tantos trabajos?" Herrera, Hist. general, loc. cit.

[16] "Dioles noticia el viejo por medio del lengua, como diez soles de alli habia un Rey muy poderoso yendo por espesas montañas, y que otro mas poderoso hijo del sol habia venido de milagro á quitarle el Reino sobre que tenian mui sangrientas batallas." (Montesinos, Annales, MS., año 1525.)   The conquest of Quito by Huayna Capac took place more than thirty years before this period in our history.   But the particulars of this revolution, its time or precise theatre, were probably but very vaguely comprehended by the rude nations in the neighborhood of Panamá; and their allusion to it in an unknown dialect was as little comprehended by the Spanish voyagers, who must have collected their information from signs much more than words.

their comrades, and Montenegro sailed into port with an ample supply of provisions for his famishing countrymen. Great was his horror at the aspect presented by the latter, their wild and haggard countenances and wasted frames,—so wasted by hunger and disease that their old companions found it difficult to recognize them. Montenegro accounted for his delay by incessant headwinds and bad weather; and he himself had also a doleful tale to tell of the distress to which he and his crew had been reduced by hunger on their passage to the Isle of Pearls. It is minute incidents like these with which we have been occupied that enable one to comprehend the extremity of suffering to which the Spanish adventurer was subjected in the prosecution of his great work of discovery.

Revived by the substantial nourishment to which they had so long been strangers, the Spanish cavaliers, with the buoyancy that belongs to men of a hazardous and roving life, forgot their past distresses in their eagerness to prosecute their enterprise. Re-embarking, therefore, on board his vessel, Pizarro bade adieu to the scene of so much suffering, which he branded with the appropriate name of *Puerto de la Hambre*, the Port of Famine, and again opened his sails to a favorable breeze that bore him onwards towards the south.

Had he struck boldly out into the deep, instead of hugging the inhospitable shore, where he had hitherto found so little to recompense him, he might have spared himself the repetition of weari-

some and unprofitable adventures and reached by
a shorter route the point of his destination.   But
the Spanish mariner groped his way along these
unknown coasts, landing at every convenient headland, as if fearful lest some fruitful region or
precious mine might be overlooked should a single
break occur in the line of survey.   Yet it should
be remembered that, though the true point of
Pizarro's destination is obvious to us, familiar with
the topography of these countries, he was wandering in the dark, feeling his way along inch by
inch, as it were, without chart to guide him, without knowledge of the seas or of the bearings of
the coast, and even with no better defined idea of
the object at which he aimed than that of a land,
teeming with gold, that lay somewhere at the
south!   It was a hunt for an *El Dorado*, on information scarcely more circumstantial or authentic than that which furnished the basis of so
many chimerical enterprises in this land of wonders.   Success only, the best argument with the
multitude, redeemed the expeditions of Pizarro
from a similar imputation of extravagance.

Holding on his southerly course under the lee
of the shore, Pizarro, after a short run, found
himself abreast of an open reach of country, or
at least one less encumbered with wood, which rose
by a gradual swell as it receded from the coast.
He landed with a small body of men, and, advancing a short distance into the interior, fell in
with an Indian hamlet.   It was abandoned by the
inhabitants, who on the approach of the invaders
had betaken themselves to the mountains;   and

the Spaniards, entering their deserted dwellings, found there a good store of maize and other articles of food, and rude ornaments of gold of considerable value. Food was not more necessary for their bodies than was the sight of gold, from time to time, to stimulate their appetite for adventure. One spectacle, however, chilled their blood with horror. This was the sight of human flesh, which they found roasting before the fire, as the barbarians had left it, preparatory to their obscene repast. The Spaniards, conceiving that they had fallen in with a tribe of Caribs, the only race in that part of the New World known to be cannibals, retreated precipitately to their vessel.[17] They were not steeled by sad familiarity with the spectacle, like the Conquerors of Mexico.

The weather, which had been favorable, now set in tempestuous, with heavy squalls, accompanied by incessant thunder and lightning, and the rain, as usual in these tropical tempests, descended not so much in drops as in unbroken sheets of water. The Spaniards, however, preferred to take their chance on the raging element rather than remain in the scene of such brutal abominations. But the fury of the storm gradually subsided, and the little vessel held on her way along the coast, till, coming abreast of a bold point of land named by Pizarro Punta Quemada, he gave orders to anchor. The margin of the shore was fringed with a deep belt of mangrove-

[17] " I en las Ollas de la comida, que estaban al Fuego, entre la Carne, que sacaban, havia Pies i Manos de Hombres, de donde conocieron, que aquellos Indios eran Caribes." Herrera, Hist. general, dec. 3, lib. 8, cap. 11.

trees, the long roots of which, interlacing one
another, formed a kind of submarine lattice-work
that made the place difficult of approach. Several avenues, opening through this tangled thicket,
led Pizarro to conclude that the country must be
inhabited, and he disembarked, with the greater
part of his force, to explore the interior.

He had not penetrated more than a league when
he found his conjecture verified by the sight of
an Indian town, of larger size than those he had
hitherto seen, occupying the brow of an eminence,
and well defended by palisades. The inhabitants,
as usual, had fled, but left in their dwellings a
good supply of provisions and some gold trinkets,
which the Spaniards made no difficulty of appro-
priating to themselves. Pizarro's flimsy bark had
been strained by the heavy gales it had of late
encountered, so that it was unsafe to prosecute the
voyage farther without more thorough repairs
than could be given to her on this desolate coast.
He accordingly determined to send her back with
a few hands to be careened at Panamá, and meanwhile to establish his quarters in his present position, which was so favorable for defence. But
first he despatched a small party under Montenegro to reconnoitre the country, and, if possible,
to open a communication with the natives.

The latter were a warlike race. They had left
their habitations in order to place their wives and
children in safety. But they had kept an eye on
the movements of the invaders, and when they
saw their forces divided they resolved to fall upon
each body singly before it could communicate

with the other. So soon, therefore, as Montenegro had penetrated through the defiles of the
lofty hills which shoot out like spurs of the Cordilleras along this part of the coast, the Indian
warriors, springing from their ambush, sent off
a cloud of arrows and other missiles that dark-
ened the air, while they made the forest ring with
their shrill war-whoop. The Spaniards, astonished at the appearance of the savages, with their
naked bodies gaudily painted, and brandishing
their weapons as they glanced among the trees
and straggling underbrush that choked up the
defile, were taken by surprise and thrown for a
moment into disarray. Three of their number
were killed and several wounded. Yet, speedily
rallying, they returned the discharge of the assail-
ants with their cross-bows,—for Pizarro's troops
do not seem to have been provided with muskets
on this expedition,—and then, gallantly charging
the enemy, sword in hand, succeeded in driving
them back into the fastnesses of the mountains.
But it only led them to shift their operations
to another quarter, and make an assault on
Pizarro before he could be relieved by his lieutenant.

Availing themselves of their superior knowledge
of the passes, they reached that commander's
quarters long before Montenegro, who had commenced a countermarch in the same direction; and,
issuing from the woods, the bold savages saluted
the Spanish garrison with a tempest of darts and
arrows, some of which found their way through
the joints of the harness and the quilted mail of

the cavaliers. But Pizarro was too well-practised
a soldier to be off his guard. Calling his men
about him, he resolved not to abide the assault
tamely in the works, but to sally out and meet the
enemy on their own ground. The barbarians, who
had advanced near the defences, fell back as the
Spaniards burst forth with their valiant leader
at their head. But, soon returning with admirable
ferocity to the charge, they singled out Pizarro,
whom by his bold bearing and air of authority they
easily recognized as the chief, and, hurling at him
a storm of missiles, wounded him, in spite of his
armor, in no less than seven places.[18]

Driven back by the fury of the assault directed
against his own person, the Spanish commander
retreated down the slope of the hill, still defend-
ing himself as he could with sword and buckler,
when his foot slipped and he fell. The enemy
set up a fierce yell of triumph, and some of the
boldest sprang forward to despatch him. But
Pizarro was on his feet in an instant, and, striking
down two of the foremost with his strong arm,
held the rest at bay till his soldiers could come to
the rescue. The barbarians, struck with admiration at his valor, began to falter, when Montenegro luckily coming on the ground at the moment, and falling on their rear, completed their
confusion; and, abandoning the field, they made
the best of their way into the recesses of the
mountains. The ground was covered with their

[18] Naharro, Relacion sumaria, MS.—Xerez, Conq. del Peru, ap.
Barcia, tom. iii. p 180.—Zarate, Conq. del Peru, lib. 1, cap. 1.—Balboa, Hist. du Pérou, chap. 15.

slain; but the victory was dearly purchased by the death of two more Spaniards and a long list of wounded.

A council of war was then called. The position had lost its charm in the eyes of the Spaniards, who had met here with the first resistance they had yet experienced on their expedition. It was necessary to place the wounded in some secure spot, where their injuries could be attended to. Yet it was not safe to proceed farther, in the crippled state of their vessel. On the whole, it was decided to return and report their proceedings to the governor; and, though the magnificent hopes of the adventurers had not been realized, Pizarro trusted that enough had been done to vindicate the importance of the enterprise and to secure the countenance of Pedrarias for the further prosecution of it.[19]

Yet Pizarro could not make up his mind to present himself, in the present state of the undertaking, before the governor. He determined, therefore, to be set on shore with the principal part of his company at Chicamá, a place on the main land, at a short distance west of Panamá. From this place, which he reached without any further accident, he despatched the vessel, and in it his treasurer, Nicholas de Ribera, with the gold he had collected, and with instructions to lay before the governor a full account of his discoveries and the result of the expedition.

While these events were passing, Pizarro's asso-

[19] Herrera, Hist. general, dec. 3, lib. 8, cap. 11.—Xerez, ubi supra.

ciate, Almagro, had been busily employed in
fitting out another vessel for the expedition at
the port of Panamá. It was not till long after
his friend's departure that he was prepared to
follow him. With the assistance of Luque, he at
length succeeded in equipping a small caravel and
embarking a body of between sixty and seventy
adventurers, mostly of the lowest order of the
colonists. He steered in the track of his comrade, with the intention of overtaking him as
soon as possible. By a signal previously con-
certed of notching the trees, he was able to identify the spots visited by Pizarro,—Puerto de
Piñas, Puerto de la Hambre, Pueblo Quemado,
—touching successively at every point of the coast
explored by his countrymen, though in a much
shorter time. At the last-mentioned place he
was received by the fierce natives with the same
hostile demonstrations as Pizarro, though in the
present encounter the Indians did not venture
beyond their defences. But the hot blood of
Almagro was so exasperated by this check that
he assaulted the place and carried it sword in
hand, setting fire to the outworks and dwellings,
and driving the wretched inhabitants into the
forests.

His victory cost him dear. A wound from a
javelin on the head caused an inflammation in one
of his eyes, which, after great anguish, ended in
the loss of it. Yet the intrepid adventurer did
not hesitate to pursue his voyage, and, after touching at several places on the coast, some of which
rewarded him with a considerable booty in gold,

he reached the mouth of the Rio de San Juan, about the fourth degree of north latitude. He was struck with the beauty of the stream, and with the cultivation on its borders, which were sprinkled with Indian cottages showing some skill in their construction, and altogether intimating a higher civilization than any thing he had yet seen.

Still his mind was filled with anxiety for the fate of Pizarro and his followers. No trace of them had been found on the coast for a long time, and it was evident they must have foundered at sea or made their way back to Panamá. This last he deemed most probable; as the vessel might have passed him unnoticed under the cover of the night or of the dense fogs that sometimes hang over the coast.

Impressed with this belief, he felt no heart to continue his voyage of discovery, for which, indeed, his single bark, with its small complement of men, was altogether inadequate. He proposed, therefore, to return without delay. On his way he touched at the Isle of Pearls, and there learned the result of his friend's expedition and the place of his present residence. He directed his course at once to Chicamá, where the two cavaliers soon had the satisfaction of embracing each other and recounting their several exploits and escapes. Almagro returned even better freighted with gold than his confederate, and at every step of his progress he had collected fresh confirmation of the existence of some great and opulent empire in the South. The confidence of the two friends was much strengthened by their discoveries; and they unhesitatingly pledged themselves to one another to die rather than abandon the enterprise.[20]

The best means of obtaining the levies requisite for so formidable an undertaking—more formidable, as it now appeared to them, than before— were made the subject of long and serious discussion. It was at length decided that Pizarro should remain in his present quarters, inconvenient and even unwholesome as they were rendered by the humidity of the climate and the pestilent swarms of insects that filled the atmosphere. Almagro would pass over to Panamá, lay the case before the governor, and secure, if possible, his good will towards the prosecution of the enterprise. If no obstacle were thrown in their way from this quarter, they might hope, with the assistance of Luque, to raise the necessary supplies; while the results of the recent expedition were sufficiently encouraging to draw adventurers to their standard in a community which had a craving for excitement that gave even danger a charm, and which held life cheap in comparison with gold.

[20] Xerez, ubi supra —Naharro, Relacion sumaria, MS —Zarate, Conq del Peru, loc. cit —Balboa, Hist du Pérou, chap 15 —Relacion del primer Descub., MS.—Herrera, Hist. general, dec. 3, lib. 8, cap 13 —Levinus Apollonius, fol. 12.—Gomara, Hist. de las Ind., cap 108.

CHAPTER III

1526–1527

ON his arrival at Panamá, Almagro found that events had taken a turn less favorable to his views than he had anticipated. Pedrarias, the governor, was preparing to lead an expedition in person against a rebellious officer in Nicaragua; and his temper, naturally not the most amiable, was still further soured by this defection of his lieutenant and the necessity it imposed on him of a long and perilous march. When, therefore, Almagro appeared before him with the request that he might be permitted to raise further levies to prosecute his enterprise, the governor received him with obvious dissatisfaction, listened coldly to the narrative of his losses, turned an incredulous ear to his magnificent promises for the future, and bluntly demanded an account of the lives which had been sacrificed by Pizarro's obstinacy, but which, had they been spared, might have stood him in good stead in his present expedition to Nicaragua. He positively declined to countenance the rash schemes of the two adventurers

any longer, and the conquest of Peru would have
been crushed in the bud, but for the efficient interposition of the remaining associate, Fernando de
Luque.

This sagacious ecclesiastic had received a very
different impression from Almagro's narrative
from that which had been made on the mind of
the irritable governor. The actual results of the
enterprises in gold and silver thus far, indeed, had
been small,—forming a mortifying contrast to the
magnitude of their expectations. But in another
point of view they were of the last importance;
since the intelligence which the adventurers had
gained at every successive stage of their progress
confirmed, in the strongest manner, the previous
accounts, received from Andagoya and others, of
a rich Indian empire at the south, which might repay the trouble of conquering it as well as Mexico
had repaid the enterprise of Cortés. Fully entering, therefore, into the feelings of his military
associates, he used all his influence with the governor to incline him to a more favorable view of
Almagro's petition; and no one in the little community of Panamá exercised greater influence
over the councils of the executive than Father
Luque, for which he was indebted no less to his
discretion and acknowledged sagacity than to his
professional station.

But while Pedrarias, overcome by the arguments or importunity of the churchman, yielded
a reluctant assent to the application, he took care
to testify his displeasure with Pizarro, on whom
he particularly charged the loss of his followers,

by naming Almagro as his equal in command in
the proposed expedition. This mortification sank
deep into Pizarro's mind. He suspected his comrade, with what reason does not appear, of solicit-
ing this boon from the governor. A temporary
coldness arose between them, which subsided, in
outward show at least, on Pizarro's reflecting that
it was better to have this authority conferred on
a friend than on a stranger, perhaps an enemy.
But the seeds of permanent distrust were left in
his bosom, and lay waiting for the due season to
ripen into a fruitful harvest of discord.[1]

Pedrarias had been originally interested in the
enterprise, at least so far as to stipulate for a share
of the gains, though he had not contributed, as it
appears, a single ducat towards the expenses. He
was at length, however, induced to relinquish all
right to a share of the contingent profits. But in
his manner of doing so he showed a mercenary
spirit better becoming a petty trader than a high
officer of the crown. He stipulated that the associates should secure to him the sum of one thousand *pesos de oro* in requital of his good will, and
they eagerly closed with his proposal, rather than
be encumbered with his pretensions. For so paltry
a consideration did he resign his portion of the
rich spoil of the Incas![2] But the governor was

[1] Xerez, Conq del Peru, ap Barcia, tom. iii. p. 180.—Montesinos,
Annales, MS., año 1526.—Herrera, Hist general, dec. 3, lib. 8,
cap. 12.

[2] Such is the account of Oviedo, who was present at the interview
between the governor and Almagro when the terms of compensation
were discussed. The dialogue, which is amusing enough, and well
told by the old Chronicler, may be found translated in Appendix
No. 5. Another version of the affair is given in the *Relacion,* often

not gifted with the eye of a prophet. His avarice was of that short-sighted kind which defeats itself. He had sacrificed the chivalrous Balboa just as that officer was opening to him the conquest of Peru, and he would now have quenched the spirit of enterprise, that was taking the same direction, in Pizarro and his associates.

Not long after this, in the following year, he was succeeded in his government by Don Pedro de los Rios, a cavalier of Cordova. It was the policy of the Castilian crown to allow no one of the great colonial officers to occupy the same station so long as to render himself formidable by his authority.[3] It had, moreover, many particular causes of disgust with Pedrarias. The function-

quoted by me, of one of the Peruvian conquerors, in which Pedrarias is said to have gone out of the partnership voluntarily, from his disgust at the unpromising state of affairs: "Vueltos con la dicha gente á Panamá, destrozados y gastados que ya no tenian haciendas para tornar con provisiones y gentes que todo lo habian gastado, el dicho Pedrarias de Avila les dijo, que ya el no queria mas hacer compañia con ellos en los gastos de la armada, que si ellos querian volver á su costa, que lo hiciesen; y ansi como gente que habia perdido todo lo que tenia y tanto habia trabajado, acordaron de tornar á proseguir su jornada y dar fin á las vidas y haciendas que les quedaba, ó descubrir aquella tierra, y ciertamente ellos tubieron grande constancia y animo." Relacion del primer Descub., MS.

[3] This policy is noticed by the sagacious Martyr: "De mutandis namque plœrisque gubernatoribus, ne longa nimis imperii assuetudine insolescant, cogitatur, qui præcipue non fuerint prouinciarum domitores, de hisce ducibus namque alia ratio ponderatur." (De Orbe Novo (Parisiis, 1587), p. 498.) One cannot but regret that the philosopher who took so keen an interest in the successive revelations of the different portions of the New World should have died before the empire of the Incas was disclosed to Europeans. He lived to learn and to record the wonders of

"Rich Mexico, the seat of Montezuma;
Not Cuzco in Peru, the richer seat of Atabalipa."

ary sent out to succeed him was fortified with
ample instructions for the good of the colony, and
especially of the natives, whose religious conversion was urged as a capital object, and whose personal freedom was unequivocally asserted, as loyal
vassals of the crown. It is but justice to the
Spanish government to admit that its provisions
were generally guided by a humane and considerate policy, which was as regularly frustrated
by the cupidity of the colonist and the capricious
cruelty of the conqueror. The few remaining
years of Pedrarias were spent in petty squabbles,
both of a personal and official nature; for he was
still continued in office, though in one of less consideration than that which he had hitherto filled.
He survived but a few years, leaving behind him
a reputation not to be envied, of one who united a
pusillanimous spirit with uncontrollable passions,
but who displayed, notwithstanding, a certain
energy of character, or, to speak more correctly,
an impetuosity of purpose, which might have led
to good results had it taken a right direction. Unfortunately, his lack of discretion was such that
the direction he took was rarely of service to his
country or to himself.

Having settled their difficulties with the governor, and obtained his sanction to their enterprise,
the confederates lost no time in making the requisite preparations for it. Their first step was to
execute the memorable contract which served as
the basis of their future arrangements; and, as
Pizarro's name appears in this, it seems probable
that the chief had crossed over to Panamá so soon

as the favorable disposition of Pedrarias had been secured.[4]   The instrument, after invoking in the most solemn manner the names of the Holy Trinity and Our Lady the Blessed Virgin, sets forth that whereas the parties have full authority to discover and subdue the countries and provinces lying south of the Gulf, belonging to the empire of Peru, and as Fernando de Luque had advanced the funds for the enterprise in bars of gold of the value of twenty thousand *pesos*, they mutually bind themselves to divide equally among them the whole of the conquered territory.   This stipulation is reiterated over and over again, particularly with reference to Luque, who, it is declared, is to be entitled to one-third of all lands, *repartimientos*, treasures of every kind, gold, silver, and precious stones,—to one-third even of all vassals, rents, and emoluments arising from such grants as may be conferred by the crown on either of his military associates, to be held for his own use, or for that of his heirs, assigns, or legal representative.

The two captains solemnly engage to devote themselves exclusively to the present undertaking until it is accomplished; and in case of failure in their part of the covenant they pledge themselves to reimburse Luque for his advances, for which all the property they possess shall be held respon-

[4] In opposition to most authorities,—but not to the judicious Quintana,—I have conformed to Montesinos, in placing the execution of the contract at the commencement of the second, instead of the first expedition. This arrangement coincides with the date of the instrument itself, which, moreover, is reported *in extenso* by no ancient writer whom I have consulted except Montesinos.

sible, and this declaration is to be a sufficient warrant for the execution of judgment against them, in the same manner as if it had proceeded from the decree of a court of justice.

The commanders, Pizarro and Almagro, made oath, in the name of God and the Holy Evangelists, sacredly to keep this covenant, swearing it on the missal, on which they traced with their own hands the sacred emblem of the cross. To give still greater efficacy to the compact, Father Luque administered the sacrament to the parties, dividing the consecrated wafer into three portions, of which each one of them partook; while the by-standers, says an historian, were affected to tears by this spectacle of the solemn ceremonial with which these men voluntarily devoted themselves to a sacrifice that seemed little short of insanity.[5]

The instrument, which was dated March 10th, 1526, was subscribed by Luque, and attested by three respectable citizens of Panamá, one of whom signed on behalf of Pizarro, and the other for Almagro; since neither of these parties, according to the avowal of the instrument, was able to subscribe his own name.[6]

Such was the singular compact by which three obscure individuals coolly carved out and partitioned among themselves an empire of whose extent, power, and resources, of whose situation, of

[5] This singular instrument is given at length by Montesinos. (Annales, MS., año 1526.) It may be found in the original in Appendix No. 6.

[6] For some investigation of the fact, which has been disputed by more than one, of Pizarro's ignorance of the art of writing, see book 4, chap. 5, of this History.

whose existence even, they had no sure or precise knowledge. The positive and unhesitating manner in which they speak of the grandeur of this empire, of its stores of wealth, so conformable to the event, but of which they could have really known so little, forms a striking contrast with the general skepticism and indifference manifested by nearly every other person, high and low, in the community of Panamá.[7]

The religious tone of the instrument is not the least remarkable feature in it, especially when we contrast this with the relentless policy pursued by the very men who were parties to it in their conquest of the country. " In the name of the Prince of Peace," says the illustrious historian of America, " they ratified a contract of which plunder and bloodshed were the objects."[8] The reflection seems reasonable. Yet, in criticising what is done, as well as what is written, we must take into account the spirit of the times.[9] The invocation of Heaven was natural, where the object of the undertaking was in part a religious one. Religion entered more or less into the theory, at least, of the

---

[7] The epithet of *loco*, or "madman," was *punningly* bestowed on Father Luque, for his spirited exertions in behalf of the enterprise; *Padre Luque ò loco*, says Oviedo of him, as if it were synonymous Historia de las Indias Islas e Tierra Firme del Mar Oceano, MS, Parte 3, lib. 8, cap 1

[8] Robertson, America, vol. iii. p. 5.

[9] " A perfect judge will read each work of wit
With the same spirit that its author writ."

says the great bard of Reason. A fair criticism will apply the same rule to action as to writing, and, in the moral estimate of conduct, will take largely into account the spirit of the age which prompted it

Spanish conquests in the New World. That motives of a baser sort mingled largely with these higher ones, and in different proportions according to the character of the individual, no one will deny. And few are they that have proposed to themselves a long career of action without the intermixture of some vulgar personal motive,— fame, honors, or emolument. Yet that religion furnishes a key to the American crusades, however rudely they may have been conducted, is evident from the history of their origin; from the sanction openly given to them by the Head of the Church; from the throng of self-devoted missionaries who followed in the track of the conquerors to garner up the rich harvest of souls; from the reiterated instructions of the crown, the great object of which was the conversion of the natives; from those superstitious acts of the iron-hearted soldiery themselves, which, however they may be set down to fanaticism, were clearly too much in earnest to leave any ground for the charge of hypocrisy. It was indeed a fiery cross that was borne over the devoted land, scathing and consuming it in its terrible progress; but it was still the cross, the sign of man's salvation, the only sign by which generations and generations yet unborn were to be rescued from eternal perdition.

It is a remarkable fact, which has hitherto escaped the notice of the historian, that Luque was not the real party to this contract. He represented another, who placed in his hands the funds required for the undertaking. This appears from an instrument signed by Luque himself and cer-

tified before the same notary that prepared the
original contract. The instrument declares that
the whole sum of twenty thousand *pesos* advanced
for the expedition was furnished by the Licentiate
Gaspar de Espinosa, then at Panamá; that the
vicar acted only as his agent and by his authority;
and that, in consequence, the said Espinosa and no
other was entitled to a third of all the profits and
acquisitions resulting from the conquest of Peru.
This instrument, attested by three persons, one of
them the same who had witnessed the original contract, was dated on the 6th of August, 1531.[10]
The Licentiate Espinosa was a respectable functionary, who had filled the office of principal al-
calde in Darien, and since taken a conspicuous
part in the conquest and settlement of Tierra
Firme. He enjoyed much consideration for his
personal character and station; and it is remarkable that so little should be known of the manner in
which the covenant so solemnly made was executed
in reference to him. As in the case of Columbus, it is probable that the unexpected magnitude of the results was such as to prevent a faithful adherence to the original stipulation; and yet,
from the same consideration, one can hardly doubt
that the twenty thousand *pesos* of the bold specu-
lator must have brought him a magnificent return.

---

[10] The instrument making this extraordinary disclosure is cited at
length in a manuscript entitled Noticia general del Perú, Tierra
Firme y Chili, by Francisco Lopez de Caravantes, a fiscal officer in
these colonies. The MS, formerly preserved in the library of the
great college of Cuenca at Salamanca, is now to be found in her
Majesty's library at Madrid. The passage is extracted by Quintana,
Españoles célebres, tom. ii. Apend. No. 2, nota

Nor did the worthy vicar of Panamá, as the history will show hereafter, go without his reward.

Having completed these preliminary arrangements, the three associates lost no time in making preparations for the voyage. Two vessels were purchased, larger and every way better than those employed on the former occasion. Stores were laid in, as experience dictated, on a larger scale than before, and proclamation was made of "an expedition to Peru." But the call was not readily answered by the skeptical citizens of Panamá. Of nearly two hundred men who had embarked on the former cruise, not more than three-fourths now remained.[11] This dismal mortality, and the emaciated, poverty-stricken aspect of the survivors, spoke more eloquently than the braggart promises and magnificent prospects held out by the adventurers. Still, there were men in the community of such desperate circumstances that any change seemed like a chance of bettering their condition. Most of the former company also, strange to say, felt more pleased to follow up the adventure to the end than to abandon it as they saw the light of a better day dawning upon them. From these sources the two captains succeeded in mustering about one hundred and sixty men, making altogether a very inadequate force for the conquest of an empire. A few horses were also purchased, and a better supply of ammuni-

---

[11] "Con ciento i diez Hombres salió de Panamà, i fue donde estaba el Capitan Piçarro con otros cinquenta de los primeros ciento i diez, que con èl salieron, i de los setenta, que el Capitan Almagro llevò, quando le fue à buscar, que los ciento i treinta ià eran muertos." Xerez, Conq del Peru, ap. Barcia, tom. iii p. 180.

tion and military stores than before, though still on a very limited scale. Considering their funds, the only way of accounting for this must be by the difficulty of obtaining supplies at Panamá, which, recently founded, and on the remote coast of the Pacific, could be approached only by crossing the rugged barrier of mountains, which made the transportation of bulky articles extremely difficult. Even such scanty stock of materials as it possessed was probably laid under heavy contribution, at the present juncture, by the governor's preparations for his own expedition to the north.

Thus indifferently provided, the two captains, each in his own vessel, again took their departure from Panamá, under the direction of Bartholomew Ruiz, a sagacious and resolute pilot, well experienced in the navigation of the Southern Ocean. He was a native of Moguer, in Andalusia, that little nursery of nautical enterprise, which furnished so many seamen for the first voyages of Columbus. Without touching at the intervening points of the coast, which offered no attraction to the voyagers, they stood farther out to sea, steering direct for the Rio de San Juan, the utmost limit reached by Almagro. The season was better selected than on the former occasion, and they were borne along by favorable breezes to the place of their destination, which they reached without accident in a few days. Entering the mouth of the river, they saw the banks well lined with Indian habitations; and Pizarro, disembarking at the head of a party of soldiers, succeeded in surprising a small village and carrying off a considerable booty of gold ornaments found in the dwellings, together with a few of the natives.[12]

Flushed with their success, the two chiefs were confident that the sight of the rich spoil so speedily obtained could not fail to draw adventurers to their standard in Panamá; and, as they felt more than ever the necessity of a stronger force to cope with the thickening population of the country which they were now to penetrate, it was decided that Almagro should return with the treasure and beat up for reinforcements, while the pilot Ruiz, in the other vessel, should reconnoitre the country towards the south, and obtain such information as might determine their future movements. Pizarro, with the rest of the force, would remain in the neighborhood of the river, as he was assured by the Indian prisoners that not far off in the interior was an open reach of country, where he and his men could find comfortable quarters. This arrangement was instantly put in execution. We will first accompany the intrepid pilot in his cruise towards the south.

Coasting along the great continent, with his canvas still spread to favorable winds, the first place at which Ruiz cast anchor was off the little island of Gallo, about two degrees north. The inhabitants, who were not numerous, were prepared to give him a hostile reception; for tidings of the invaders had preceded them along the country, and even reached this insulated spot. As the

[12] Xerez, Conq. del Peru, ap. Barcia, tom. iii. pp. 180, 181.—Naharro, Relacion sumaria, MS —Zarate, Conq. del Peru, lib. 1, cap. 1.—Herrera, Hist. general, dec. 3, lib. 8, cap. 13.

object of Ruiz was to explore, not to conquer, he did not care to entangle himself in hostilities with the natives: so, changing his purpose of landing, he weighed anchor, and ran down the coast as far as what is now called the Bay of St. Matthew. The country, which, as he advanced, continued to exhibit evidence of a better culture as well as of a more dense population than the parts hitherto seen, was crowded, along the shores, with spectators, who gave no signs of fear or hostility. They stood gazing on the vessel of the white men as it glided smoothly into the crystal waters of the bay, fancying it, says an old writer, some mysterious being descended from the skies.

Without staying long enough on this friendly coast to undeceive the simple people, Ruiz, standing off shore, struck out into the deep sea; but he had not sailed far in that direction when he was surprised by the sight of a vessel, seeming in the distance like a caravel of considerable size, traversed by a large sail that carried it sluggishly over the waters. The old navigator was not a little perplexed by this phenomenon, as he was confident no European bark could have been before him in these latitudes, and no Indian nation yet discovered, not even the civilized Mexican, was acquainted with the use of sails in navigation. As he drew near, he found it was a large vessel, or rather raft, called *balsa* by the natives, consisting of a number of huge timbers of a light, porous wood, tightly lashed together, with a frail flooring of reeds raised on them by way of deck. Two masts or sturdy poles, erected in the middle of the vessel, sustained a large square sail of cotton, while a rude kind of rudder and a movable keel, made of plank inserted between the logs, enabled the mariner to give a direction to the floating fabric, which held on its course without the aid of oar or paddle.[13]   The simple architecture of this craft was sufficient for the purposes of the natives, and indeed has continued to answer them to the present day; for the *balsa*, surmounted by small thatched huts or cabins, still supplies the most commodious means for the transportation of passengers and luggage on the streams and along the shores of this part of the South American continent.

On coming alongside, Ruiz found several Indians, both men and women, on board, some with rich ornaments on their persons, besides several articles wrought with considerable skill in gold and silver, which they were carrying for purposes of traffic to the different places along the coast. But what most attracted his attention was the woollen cloth of which some of their dresses were made. It was of a fine texture, delicately embroidered with figures of birds and flowers, and dyed in brilliant colors. He also observed in the boat a pair of balances made to weigh the precious metals.[14]   His astonishment at these proofs of

[13] "Traia sus manteles y antenas de muy fina madera y velas de algodon del mismo talle de manera que los nuestros navios." Relacion de los primeros Descubrimientos de F Pizarro y Diego de Almagro, sacada del Codice No. 120 de la Biblioteca Imperial de Vienna, MS

[14] In a short notice of this expedition, written apparently at the time of it, or soon after, a minute specification is given of the several articles found in the *balsa;* among them are mentioned vases

ingenuity and civilization, so much higher than
any thing he had ever seen in the country, was
heightened by the intelligence which he collected
from some of these Indians. Two of them had
come from Tumbez, a Peruvian port, some degrees to the south; and they gave him to understand that in their neighborhood the fields were
covered with large flocks of the animals from
which the wool was obtained, and that gold and
silver were almost as common as wool in the
palaces of their monarch. The Spaniards listened
greedily to reports which harmonized so well with
their fond desires. Though half distrusting the
exaggeration, Ruiz resolved to detain some of the
Indians, including the natives of Tumbez, that
they might repeat the wondrous tale to his commander, and at the same time, by learning the
Castilian, might hereafter serve as interpreters
with their countrymen. The rest of the party
he suffered to proceed without further interrup-
tion on their voyage. Then, holding on his course,
the prudent pilot, without touching at any other
point of the coast, advanced as far as the Punta
de Pasado, about half a degree south, having the
glory of being the first European who, sailing in

and mirrors of burnished silver, and curious fabrics both cotton and
woollen: "Espejos guarnecidos de la dicha plata, y tasas y otras
vasijas para beber, trahian muchas mantas de lana y de algodon, y
camisas y aljubas y alcaçeres y alaremes, y otras muchas ropas, todo
lo mas de ello muy labrado de labores muy ricas de colores de grana
y carmisi y azul y amarillo, y de todas otras colores de diversas
maneras de labores y figuras de aves y animales, y Pescados, y
arbolesas y trahian unos pesos chiquitos de pesar oro como hechura
de Romana, y otras muchas cosas" Relacion sacada de la Biblioteca Imperial de Vienna, MS

this direction on the Pacific, had crossed the equinoctial line. This was the limit of his discoveries; on reaching which he tacked about, and, standing away to the north, succeeded, after an absence of several weeks, in regaining the spot where he had left Pizarro and his comrades.[15]

It was high time; for the spirits of that little band had been sorely tried by the perils they had encountered. On the departure of his vessels, Pizarro marched into the interior, in the hope of finding the pleasant champaign country which had been promised him by the natives. But at every step the forests seemed to grow denser and darker, and the trees towered to a height such as he had never seen, even in these fruitful regions, where Nature works on so gigantic a scale.[16] Hill continued to rise above hill, as he advanced, rolling onward, as it were, by successive waves to join that colossal barrier of the Andes, whose frosty sides, far away above the clouds, spread out like a curtain of burnished silver, that seemed to connect the heavens with the earth.

On crossing these woody eminences, the forlorn adventurers would plunge into ravines of frightful depth, where the exhalations of a humid soil

---

[15] Xerez, Conq. del Peru, ap. Barcia, tom. iii. p. 181.—Relacion sacada de la Biblioteca Imperial de Vienna, MS.—Herrera, Hist. general, dec. 3, lib. 8, cap. 13.—One of the authorities speaks of his having been sixty days on this cruise. I regret not to be able to give precise dates of the events in these early expeditions. But chronology is a thing beneath the notice of these ancient chroniclers, who seem to think that the date of events so fresh in their own memory must be so in that of every one else.

[16] "Todo era montañas, con arboles hasta el cielo!" Herrera, Hist. general, ubi supra.

steamed up amidst the incense of sweet-scented flowers, which shone through the deep gloom in every conceivable variety of color. Birds, especially of the parrot tribe, mocked this fantastic variety of nature with tints as brilliant as those of the vegetable world. Monkeys chattered in crowds above their heads, and made grimaces like the fiendish spirits of these solitudes; while hideous reptiles, engendered in the slimy depths of the pools, gathered round the footsteps of the wanderers. Here was seen the gigantic boa, coiling his unwieldy folds about the trees, so as hardly to be distinguished from their trunks, till he was ready to dart upon his prey; and alligators lay basking on the borders of the streams, or, gliding under the waters, seized their incautious victim before he was aware of their approach.[17] Many of the Spaniards perished miserably in this way, and others were waylaid by the natives, who kept a jealous eye on their movements and availed themselves of every opportunity to take them at advantage. Fourteen of Pizarro's men were cut off at once in a canoe which had stranded on the bank of a stream.[18]

Famine came in addition to other troubles, and it was with difficulty that they found the means of sustaining life on the scanty fare of the forest, —occasionally the potato, as it grew without cultivation, or the wild cocoanut, or, on the shore, the salt and bitter fruit of the mangrove; though

[17] Ibid., ubi supra.
[18] Herrera, loc. cit—Gomara, Hist. de las Ind, cap. 108—Naharro, Relacion sumaria, MS.

the shore was less tolerable than the forest, from the swarms of mosquitos which compelled the wretched adventurers to bury their bodies up to their very faces in the sand. In this extremity of suffering, they thought only of return; and all schemes of avarice and ambition—except with Pizarro and a few dauntless spirits—were exchanged for the one craving desire to return to Panamá.

It was at this crisis that the pilot Ruiz returned with the report of his brilliant discoveries; and, not long after, Almagro sailed into port with his vessel laden with provisions and a considerable reinforcement of volunteers. The voyage of that commander had been prosperous. When he arrived at Panamá, he found the government in the hands of Don Pedro de los Rios; and he came to anchor in the harbor, unwilling to trust himself on shore till he had obtained from Father Luque some account of the dispositions of the executive. These were sufficiently favorable; for the new governor had particular instructions fully to carry out the arrangements made by his predecessor with the associates. On learning Almagro's arrival, he came down to the port to welcome him, professing his willingness to afford every facility for the execution of his designs. Fortunately, just before this period a small body of military adventurers had come to Panamá from the mother-country, burning with desire to make their fortunes in the New World. They caught much more eagerly than the old and wary colonists at the golden bait held out to them; and with their

addition, and that of a few supernumerary strag-
glers who hung about the town, Almagro found
himself at the head of a reinforcement of at least
eighty men, with which, having laid in a fresh
supply of stores, he again set sail for the Rio de
San Juan.

The arrival of the new recruits all eager to follow up the expedition, the comfortable change in
their circumstances produced by an ample supply
of provisions, and the glowing pictures of the
wealth that awaited them in the south, all had their
effect on the dejected spirits of Pizarro's followers. Their late toils and privations were speedily
forgotten, and, with the buoyant and variable feelings incident to a freebooter's life, they now called
as eagerly on their commander to go forward in
the voyage as they had before called on him to
abandon it. Availing themselves of the renewed
spirit of enterprise, the captains embarked on
board their vessels, and, under the guidance of
the veteran pilot, steered in the same track he had
lately pursued.

But the favorable season for a southern course,
which in these latitudes lasts but a few months in
the year, had been suffered to escape. The breezes
blew steadily towards the north, and a strong current, not far from shore, set in the same direction.
The winds frequently rose into tempests, and the
unfortunate voyagers were tossed about, for many
days, in the boiling surges, amidst the most awful
storms of thunder and lightning, until at length
they found a secure haven in the island of Gallo,
already visited by Ruiz. As they were now too

strong in numbers to apprehend an assault, the crews landed, and, experiencing no molestation from the natives, they continued on the island for a fortnight, refitting their damaged vessels, and recruiting themselves after the fatigues of the ocean. Then, resuming their voyage, the captains stood towards the south until they reached the bay of St. Matthew. As they advanced along the coast, they were struck, as Ruiz had been before, with the evidences of a higher civilization constantly exhibited in the general aspect of the country and its inhabitants. The hand of cultivation was visible in every quarter. The natural appearance of the coast, too, had something in it more inviting; for instead of the eternal labyrinth of mangrove-trees, with their complicated roots snarled into formidable coils under the water, as if to waylay and entangle the voyager, the low margin of the sea was covered with a stately growth of ebony, and with a species of mahogany, and other hard woods that take the most brilliant and variegated polish. The sandal-wood, and many balsamic trees of unknown names, scattered their sweet odors far and wide, not in an atmosphere tainted with vegetable corruption, but on the pure breezes of the ocean, bearing health as well as fragrance on their wings. Broad patches of cultivated land intervened, disclosing hill-sides covered with the yellow maize and the potato, or checkered, in the lower levels, with blooming plantations of cacao.[19]

[19] Xerez, Conq. del Peru, ap. Barcia, tom. iii. p. 181.—Relacion sacada de la Biblioteca Imperial de Vienna, MS.—Naharro, Rela-

The villages became more numerous; and, as
the vessels rode at anchor off the port of Tacamez,
the Spaniards saw before them a town of two
thousand houses or more, laid out into streets, with
a numerous population clustering around it in the
suburbs.[20] The men and women displayed many
ornaments of gold and precious stones about their
persons, which may seem strange, considering that
the Peruvian Incas claimed a monopoly of jewels
for themselves and the nobles on whom they condescended to bestow them.   But, although the
Spaniards had now reached the outer limits of the
Peruvian empire, it was not Peru, but Quito, and
that portion of it but recently brought under the
sceptre of the Incas, where the ancient usages of
the people could hardly have been effaced under
the oppressive system of the American despots.
The adjacent country was, moreover, particularly
rich in gold, which, collected from the washings
of the streams, still forms one of the staple products of Barbacoas. Here, too, was the fair River
of Emeralds, so called from the quarries of the
beautiful gem on its borders, from which the
Indian monarchs enriched their treasury.[21]

cion sumaria, MS—Montesinos, Annales, MS, año 1526—Zarate,
Conq del Peru, lib 1, cap 1.—Relacion del primer Descub, MS.

[20] Pizarro's secretary speaks of one of the towns as containing
3000 houses: "En esta Tierra havia muchos Mantenimientos, i la
Gente tenia mui buena orden de vivir, los Pueblos con sus Calles, i
Plaças: Pueblo havia que tenia mas de tres mil Casas, i otros havia
menores." Conq. del Peru, ap. Barcia, tom. iii. p. 181.

[21] Stevenson, who visited this part of the coast early in the present
century, is profuse in his description of its mineral and vegetable
treasures. The emerald-mine in the neighborhood of Las Esmeraldas, once so famous, is now placed under the ban of a superstition more befitting the times of the Incas. " I never visited it," says

The Spaniards gazed with delight on these un-
deniable evidences of wealth, and saw in the careful cultivation of the soil a comfortable assurance
that they had at length reached the land which had
so long been seen in brilliant, though distant, per-
spective before them.   But here again they were
doomed to be disappointed by the warlike spirit of
the people, who, conscious of their own strength,
showed no disposition to quail before the invaders.
On the contrary, several of their canoes shot out,
loaded with warriors, who, displaying a gold mask
as their ensign, hovered round the vessels with
looks of defiance, and, when pursued, easily took
shelter under the lee of the land.[22]

A more formidable body mustered along the
shore, to the number, according to the Spanish
accounts, of at least ten thousand warriors, eager,
apparently, to come to close action with the invaders.   Nor could Pizarro, who had landed with
a party of his men in the hope of a conference
with the natives, wholly prevent hostilities; and it
might have gone hard with the Spaniards, hotly
pressed by their resolute enemy so superior in
numbers, but for a ludicrous accident reported by

the traveller, "owing to the superstitious dread of the natives, who
assured me that it was enchanted, and guarded by an enormous
dragon, which poured forth thunder and lightning on those who
dared to ascend the river." Residence in South America, vol. ii.
p. 406.

[22] " Salieron á los dichos navios quatorce canoas grandes con muchos Indios dos armados de oro y plata, y trahian en la una canoa ó
en estandarte y encima de él un bolto de un mucho desio de oro, y
dieron una suelta á los navios por avisarlos en manera que no los pudiese enojar, y asi dieron vuelta acia á su pueblo, y los navios no los
pudieron tomar porque se metieron en los baxos junto á la tierra."
Relacion sacada de la Biblioteca Imperial de Vienna, MS.

the historians as happening to one of the cavaliers.
This was a fall from his horse, which so astonished
the barbarians, who were not prepared for this
division of what seemed one and the same being
into two, that, filled with consternation, they fell
back, and left a way open for the Christians to
regain their vessels! [23]

A council of war was now called. It was evident that the forces of the Spaniards were unequal
to a contest with so numerous and well-appointed
a body of natives; and, even if they should pre-
vail here, they could have no hope of stemming
the torrent which must rise against them in their
progress,—for the country was becoming more
and more thickly settled, and towns and hamlets
started into view at every new headland which they
doubled. It was better, in the opinion of some,
—the faint-hearted,—to abandon the enterprise
at once, as beyond their strength. But Almagro
took a different view of the affair. "To go
home," he said, "with nothing done, would be
ruin, as well as disgrace. There was scarcely one
but had left creditors at Panamá, who looked for
payment to the fruits of this expedition. To go
home now would be to deliver themselves at once

---

[23] "Al tiempo del romper los unos con los otros, uno de aquellos
de caballo cayó del caballo abajo; y como los Indios vieron dividirse
aquel animal en dos partes, teniendo por cierto que todo era una cosa,
fué tanto el miedo que tubieron que volvieron las espaldas dando
voces á los suyos, diciendo, que se habia hecho dos haciendo admiracion dello: lo cual no fué sin misterio; porque á no acaecer esto se
presume, que mataran todos los cristianos." (Relation del primer
Descub, MS.) This way of accounting for the panic of the barbarians is certainly quite as credible as the explanation, under
similar circumstances, afforded by the apparition of the militant
apostle St. James, so often noticed by the historians of these wars.

into their hands. It would be to go to prison. Better to roam a freeman, though in the wilderness, than to lie bound with fetters in the dungeons of Panamá.[24] The only course for them," he concluded, " was the one lately pursued. Pizarro might find some more commodious place where he could remain with part of the force while he himself went back for recruits to Panamá. The story they had now to tell of the riches of the land, as they had seen them with their own eyes, would put their expedition in a very different light, and could not fail to draw to their banner as many volunteers as they needed."

But this recommendation, however judicious, was not altogether to the taste of the latter commander, who did not relish the part, which constantly fell to him, of remaining behind in the swamps and forests of this wild country. " It is all very well," he said to Almagro, " for you, who pass your time pleasantly enough, careering to and fro in your vessel, or snugly sheltered in a land of plenty at Panamá; but it is quite another matter for those who stay behind to droop and die of hunger in the wilderness." [25] To this Almagro

---

[24] " No era bien bolver pobres, á pedir limosna, i morir en las Carceles, los que tenian deudas." Herrera, Hist. general, dec. 3, lib. 10, cap. 2.

[25] " Como iba, i venia en los Navios, adonde no le faltaba Vitualla, no padecia la miseria de la hambre, i otras angustias que tenian, i ponian á todos en estrema congoja." (Herrera, Hist. general, dec. 3, lib. 10, cap. 2.) The cavaliers of Cortés and Pizarro, however doughty their achievements, certainly fell short of those knights-errant, commemorated by Hudibras, who,

> " As some think,
> Of old did neither eat nor drink;

retorted with some heat, professing his own willingness to take charge of the brave men who would remain with him, if Pizarro declined it. The controversy assuming a more angry and menacing tone, from words they would have soon come to blows, as both, laying their hands on their swords, were preparing to rush on each other, when the treasurer Ribera, aided by the pilot Ruiz, succeeded in pacifying them. It required but little effort on the part of these cooler counsellors to convince the cavaliers of the folly of a conduct which must at once terminate the expedition in a manner little creditable to its projectors. A reconciliation consequently took place, sufficient, at least in outward show, to allow the two commanders to act together in concert. Almagro's plan was then adopted; and it only remained to find out the most secure and convenient spot for Pizarro's quarters.

Several days were passed in touching at different parts of the coast, as they retraced their course; but everywhere the natives appeared to have caught the alarm, and assumed a menacing, and from their numbers a formidable, aspect. The more northerly region, with its unwholesome fens and forests, where nature wages a war even more relentless than man, was not to be thought of. In this perplexity, they decided on the little island of Gallo, as being, on the whole, from its distance

Because, when thorough deserts vast
And regions desolate they past,
Unless they grazed, there's not one word
Of their provision on record :
Which made some confidently write,
They had no stomachs but to fight."

from the shore, and from the scantiness of its population, the most eligible spot for them in their forlorn and destitute condition.[26]

But no sooner was the resolution of the two captains made known than a feeling of discontent broke forth among their followers, especially those who were to remain with Pizarro on the island. "What!" they exclaimed, "were they to be dragged to that obscure spot to die by hunger? The whole expedition had been a cheat and a failure, from beginning to end. The golden countries, so much vaunted, had seemed to fly before them as they advanced; and the little gold they had been fortunate enough to glean had all been sent back to Panamá to entice other fools to follow their example. What had they got in return for all their sufferings? The only treasures they could boast were their bows and arrows, and they were now to be left to die on this dreary island, without so much as a rood of consecrated ground to lay their bones in!"[27]

In this exasperated state of feeling, several of the soldiers wrote back to their friends, informing

[26] Pedro Pizarro, Descub. y Conq, MS.—Relacion sacada de la Biblioteca Imperial de Vienna, MS.—Naharro, Relacion sumaria, MS.—Zarate, Conq. del Peru, lib. 1, cap. 1.—Herrera, Hist. general, dec. 3, lib 10, cap 2—It was singularly unfortunate that Pizarro, instead of striking farther south, should have so long clung to the northern shores of the continent. Dampier notices them as afflicted with incessant rain, while the inhospitable forests and the particularly ferocious character of the natives continued to make these regions but little known down to his time See his Voyages and Adventures (London, 1776), vol i. chap. 14.

[27] "Miserablemente morir adonde aun no havia lugar Sagrado, para sepultura de sus cuerpos." Herrera, Hist. general, dec. 3, lib. 10, cap. 3.

them of their deplorable condition, and complaining of the cold-blooded manner in which they were to be sacrificed to the obstinate cupidity of their leaders. But the latter were wary enough to anticipate this movement, and Almagro defeated it by seizing all the letters in the vessels and thus cutting off at once the means of communication with their friends at home. Yet this act of unscrupulous violence, like most other similar acts, fell short of its purpose; for a soldier named Sarabia had the ingenuity to evade it by introducing a letter into a ball of cotton, which was to be taken to Panamá as a specimen of the products of the country and presented to the governor's lady.[28]

The letter, which was signed by several of the disaffected soldiery besides the writer, painted in gloomy colors the miseries of their condition, accused the two commanders of being the authors of this, and called on the authorities at Panamá to interfere by sending a vessel to take them from the desolate spot while some of them might still be found surviving the horrors of their confinement. The epistle concluded with a stanza, in which the two leaders were stigmatized as partners in a slaughter-house,—one being employed to drive in the cattle for the other to butcher. The verses, which had a currency in their day among the colonists to which they were certainly not

---

[28] " Metieron en un ovillo de algodon una carta firmada de muchos en que sumariamente daban cuenta de las hambres, muertes y desnudez que padecian, y que era cosa de risa todo, pues las riquezas se habian convertido en flechas, y no havia otra cosa " Montesinos, Annales, MS, año 1527.

entitled by their poetical merits, may be thus rendered into corresponding doggerel:

> "Look out, Señor Governor,
> For the drover while he's near;
> Since he goes home to get the sheep
> For the butcher, who stays here." [29] *

[29] Xerez, Conq. del Peru, ap. Barcia, tom. iii p. 181 —Naharro, Relacion sumaria, MS —Balboa, Hist. du Pérou, chap. 15.—" Al fin de la peticion que hacian en la carta al Governador puso Juan de Sarabia, natural de Trujillo, esta cuarteta:

> "Pues Señor Gobernador,
> Mírelo bien por entero
> que allá va el recogedor,
> y acá queda el carnicero."

Montesinos, Annales, MS., año 1527.

* [Helps translates these lines as follows:

> "My good Lord Governor,
> Have pity on our woes,
> For here remains the butcher,
> To Panamá the salesman goes."—M]

CHAPTER IV

INDIGNATION OF THE GOVERNOR — STERN RESOLU-
TION OF PIZARRO — PROSECUTION OF THE VOYAGE
— BRILLIANT ASPECT OF TUMBEZ — DISCOVERIES
ALONG THE COAST — RETURN TO PANAMÁ —
PIZARRO EMBARKS FOR SPAIN

1527–1528

NOT long after Almagro's departure, Pizarro sent off the remaining vessel, under the pretext of its being put in repair at Panamá. It probably relieved him of a part of his followers, whose mutinous spirit made them an obstacle rather than a help in his forlorn condition, and with whom he was the more willing to part from the difficulty of finding subsistence on the barren spot which he now occupied.

Great was the dismay occasioned by the return of Almagro and his followers in the little community of Panamá; for the letter surreptitiously conveyed in the ball of cotton fell into the hands for which it was intended, and the contents soon got abroad, with the usual quantity of exaggeration. The haggard and dejected mien of the adventurers, of itself, told a tale sufficiently disheartening, and it was soon generally believed that the few ill-fated survivors of the expedition were detained against their will by Pizarro, to end their

days with their disappointed leader on his desolate
island.

Pedro de los Rios, the governor, was so much
incensed at the result of the expedition, and the
waste of life it had occasioned to the colony, that
he turned a deaf ear to all the applications of
Luque and Almagro for further countenance in
the affair; he derided their sanguine anticipations
of the future, and finally resolved to send an
officer to the isle of Gallo, with orders to bring
back every Spaniard whom he should find still
living in that dreary abode. Two vessels were immediately despatched for the purpose, and placed
under charge of a cavalier named Tafur, a native
of Cordova.

Meanwhile, Pizarro and his followers were experiencing all the miseries which might have been
expected from the character of the barren spot
on which they were imprisoned. They were, indeed, relieved from all apprehensions of the natives, since these had quitted the island on its occupation by the white men; but they had to endure
the pains of hunger even in a greater degree than
they had formerly experienced in the wild woods
of the neighboring continent. Their principal
food was crabs and such shell-fish as they could
scantily pick up along the shores. Incessant
storms of thunder and lightning, for it was the
rainy season, swept over the devoted island and
drenched them with a perpetual flood. Thus, half
naked, and pining with famine, there were few in
that little company who did not feel the spirit of
enterprise quenched within them, or who looked

for any happier termination of their difficulties than that afforded by a return to Panamá. The appearance of Tafur, therefore, with his two vessels, well stored with provisions, was greeted with all the rapture that the crew of a sinking wreck might feel on the arrival of some unexpected succor; and the only thought, after satisfying the immediate cravings of hunger, was to embark and leave the detested isle forever.

But by the same vessel letters came to Pizarro from his two confederates, Luque and Almagro, beseeching him not to despair in his present extremity, but to hold fast to his original purpose. To return under the present circumstances would be to seal the fate of the expedition; and they solemnly engaged, if he would remain firm at his post, to furnish him in a short time with the necessary means for going forward.[1]

A ray of hope was enough for the courageous spirit of Pizarro. It does not appear that he himself had entertained, at any time, thoughts of returning. If he had, these words of encouragement entirely banished them from his bosom, and he prepared to stand the fortune of the cast on which he had so desperately ventured. He knew, however, that solicitations or remonstrances would avail little with the companions of his enterprise; and he probably did not care to win over the more timid spirits who, by perpetually looking back,

---

[1] Xerez, Conq. del Peru, ap. Barcia. tom iii p 182.—Zarate, Conq. del Peru, lib. 1, cap. 2.—Montesinos, Annales, MS., año 1527.—Herrera, Hist. general, dec. 3, lib. 10, cap. 3.—Naharro, Relacion sumaria, MS.

would only be a clog on his future movements. He announced his own purpose, however, in a laconic but decided manner, characteristic of a man more accustomed to act than to talk, and well calculated to make an impression on his rough followers.

Drawing his sword, he traced a line with it on the sand from east to west. Then, turning towards the south, "Friends and comrades!" he said, "on that side are toil, hunger, nakedness, the drenching storm, desertion, and death; on this side, ease and pleasure. There lies Peru with its riches; here, Panamá and its poverty. Choose, each man, what best becomes a brave Castilian. For my part, I go to the south." So saying, he stepped across the line.[2] He was followed by the brave pilot Ruiz; next by Pedro de Candia, a cavalier, born, as his name imports, in one of the isles of Greece. Eleven others successively crossed the line, thus intimating their willingness to abide the fortunes of their leader, for good or for evil.[3]

[2] "Obedeciola Pizarro y antes que se egecutase sacó un Puñal, y con notable animo hizo con la punta una raya de Oriente á Poniente; y señalando al medio dia, que era la parte de su noticia, y derrotero dijo; Camaradas y amigos, esta parte es la de la muerte, de los trabajos, de las hambres, de la desnudez, de los aguaceros, y desamparos; la otra la del gusto: Por aquí se ba á Panama á ser pobres, por allá al Peru á ser ricos. Escoja el que fuere buen Castellano lo que mas bien le estubiere. Diciendo esto pasó la raya: siguieronle Barthome Ruiz natural de Moguer, Pedro de Candi Griego, natural de Candia." Montesinos, Annales, MS., año 1527.

[3] The names of these thirteen faithful companions are preserved in the convention made with the crown two years later, where they are suitably commemorated for their loyalty. Their names should not be omitted in a history of the Conquest of Peru. They were "Bartolomé Ruiz, Cristoval de Peralta, Pedro de Candia, Domingo de Soria Luce, Nícolas de Ribera, Francisco de Cuellar, Alonso de

Fame, to quote the enthusiastic language of an ancient chronicler, has commemorated the names

Molina, Pedro Alcon, Garcia de Jerez, Anton de Carrion, Alonso Briceño, Martin de Paz, Joan de la Torre." *

* [Bartolomé Ruiz, of Moguer, the pilot.

Cristoval de Peralta, of Baeza, in Andalusia, one of the founders of Lima, 1535.

Pedro de Candia, a Greek, in charge of the artillery, killed, because of suspected treachery, by the younger Almagro, at Chupás.

Domingo de Soria Luce, a Basque, probably of Guipuzcoa.

Nícolas de Ribera, the treasurer, an Andalusian from Olvera, one of the founders of Lima, 1535. Died on his estates at Cuzco after the civil wars.

Francisco de Cuellar. Nothing is known of him.

Alonso de Molina. Born at Ubeda; was landed at Tumbez to await Pizarro's return, but died before his chief came back.

Pedro Alcon. Fell in love with a Peruvian woman and refused to return to the ship. Because he drew his sword against his companions, Ruiz knocked him down with an oar He was then placed in irons on the lower deck. Nothing more is known of him.

Garcia de Jerez. Helps quotes Garcia de *Jaren* (Documentos Ineditos, tom. 26, p. 260), vol III. p. 446.

Anton de Carrion. Nothing more is known of him.

Alonso Briceño, of Benevente. Received the share of a captain of cavalry from Atahualpa's ransom.

Martin de Paz Nothing more is known of him.

Joan de la Torre, of Benevente. Married the daughter of an Indian chief and became very wealthy. He was a man of most ferocious temper He embraced the cause of Gonzalo Pizarro and was hanged by order of Gasca, a man who rarely made a mistake, in 1548.

Of these men, Pedro de Candia, Nícolas de Ribera, and Joan de la Torre left children. Of five others, as stated above, nothing but the names and probable birthplaces are known. Herrera says one of the thirteen was a mulatto This lack of knowledge concerning their antecedent and subsequent history is not at all remarkable when we consider the class of adventurers engaged in the expeditions of discovery and conquest. Garcilasso writes always of thirteen men, and speaks of three whom he knew personally, whose names are not specified in the "convention" These men were Diego of Truxillo, known to Garcilasso in Cuzco; Alonso (or Geronimo) Ribera, who, with his children, lived at Lima; and Francisco Rodriguez de Villa Fuerte, who, according to tradition, was first to cross the line drawn by Pizarro In 1560 he was living at Cuzco, rich and prosperous Zarate speaks of Alonzo of Truxillo, probably the Diego of Garcilasso. Xerez says there were sixteen men. See Kirk's note, vol. ii., p. 8.—M]

of this little band, " who thus, in the face of difficulties unexampled in history, with death rather
than riches for their reward, preferred it all to
abandoning their honor, and stood firm by their
leader as an example of loyalty to future ages." [4]
But the act excited no such admiration in the
mind of Tafur, who looked on it as one of gross
disobedience to the commands of the governor,
and as little better than madness, involving the
certain destruction of the parties engaged in it.
He refused to give any sanction to it himself by
leaving one of his vessels with the adventurers to
prosecute their voyage, and it was with great difficulty that he could be persuaded even to allow
them a part of the stores which he had brought
for their support. This had no influence on their
determination, and the little party, bidding adieu
to their returning comrades, remained unshaken in
their purpose of abiding the fortunes of their
commander.[5]

There is something striking to the imagination
in the spectacle of these few brave spirits thus consecrating themselves to a daring enterprise, which
seemed as far above their strength as any recorded
in the fabulous annals of knight-errantry. A
handful of men, without food, without clothing,

[4] " Estos fueron los trece de la fama. Estos los que cercados de
los mayores trabajos que pudo el Mundo ofrecer á hombres, y los
que estando mas para esperar la muerte que las riquezas que se les
prometian, todo lo pospusieron á la honra, y siguieron á su capitan
y caudillo para egemplo de lealtad en lo futuro." Montesinos, Annales, MS., año 1527.

[5] Zarate, Conq. del Peru, lib. 1, cap. 2.—Montesinos, Annales, MS.,
año 1527.—Naharro, Relacion sumaria, MS.—Herrera, Hist. general, dec. 3, lib. 10, cap. 3.

almost without arms, without knowledge of the
land to which they were bound, without vessel to
transport them, were here left on a lonely rock in
the ocean with the avowed purpose of carrying on
a crusade against a powerful empire, staking their
lives on its success. What is there in the legends
of chivalry that surpasses it? This was the crisis
of Pizarro's fate. There are moments in the lives
of men, which, as they are seized or neglected, decide their future destiny.[6] Had Pizarro faltered
from his strong purpose, and yielded to the occasion, now so temptingly present, for extricating
himself and his broken band from their desperate
position, his name would have been buried with
his fortunes, and the conquest of Peru would have
been left for other and more successful adventurers. But his constancy was equal to the occasion,
and his conduct here proved him competent to the
perilous post he had assumed, and inspired others
with a confidence in him which was the best assurance of success.

In the vessel that bore back Tafur and those
who seceded from the expedition the pilot Ruiz

---

[6] This common sentiment is expressed with uncommon beauty by
the fanciful Boiardo, where he represents Rinaldo as catching Fortune, under the guise of the fickle fairy Morgana, by the forelock.
The Italian reader may not be displeased to refresh his memory
with it:

"Chi cerca in questo mondo aver tesoro,
O diletto, e piacere, honore, e stato,
Ponga la mano a questa chioma d' oro,
Ch' io porto in fronte, e lo farò beato,
Ma quando ha in destro sì fatto lavoro
Non prenda indugio, che 'l tempo passato
Perduto è tutto, e non ritorna mai,
Ed io mi volto, e lui lascio con guai"
  Orlando Innamorato, lib 2, canto 8.

was also permitted to return, in order to co-oper-
ate with Luque and Almagro in their application
for further succor.

Not long after the departure of the ships, it
was decided by Pizarro to abandon his present
quarters, which had little to recommend them, and
which, he reflected, might now be exposed to annoyance from the original inhabitants, should they
take courage and return on learning the diminished number of the white men. The Spaniards,
therefore, by his orders, constructed a rude boat or
raft, on which they succeeded in transporting
themselves to the little island of Gorgona, twenty-
five leagues to the north of their present residence.
It lay about five leagues from the continent, and
was uninhabited. It had some advantages over
the isle of Gallo; for it stood higher above the
sea, and was partially covered with wood, which
afforded shelter to a species of pheasant, and the
hare or rabbit of the country, so that the Spaniards, with their cross-bows, were enabled to procure a tolerable supply of game. Cool streams
that issued from the living rock furnished abundance of water, though the drenching rains that
fell without intermission left them in no danger
of perishing by thirst. From this annoyance they
found some protection in the rude huts which they
constructed; though here, as in their former residence, they suffered from the no less intolerable
annoyance of venomous insects, which multiplied
and swarmed in the exhalations of the rank and
stimulated soil. In this dreary abode Pizarro
omitted no means by which to sustain the drooping

spirits of his men. Morning prayers were duly said, and the evening hymn to the Virgin was regularly chanted; the festivals of the Church were carefully commemorated, and every means taken by their commander to give a kind of religious character to his enterprise, and to inspire his rough followers with a confidence in the protection of Heaven, that might support them in their perilous circumstances.[7]

In these uncomfortable quarters, their chief employment was to keep watch on the melancholy ocean, that they might hail the first signal of the anticipated succor. But many a tedious month passed away, and no sign of it appeared. All around was the same wide waste of waters, except to the eastward, where the frozen crest of the Andes, touched with the ardent sun of the equator, glowed like a ridge of fire along the whole extent of the great continent. Every speck in the distant horizon was carefully noticed, and the drifting timber or masses of sea-weed, heaving to and fro on the bosom of the waters, was converted by their imaginations into the promised vessel; till, sinking under successive disappointments, hope gradually gave way to doubt, and doubt settled into despair.[8]

Meanwhile the vessel of Tafur had reached the

---

[7] "Cada Mañana daban gracias á Dios: á las tardes decian la Salve, i otras Oraciones, por las Horas: sabian las Fiestas, i tenian cuenta con los Viernes, i Domingos." Herrera, Hist. general, dec. 3, lib. 10, cap. 3

[8] "Al cabo de muchos Dias aguardando, estaban tan angustiados, que los salages, que se hacian bien dentro de la Mar, les parecia, que era el Navio." Herrera, Hist. general, dec. 3, lib. 10, cap 4

port of Panamá. The tidings which she brought
of the inflexible obstinacy of Pizarro and his followers filled the governor with indignation. He
could look on it in no other light than as an act
of suicide, and steadily refused to send further
assistance to men who were obstinately bent on
their own destruction. Yet Luque and Almagro
were true to their engagements. They represented
to the governor that, if the conduct of their comrade was rash, it was at least in the service of the
crown and in prosecuting the great work of discovery. Rios had been instructed, on his taking
the government, to aid Pizarro in the enterprise;
and to desert him now would be to throw away
the remaining chance of success, and to incur the
responsibility of his death and that of the brave
men who adhered to him. These remonstrances,
at length, so far operated on the mind of that
functionary that he reluctantly consented that a
vessel should be sent to the island of Gorgona, but
with no more hands than were necessary to work
her, and with positive instructions to Pizarro to
return in six months and report himself at Panamá, whatever might be the future results of his
expedition.

Having thus secured the sanction of the executive, the two associates lost no time in fitting out
a small vessel with stores and a supply of arms
and ammunition, and despatched it to the island.
The unfortunate tenants of this little wilderness,
who had now occupied it for seven months,[9] hardly

[9] "Estubieron con estos trabajos con igualdad de animo siete
meses." Montesinos, Annales, MS., año 1527.

dared to trust their senses when they descried the white sails of the friendly bark coming over the waters. And although, when the vessel anchored off the shore, Pizarro was disappointed to find that it brought no additional recruits for the enterprise, yet he greeted it with joy, as affording the means of solving the great problem of the existence of the rich southern empire, and of thus opening the way for its future conquest. Two of his men were so ill that it was determined to leave them in the care of some of the friendly Indians who had continued with him through the whole of his sojourn, and to call for them on his return. Taking with him the rest of his hardy followers and the natives of Tumbez, he embarked, and, speedily weighing anchor, bade adieu to the "Hell," as it was called by the Spaniards, which had been the scene of so much suffering and such undaunted resolution.[10]

Every heart was now elated with hope, as they found themselves once more on the waters, under the guidance of the good pilot Ruiz, who, obeying the directions of the Indians, proposed to steer for the land of Tumbez, which would bring them at once into the golden empire of the Incas,— the El Dorado of which they had been so long in pursuit. Passing by the dreary isle of Gallo, which they had such good cause to remember, they stood farther out to sea until they made Point Tacumez, near which they had landed on their

[10] Xerez, Conq. del Peru, ap Barcia, tom iii p. 182.—Montesinos, Annales, MS, año 1527 —Naharro, Relacion sumaria, MS —Herrera, Hist. general, dec. 3, lib. 10, cap. 4 —Pedro Pizarro, Descub. y Conq., MS

previous voyage. They did not touch at any part
of the coast, but steadily held on their way, though
considerably impeded by the currents, as well as
by the wind, which blew with little variation from
the south. Fortunately, the wind was light, and,
as the weather was favorable, their voyage, though
slow, was not uncomfortable. In a few days they
came in sight of Point Pasado, the limit of the
pilot's former navigation; and, crossing the line,
the little bark entered upon those unknown seas
which had never been ploughed by European keel
before. The coast, they observed, gradually declined from its former bold and rugged character,
gently sloping towards the shore, and spreading
out into sandy plains, relieved here and there by
patches of uncommon richness and beauty; while
the white cottages of the natives glistening along
the margin of the sea, and the smoke that rose
among the distant hills, intimated the increasing
population of the country.

At length, after the lapse of twenty days from
their departure from the island, the adventurous
vessel rounded the point of St. Helena and glided
smoothly into the waters of the beautiful gulf of
Guayaquil. The country was here studded along
the shore with towns and villages, though the
mighty chain of the Cordilleras, sweeping up
abruptly from the coast, left but a narrow strip
of emerald verdure, through which numerous
rivulets, spreading fertility around them, wound
their way to the sea.

The voyagers were now abreast of some of
the most stupendous heights of this magnificent

range; Chimborazo, with its broad round summit, towering like the dome of the Andes, and Cotopaxi, with its dazzling cone of silvery white, that knows no change except from the action of its own volcanic fires; for this mountain is the most terrible of the American volcanoes, and was in formidable activity at no great distance from the period of our narrative. Well pleased with the signs of civilization that opened on them at every league of their progress, the Spaniards at length came to anchor, off the island of Santa Clara, lying at the entrance of the bay of Tumbez.[11]

The place was uninhabited, but was recognized by the Indians on board as occasionally resorted to by the warlike people of the neighboring island of Puná for purposes of sacrifice and worship. The Spaniards found on the spot a few bits of gold rudely wrought into various shapes, and probably designed as offerings to the Indian deity. Their hearts were cheered, as the natives assured them they would see abundance of the same precious metal in their own city of Tumbez.

The following morning they stood across the bay for this place. As they drew near, they beheld a town of considerable size, with many of the buildings apparently of stone and plaster, situ-

---

[11] According to Garcilasso, two years elapsed between the departure from Gorgona and the arrival at Tumbez. (Com. Real., Parte 2, lib. 1, cap. 11.) Such gross defiance of chronology is rather common even in the narratives of these transactions, where it is as difficult to fix a precise date, amidst the silence, rather than the contradictions, of contemporary statements, as if the events had happened before the deluge.

ated in the bosom of a fruitful meadow, which seemed to have been redeemed from the sterility of the surrounding country by careful and minute irrigation. When at some distance from shore, Pizarro saw standing towards him several large balsas, which were found to be filled with warriors going on an expedition against the island of Puná. Running alongside of the Indian flotilla, he invited some of the chiefs to come on board of his vessel. The Peruvians gazed with wonder on every object which met their eyes, and especially on their own countrymen, whom they had little expected to meet there. The latter informed them in what manner they had fallen into the hands of the strangers, whom they described as a wonderful race of beings, that had come thither for no harm, but solely to be made acquainted with the country and its inhabitants. This account was confirmed by the Spanish commander, who persuaded the Indians to return in their balsas and report what they had learned to their townsmen, requesting them at the same time to provide his vessel with refreshments, as it was his desire to enter into friendly intercourse with the natives.

The people of Tumbez were gathered along the shore, and were gazing with unutterable amazement on the floating castle, which, now having dropped anchor, rode lazily at its moorings in their bay. They eagerly listened to the accounts of their countrymen, and instantly reported the affair to the *curaca* or ruler of the district, who, conceiving that the strangers must be beings of a superior order, prepared at once to comply with

their request. It was not long before several
balsas were seen steering for the vessel, laden with
bananas, plantains, yuca, Indian corn, sweet po-
tatoes, pine-apples, cocoanuts, and other rich
products of the bountiful vale of Tumbez. Game
and fish, also, were added, with a number of
llamas, of which Pizarro had seen the rude drawings belonging to Balboa, but of which till now
he had met with no living specimen. He examined
this curious animal, the Peruvian sheep,—or, as
the Spaniards called it, the " little camel " of the
Indians,—with much interest, greatly admiring
the mixture of wool and hair which supplied the
natives with the materials for their fabrics.

At that time there happened to be at Tumbez an
Inca noble, or *orejon*,—for so, as I have already
noticed, men of his rank were called by the Spaniards, from the huge ornaments of gold attached
to their ears. He expressed great curiosity to see
the wonderful strangers, and had, accordingly,
come out with the balsas for the purpose. It was
easy to perceive from the superior quality of his
dress, as well as from the deference paid to him
by the others, that he was a person of consideration; and Pizarro received him with marked distinction. He showed him the different parts of
the ship, explaining to him the uses of whatever
engaged his attention, and answering his numerous queries, as well as he could, by means of the
Indian interpreters. The Peruvian chief was especially desirous of knowing whence and why Pizarro and his followers had come to these shores.
The Spanish captain replied that he was the vassal

of a great prince, the greatest and most powerful in the world, and that he had come to this country to assert his master's *lawful supremacy* over it. He had further come to rescue the inhabitants from the darkness of unbelief in which they were now wandering. They worshipped an evil spirit, who would sink their souls into everlasting perdition; and he would give them the knowledge of the true and only God, Jesus Christ, since to believe in Him was eternal salvation.[12]

The Indian prince listened with deep attention and apparent wonder, but answered nothing. It may be that neither he nor his interpreters had any very distinct ideas of the doctrines thus abruptly revealed to them. It may be that he did not believe there was any other potentate on earth greater than the Inca; none, at least, who had a better right to rule over his dominions. And it is very possible he was not disposed to admit that the great luminary whom he worshipped was inferior to the God of the Spaniards. But whatever may have passed in the untutored mind of the barbarian, he did not give vent to it, but maintained a discreet silence, without any attempt to controvert or to convince his Christian antagonist.

He remained on board the vessel till the hour of dinner, of which he partook with the Spaniards, expressing his satisfaction at the strange dishes, and especially pleased with the wine, which he

[12] The text abridges somewhat the discourse of the military polemic; which is reported at length by Herrera, Hist. general, dec. 3, lib. 10, cap. 4.—See also Montesinos, Annales, MS., año 1527.—Conq. i Pob. del Piru, MS.—Naharro, Relacion sumaria, MS.—Relacion del primer Descub., MS.

pronounced far superior to the fermented liquors of his own country. On taking leave, he courteously pressed the Spaniards to visit Tumbez, and Pizarro dismissed him with the present among other things, of an iron hatchet, which had greatly excited his admiration; for the use of iron, as we have seen, was as little known to the Peruvians as to the Mexicans.

On the day following, the Spanish captain sent one of his own men, named Alonso de Molina, on shore, accompanied by a negro who had come in the vessel from Panamá, together with a present for the curaca of some swine and poultry, neither of which were indigenous to the New World. Towards evening his emissary returned with a fresh supply of fruits and vegetables, that the friendly people sent to the vessel. Molina had a wondrous tale to tell. On landing, he was surrounded by the natives, who expressed the greatest astonishment at his dress, his fair complexion, and his long beard. The women, especially, manifested great curiosity in respect to him, and Molina seemed to be entirely won by their charms and captivating manners. He probably intimated his satisfaction by his demeanor, since they urged him to stay among them, promising in that case to provide him with a beautiful wife.

Their surprise was equally great at the complexion of his sable companion. They could not believe it was natural, and tried to rub off the imaginary dye with their hands. As the African bore all this with characteristic good humor, displaying at the same time his rows of ivory teeth, they were prodigiously delighted.[13] The animals were no less above their comprehension; and, when the cock crew, the simple people clapped their hands and inquired what he was saying.[14] Their intellects were so bewildered by sights so novel that they seemed incapable of distinguishing between man and brute.

Molina was then escorted to the residence of the curaca, whom he found living in much state, with porters stationed at his doors, and with a quantity of gold and silver vessels, from which he was served. He was then taken to different parts of the Indian city, and saw a fortress built of rough stone, and, though low, spreading over a large extent of ground.[15] Near this was a temple; and the Spaniard's description of its decorations, blazing with gold and silver, seemed so extravagant that Pizarro, distrusting his whole account, resolved to send a more discreet and trustworthy emissary on the following day.[16]

The person selected was Pedro de Candia, the Greek cavalier mentioned as one of the first who intimated his intention to share the fortunes of his commander. He was sent on shore, dressed

[13] " No se cansaban de mirarle, hacianle labar, para vèr si se le quitaba la Tinta negra, i èl lo hacia de buena gana, riendose, i mostrando sus Dientes blancos." Herrera, Hist. general, dec. 3, lib. 10, cap. 5.

[14] Ibid., ubi supra.

[15] " Cerca del solia estar una fortaleza muy fuerte y de linda obra, hecha por los Yngas reyes del Cuzco y señores de todo el Peru. . . . Ya esta el edificio desta fortaleza muy gastado y deshecho: mas no para que dexe de dar muestra de lo mucho que fue." Cieza de Leon, Cronica, cap. 4.

[16] Conq. i Pob. del Piru, MS.—Herrera, Hist. general, loc. cit.— Zarate, Conq. del Peru, lib. 1, cap. 2.

in complete mail, as became a good knight, with his sword by his side, and his arquebuse on his shoulder. The Indians were even more dazzled by his appearance than by Molina's, as the sun fell brightly on his polished armor and glanced from his military weapons. They had heard much of the formidable arquebuse from their townsmen who had come in the vessel, and they besought Candia " to let it speak to them." He accordingly set up a wooden board as a target, and, taking deliberate aim, fired off the musket. The flash of the powder and the startling report of the piece, as the board, struck by the ball, was shivered into splinters, filled the natives with dismay. Some fell on the ground, covering their faces with their hands, and others approached the cavalier with feelings of awe, which were gradually dispelled by the assurance they received from the smiling expression of his countenance.[17]

They then showed him the same hospitable at-

[17] It is moreover stated that the Indians, desirous to prove still further the superhuman nature of the Spanish cavalier, let loose on him a tiger—a jaguar probably—which was caged in the royal fortress. But Don Pedro was a good Catholic, and he gently laid the cross which he wore round his neck on the animal's back, who, instantly forgetting his ferocious nature, crouched at the cavalier's feet and began to play round him in innocent gambols The Indians, now more amazed than ever, nothing doubted of the sanctity of their guest, and bore him in triumph on their shoulders to the temple This credible anecdote is repeated, without the least qualification or distrust, by several contemporary writers (See Naharro, Relacion sumaria, MS.—Herrera, Hist general, dec 3, lib. 10, cap 5 —Cieza de Leon, Cronica, cap. 54.—Garcilasso, Com. Real., Parte 2, lib. 1, cap. 12.) This last author may have had his version from Candia's own son, with whom he tells us he was brought up at school. It will no doubt find as easy admission with those of the present day who conceive that the age of miracles has not yet passed.

tentions which they had paid to Molina; and his
description of the marvels of the place, on his
return, fell nothing short of his predecessor's.
The fortress, which was surrounded by a triple
row of wall, was strongly garrisoned. The temple he described as literally tapestried with plates
of gold and silver. Adjoining this structure was
a sort of convent appropriated to the Inca's destined brides, who manifested great curiosity to
see him. Whether this was gratified is not clear;
but Candia described the gardens of the convent,
which he entered, as glowing with imitations of
fruits and vegetables all in pure gold and silver.[18]
He had seen a number of artisans at work, whose
sole business seemed to be to furnish these gorgeous decorations for the religious houses.

The reports of the cavalier may have been somewhat overcolored.[19] It was natural that men
coming from the dreary wilderness in which they
had been buried the last six months should have
been vividly impressed by the tokens of civiliza-

[18] " Que habia visto un jardin donde las yerbas eran de oro imitando
en un todo á las naturales, arboles con frutas de lo mismo, y otras
muchas cosas á este modo, con que aficionó grandemente á sus compañeros á esta conquista." Montesinos, Annales, año 1527.

[19] The worthy knight's account does not seem to have found favor
with the old Conqueror, so often cited in these pages, who says that,
when they afterwards visited Tumbez, the Spaniards found Candia's
relation a lie from beginning to end, except, indeed, in respect to the
temple; though the veteran acknowledges that what was deficient in
Tumbez was more than made up by the magnificence of other places
in the empire not then visited. " Lo cual fué mentira; porque despues que todos los Españoles entramos en ella, se vió por vista de
ojos haber mentido en todo, salvo en lo del templo, que este era cosa
de ver, aunque mucho mas de lo que aquel encareció, lo que faltó en
esta ciudad, se halló despues en otras que muchas leguas mas adelante
se descubrieron." Relacion del primer Descub., MS.

tion which met them on the Peruvian coast. But
Tumbez was a favorite city of the Peruvian
princes. It was the most important place on the
northern borders of the empire, contiguous to the
recent acquisition of Quito. The great Tupac
Yupanqui had established a strong fortress there,
and peopled it with a colony of *mitimaes*. The
temple, and the house occupied by the Virgins of
the Sun, had been erected by Huayna Capac, and
were liberally endowed by that Inca, after the
sumptuous fashion of the religious establishments
of Peru. The town was well supplied with water
by numerous aqueducts; and the fruitful valley
in which it was embosomed, and the ocean which
bathed its shores, supplied ample means of subsistence to a considerable population. But the
cupidity of the Spaniards, after the Conquest, was
not slow in despoiling the place of its glories; and
the site of its proud towers and temples, in less
than half a century after that fatal period, was
to be traced only by the huge mass of ruins that
encumbered the ground.[20]

The Spaniards were nearly mad with joy, says
an old writer, at receiving these brilliant tidings
of the Peruvian city. All their fond dreams were
now to be realized, and they had at length reached
the realm which had so long flitted in visionary
splendor before them. Pizarro expressed his gratitude to Heaven for having crowned his labors with
so glorious a result; but he bitterly lamented the

[20] Cieza de Leon, who crossed this part of the country in 1548, mentions the wanton manner in which the hand of the Conqueror had
fallen on the Indian edifices, which lay in ruins even at that early
period. Cronica, cap. 67.

hard fate which, by depriving him of his followers, denied him, at such a moment, the means of availing himself of his success. Yet he had no cause for lamentation; and the devout Catholic saw in this very circumstance a providential interposition which prevented the attempt at conquest while such attempts would have been premature. Peru was not yet torn asunder by the dissensions of rival candidates for the throne; and, united and strong under the sceptre of a warlike monarch, she might well have bid defiance to all the forces that Pizarro could muster. " It was manifestly the work of Heaven," exclaims a devout son of the Church, " that the natives of the country should have received him in so kind and loving a spirit as best fitted to facilitate the conquest; for it was the Lord's hand which led him and his followers to this remote region for the extension of the holy faith, and for the salvation of souls." [21]

Having now collected all the information essential to his object, Pizarro, after taking leave of the natives of Tumbez and promising a speedy return, weighed anchor, and again turned his prow towards the south. Still keeping as near as possible to the coast, that no place of importance might escape his observation, he passed Cape Blanco, and, after sailing about a degree and a half, made the port of Payta. The inhabitants, who had notice of his approach, came out in their balsas to get sight of the wonderful strangers,

[21] " I si le recibiesen con amor, hiciese su Mrd. lo que mas conveniente le pareciese al efecto de su conquista: porque tenia entendido, que el haverlos traido Dios erá para que su santa fé se dilatase i aquellas almas se salvasen." Naharro, Relacion sumaria, MS.

bringing with them stores of fruits, fish, and vegetables, with the same hospitable spirit shown by their countrymen at Tumbez.

After staying here a short time, and interchanging presents of trifling value with the natives, Pizarro continued his cruise; and, sailing by the sandy plains of Sechura for an extent of near a hundred miles, he doubled the Punta de Aguja, and swept down the coast as it fell off towards the east, still carried forward by light and somewhat variable breezes. The weather now became unfavorable, and the voyagers encountered a succession of heavy gales, which drove them some distance out to sea and tossed them about for many days. But they did not lose sight of the mighty ranges of the Andes, which, as they proceeded towards the south, were still seen, at nearly the same distance from the shore, rolling onwards, peak after peak, with their stupendous surges of ice, like some vast ocean that had been suddenly arrested and frozen up in the midst of its wild and tumultuous career. With this landmark always in view, the navigator had little need of star or compass to guide his bark on her course.

As soon as the tempest had subsided, Pizarro stood in again for the continent, touching at the principal points as he coasted along. Everywhere he was received with the same spirit of generous hospitality, the natives coming out in their balsas to welcome him, laden with their little cargoes of fruits and vegetables, of all the luscious varieties that grow in the *tierra caliente*. All were eager to have a glimpse of the strangers, the " Children of the Sun," as the Spaniards began already to be called, from their fair complexions, brilliant armor, and the thunderbolts which they bore in their hands.[22]   The most favorable reports, too, had preceded them, of the urbanity and gentleness of their manners, thus unlocking the hearts of the simple natives and disposing them to confidence and kindness.   The iron-hearted soldier had not yet disclosed the darker side of his character. He was too weak to do so.   The hour of conquest had not yet come.

In every place Pizarro received the same accounts of a powerful monarch who ruled over the land, and held his court on the mountain plains of the interior, where his capital was depicted as blazing with gold and silver and displaying all the profusion of an Oriental satrap.   The Spaniards, except at Tumbez, seem to have met with little of the precious metals among the natives on the coast.   More than one writer asserts that they did not covet them, or at least, by Pizarro's orders, affected not to do so.   He would not have them betray their appetite for gold, and actually refused gifts when they were proffered![23]   It is more probable that they saw little display of wealth, except in the embellishments of the temples and other sacred buildings, which they did

---

[22] " Que resplandecian como el Sol. Llamabanles hijos del Sol por esto." Montesinos, Annales, MS., año 1528.

[23] Pizarro wished the natives to understand, says Father Naharro, that their good alone, and not the love of gold, had led him to their distant land! " Sin haver querido recibir el oro, plata i perlas que les ofrecieron, á fin de que conociesen no era codicia, sino deseo de su bien el que les habia traido de tan lejas tierras á las suyas." Relacion sumaria, MS.

not dare to violate. The precious metals, reserved
for the uses of religion and for persons of high
degree, were not likely to abound in the remote
towns and hamlets on the coast.

Yet the Spaniards met with sufficient evidence
of general civilization and power to convince them
that there was much foundation for the reports
of the natives. Repeatedly they saw structures of
stone and plaster, occasionally showing architectural skill in the execution, if not elegance of design. Wherever they cast anchor, they beheld
green patches of cultivated country redeemed
from the sterility of nature and blooming with
the variegated vegetation of the tropics; while
a refined system of irrigation, by means of aqueducts and canals, seemed to be spread like a net-
work over the surface of the country, making
even the desert to blossom as the rose. At many
places where they landed they saw the great road
of the Incas which traversed the sea-coast, often,
indeed, lost in the volatile sands, where no road
could be maintained, but rising into a broad and
substantial causeway as it emerged on a firmer
soil. Such a provision for internal communication
was in itself no slight monument of power and
civilization.

Still beating to the south, Pizarro passed the
site of the future flourishing city of Truxillo,
founded by himself some years later, and pressed
on till he rode off the port of Santa. It stood on
the banks of a broad and beautiful stream; but
the surrounding country was so exceedingly arid
that it was frequently selected as a burial-place

by the Peruvians, who found the soil most favorable for the preservation of their mummies. So numerous, indeed, were the Indian *huacas* that the place might rather be called the abode of the dead than of the living.[24]

Having reached this point, about the ninth degree of southern latitude, Pizarro's followers besought him not to prosecute the voyage farther. Enough and more than enough had been done, they said, to prove the existence and actual position of the great Indian empire of which they had so long been in search. Yet, with their slender force, they had no power to profit by the discovery. All that remained, therefore, was to return and report the success of their enterprise to the governor of Panamá. Pizarro acquiesced in the reasonableness of this demand. He had now penetrated nine degrees farther than any former navigator in these southern seas, and, instead of the blight which, up to this hour, had seemed to hang over his fortunes, he could now return in triumph to his countrymen. Without hesitation, therefore, he prepared to retrace his course, and stood again towards the north.

On his way he touched at several places where he had before landed. At one of these, called by the Spaniards Santa Cruz, he had been invited on

---

[24] "Lo que mas me admiro, quando passe por este valle, fue ver la muchedumbre que tienen de sepolturas: y que por todas las sierras y secadales en los altos del valle ay numero grande de apartados, hechos a su usança, todo cubiertas de huessos de muertos. De manera que lo que ay en este valle mas que ver, es las sepolturas de los muertos, y los campos que labraron siendo vivos." Cieza de Leon, Cronica, cap. 70.

shore by an Indian woman of rank, and had
promised to visit her on his return. No sooner
did his vessel cast anchor off the village where
she lived, than she came on board, followed by a
numerous train of attendants. Pizarro received
her with every mark of respect, and on her departure presented her with some trinkets which had a
real value in the eyes of an Indian princess. She
urged the Spanish commander and his companions to return the visit, engaging to send a number
of hostages on board as security for their good
treatment. Pizarro assured her that the frank
confidence she had shown towards them proved
that this was unnecessary. Yet no sooner did he
put off in his boat, the following day, to go on
shore, than several of the principal persons in the
place came alongside of the ship to be received as
hostages during the absence of the Spaniards,—a
singular proof of consideration for the sensitive
apprehensions of her guests.

Pizarro found that preparations had been made
for his reception in a style of simple hospitality
that evinced some degree of taste. Arbors were
formed of luxuriant and wide-spreading branches,
interwoven with fragrant flowers and shrubs that
diffused a delicious perfume through the air. A
banquet was provided, teeming with viands prepared in the style of the Peruvian cookery, and
with fruits and vegetables of tempting hue and
luscious to the taste, though their names and nature were unknown to the Spaniards. After the
collation was ended, the guests were entertained
with music and dancing by a troop of young men

and maidens simply attired, who exhibited in their
favorite national amusement all the agility and
grace which the supple limbs of the Peruvian
Indians so well qualified them to display. Before
his departure, Pizarro stated to his kind hostess the
motives of his visit to the country, in the same
manner as he had done on other occasions, and he
concluded by unfurling the royal banner of Castile, which he had brought on shore, requesting her
and her attendants to raise it in token of their
allegiance to his sovereign. This they did with
great good humor, laughing all the while, says the
chronicler, and making it clear that they had a
very imperfect conception of the serious nature
of the ceremony. Pizarro was contented with this
outward display of loyalty, and returned to his
vessel well satisfied with the entertainment he had
received, and meditating, it may be, on the best
mode of repaying it, hereafter, by the subjugation
and conversion of the country.

The Spanish commander did not omit to touch
also at Tumbez on his homeward voyage. Here
some of his followers, won by the comfortable
aspect of the place and the manners of the people,
intimated a wish to remain, conceiving, no doubt,
that it would be better to live where they would
be persons of consequence than to return to an
obscure condition in the community of Panamá.
One of these men was Alonso de Molina, the same
who had first gone on shore at this place and been
captivated by the charms of the Indian beauties.
Pizarro complied with their wishes, thinking it
would not be amiss to find, on his return, some of

his own followers who would be instructed in the language and usages of the natives. He was also allowed to carry back in his vessel two or three Peruvians, for the similar purpose of instructing them in the Castilian. One of them, a youth named by the Spaniards Felipillo, plays a part of some importance in the history of subsequent events.

On leaving Tumbez, the adventurers steered directly for Panamá, touching only, on their way, at the ill-fated island of Gorgona, to take on board their two companions who were left there too ill to proceed with them. One had died; and, receiving the other, Pizarro and his gallant little band continued their voyage, and, after an absence of at least eighteen months, found themselves once more safely riding at anchor in the harbor of Panamá.[25]

The sensation caused by their arrival was great, as might have been expected. For there were few, even among the most sanguine of their friends, who did not imagine that they had long since paid for their temerity, and fallen victims to the climate or the natives, or miserably perished in a watery grave. Their joy was proportionably great, therefore, as they saw the wanderers now returned, not only in health and safety, but with certain tidings of the fair countries which had so long eluded their grasp. It was a moment of

[25] Conq. i Pob. del Piru, MS.—Montesinos, Annales, MS , año 1528.—Naharro, Relacion sumaria, MS.—Pedro Pizarro, Descub. y Conq., MS —Herrera, Hist. general, dec. 4, lib. 2, cap. 6, 7.—Relacion del primer Descub , MS.

proud satisfaction to the three associates, who, in
spite of obloquy, derision, and every impediment
which the distrust of friends or the coldness of
government could throw in their way, had persevered in their great enterprise until they had established the truth of what had been so generally
denounced as a chimera. It is the misfortune of
those daring spirits who conceive an idea too vast
for their own generation to comprehend, or, at
least, to attempt to carry out, that they pass for
visionary dreamers. Such had been the fate of
Luque and his associates. The existence of a rich
Indian empire at the south, which in their minds,
dwelling long on the same idea and alive to all the
arguments in its favor, had risen to the certainty
of conviction, had been derided by the rest of their
countrymen as a mere *mirage* of the fancy, which,
on nearer approach, would melt into air; while
the projectors who staked their fortunes on the
adventure were denounced as madmen. But their
hour of triumph, their slow and hard-earned triumph, had now arrived.

Yet the governor, Pedro de los Rios, did not
seem, even at this moment, to be possessed with
a conviction of the magnitude of the discovery,
—or perhaps he was discouraged by its very
magnitude. When the associates now with more
confidence applied to him for patronage in an
undertaking too vast for their individual resources, he coldly replied, " He had no desire to
build up other states at the expense of his own;
nor would he be led to throw away more lives
than had already been sacrificed by the cheap

display of gold and silver toys and a few Indian
sheep!"[26]

Sorely disheartened by this repulse from the
only quarter whence effectual aid could be expected, the confederates, without funds, and with
credit nearly exhausted by their past efforts, were
perplexed in the extreme. Yet to stop now,—
what was it but to abandon the rich mine which
their own industry and perseverance had laid open,
for others to work at pleasure? In this extremity
the fruitful mind of Luque suggested the only
expedient by which they could hope for success.
This was to apply to the crown itself. No one was
so much interested in the result of the expedition.
It was for the government, indeed, that discoveries
were to be made, that the country was to be conquered. The government alone was competent to
provide the requisite means, and was likely to take
a much broader and more liberal view of the matter
than a petty colonial officer.

But who was there qualified to take charge of
this delicate mission? Luque was chained by his
professional duties to Panamá; and his associates,
unlettered soldiers, were much better fitted for
the business of the camp than of the court. Almagro, blunt, though somewhat swelling and os-
tentatious in his address, with a diminutive stature
and a countenance naturally plain, now much disfigured by the loss of an eye, was not so well

---

[26] "No entendia de despoblar su Governacion, para que se fuesen
à poblar nuevas Tierras, muriendo en tal demanda mas Gente de la
que havia muerto, cebando à los Hombres con la muestra de las
Ovejas, Oro, i Plata, que havian traido." Herrera, Hist. general, dec.
4, lib. 3, cap. 1.

qualified for the mission as his companion in arms,
who, possessing a good person and altogether a
commanding presence, was plausible, and, with all
his defects of education, could, where deeply interested, be even eloquent in discourse. The ecclesiastic, however, suggested that the negotiation
should be committed to the Licentiate Corral, a
respectable functionary, then about to return on
some public business to the mother-country. But
to this Almagro strongly objected. No one, he
said, could conduct the affair so well as the party
interested in it. He had a high opinion of Pizarro's prudence, his discernment of character, and
his cool, deliberate policy.[27] He knew enough of
his comrade to have confidence that his presence of
mind would not desert him even in the new, and
therefore embarrassing, circumstances in which he
would be placed at court. No one, he said, could
tell the story of their adventures with such effect
as the man who had been the chief actor in them.
No one could so well paint the unparalleled sufferings and sacrifices which they had encountered;
no other could tell so forcibly what had been done,
what yet remained to do, and what assistance
would be necessary to carry it into execution.
He concluded, with characteristic frankness, by
strongly urging his confederate to undertake the
mission.

Pizarro felt the force of Almagro's reasoning,
and, though with undisguised reluctance, acqui-

---

[27] " É por pura importunacion de Almagro cupole á Pizarro, porque siempre Almagro le tubo respeto, é deseó honrarle." Oviedo,
Hist. de las Indias, MS., Parte 3, lib. 8, cap. 1.

esced in a measure which was less to his taste than an expedition to the wilderness. But Luque came into the arrangement with more difficulty. " God grant, my children," exclaimed the ecclesiastic, " that one of you may not defraud the other of his blessing!"[28] Pizarro engaged to consult the interests of his associates equally with his own. But Luque, it is clear, did not trust Pizarro.

There was some difficulty in raising the funds necessary for putting the envoy in condition to make a suitable appearance at court; so low had the credit of the confederates fallen, and so little confidence was yet placed in the result of their splendid discoveries. Fifteen hundred ducats were at length raised; and Pizarro, in the spring of 1528, bade adieu to Panamá, accompanied by Pedro de Candia.[29] He took with him, also, some of the natives, as well as two or three llamas, various nice fabrics of cloth, with many ornaments and vases of gold and silver, as specimens of the civilization of the country, and vouchers for his wonderful story.

Of all the writers on ancient Peruvian history, no one has acquired so wide celebrity, or been so largely referred to by later compilers, as the Inca Garcilasso de la Vega. He was born in Cuzco, in 1540, and was a *mestizo*, that is, of mixed descent, his father being European and his mother Indian. His father, Garcilasso de la Vega, was one of that illustrious family whose achievements, both in arms and letters, shed such lustre over the proudest period of the Castilian annals. He came to Peru, in the suite of Pedro de Alvarado, soon

[28] " Plegue à Dios, Hijos, que no os hurteis la bendicion el uno al otro que yo todavia holgaria, que à lo menos fuerades entrambos." Herrera, Hist. general, dec. 4, lib 3, cap 1.

[29] " Juntaronle mil y quinientos pesos de oro, que dió de buena voluntad Dⁿ Fernando de Luque." Montesinos, Annales, MS, año 1528.

after the country had been gained by Pizarro Garcilasso attached himself to the fortunes of this chief, and, after his death, to those of his brother Gonzalo,—remaining constant to the latter, through his rebellion, up to the hour of his rout at Xaquixaguana, when Garcilasso took the same course with most of his faction, and passed over to the enemy. But this demonstration of loyalty, though it saved his life, was too late to redeem his credit with the victorious party; and the obloquy which he incurred by his share in the rebellion threw a cloud over his subsequent fortunes, and even over those of his son, as it appears, in after-years.

The historian's mother was of the Peruvian blood royal. She was niece of Huayna Capac, and granddaughter of the renowned Tupac Inca Yupanqui. Garcilasso, while he betrays obvious satisfaction that the blood of the civilized European flows in his veins, shows himself not a little proud of his descent from the royal dynasty of Peru; and this he intimated by combining with his patronymic the distinguishing title of the Peruvian princes,—subscribing himself always Garcilasso Inca de la Vega.

His early years were passed in his native land, where he was reared in the Roman Catholic faith, and received the benefit of as good an education as could be obtained amidst the incessant din of arms and civil commotion. In 1560, when twenty years of age, he left America, and from that time took up his residence in Spain. Here he entered the military service, and held a captain's commission in the war against the Moriscos, and, afterwards, under Don John of Austria. Though he acquitted himself honorably in his adventurous career, he does not seem to have been satisfied with the manner in which his services were requited by the government. The old reproach of the father's disloyalty still clung to the son, and Garcilasso assures us that this circumstance defeated all his efforts to recover the large inheritance of landed property belonging to his mother, which had escheated to the crown. "Such were the prejudices against me," says he, "that I could not urge my ancient claims or expectations; and I left the army so poor and so much in debt that I did not care to show myself again at court, but was obliged to withdraw into an obscure solitude, where I lead a tranquil life for the brief space that remains to me, no longer deluded by the world or its vanities."

The scene of this obscure retreat was not, however, as the reader might imagine from this tone of philosophic resignation in the depths of some rural wilderness, but in Cordova, once the gay capital of Moslem science, and still the busy haunt of men. Here our philosopher occupied himself with literary labors, the more sweet and soothing to his wounded spirit that they tended to illustrate the faded glories of his native land and exhibit them in their primitive splendor to the eyes of his adopted countrymen. "And I have no reason to regret," he says in his Preface to his account of Florida, "that Fortune has not smiled on me, since this circumstance has opened a literary career which, I trust, will secure to me a wider and more enduring fame than could flow from any worldly prosperity."

In 1609 he gave to the world the First Part of his great work, the *Commentarios Reales*, devoted to the history of the country under the Incas; and in 1616, a few months before his death, he finished the Second Part, embracing the story of the Conquest, which was published at Cordova the following year. The chronicler, who thus closed his labors with his life, died at the ripe old age of seventy-six. He left a considerable sum for the purchase of masses for his soul, showing that the complaints of his poverty are not to be taken literally His remains were interred in the cathedral church of Cordova, in a chapel which bears the name of Garcilasso; and an inscription was placed on his monument, intimating the high respect in which the historian was held both for his moral worth and his literary attainments.

The First Part of the *Commentarios Reales* is occupied, as already noticed, with the ancient history of the country, presenting a complete picture of its civilization under the Incas,—far more complete than has been given by any other writer. Garcilasso's mother was but ten years old at the time of her cousin Atahuallpa's accession, or rather usurpation, as it is called by the party of Cuzco. She had the good fortune to escape the massacre which, according to the chronicler, befell most of her kindred, and, with her brother, continued to reside in their ancient capital after the Conquest. Their conversations naturally turned to the good old times of the Inca rule, which, colored by their fond regrets, may be presumed to have lost nothing as seen through the magnifying medium of the past. The young Garcilasso listened greedily to the stories which recounted the magnificence and prowess of his royal ancestors, and, though he made no use of them at the time, they sank deep into his memory, to be treasured up for a future occasion. When he prepared, after the lapse of many years, in his retirement at Cordova, to compose the history of his country, he wrote to his old companions and schoolfellows of the Inca family, to obtain fuller information than he could get in Spain on various matters of historical interest He had witnessed in his youth the ancient ceremonies and usages of his countrymen, understood the science of their quipus, and mastered many of their primitive traditions. With the assistance he now obtained from his Peruvian kindred, he acquired a familiarity with the history of the great Inca race, and of their national institutions, to an extent that no person could have possessed unless educated in the midst of them, speaking the same language, and with the same Indian blood flowing in his veins Garcilasso, in short, was the representative of the conquered race; and we might expect to find the light and shadows of the picture disposed under his pencil so as to produce an effect very different from that which they had hitherto exhibited under the hands of the Conquerors

Such, to a certain extent, is the fact; and this circumstance affords a means of comparison which alone would render his works of great value in arriving at just historic conclusions. But Garcilasso wrote late in life, after the story had been often told by Castilian writers. He naturally deferred much to men, some of whom enjoyed high credit on the score both of their scholarship and their social position. His object, he professes, was not so much to add any thing new of his own, as to correct their errors and the misconceptions into which they had been brought by their ignorance of the Indian languages and the usages of his people. He does, in fact, however, go far beyond this; and the stores of information which he has collected have made his work a large repository, whence later laborers in the same field have drawn copious materials. He writes from the fulness of his heart, and illuminates every topic that he touches with a variety and richness of illustration that leave little to be desired by the most importunate curiosity. The difference between reading his commentaries and the accounts of European writers is the difference that exists between reading a work in the original and in a bald translation. Garcilasso's writings are an emanation from the Indian mind.

Yet his Commentaries are open to a grave objection,—and one naturally suggested by his position. Addressing himself to the cultivated European, he was most desirous to display the ancient glories of his people, and still more of the Inca race, in their most imposing form. This, doubtless, was the great spur to his literary labors, for which previous education, however good for the evil time on which he was cast, had far from qualified him. Garcilasso, therefore, wrote to effect a particular object. He stood forth as counsel for his unfortunate countrymen, pleading the cause of that degraded race before the tribunal of posterity. The exaggerated tone of panegyric consequent on this becomes apparent in every page of his work. He pictures forth a state of society such as an Utopian philosopher would hardly venture to depict. His royal ancestors became the types of every imaginary excellence, and the golden age is revived for a nation which, while the war of proselytism is raging on its borders, enjoys within all the blessings of tranquillity and peace. Even the material splendors of the monarchy, sufficiently great in this land of gold, become heightened, under the glowing imagination of the Inca chronicler, into the gorgeous illusions of a fairy-tale.

Yet there is truth at the bottom of his wildest conceptions, and it would be unfair to the Indian historian to suppose that he did not himself believe most of the magic marvels which he describes. There is no credulity like that of a Christian convert,—one newly converted to the faith. From long dwelling in the darkness of paganism, his eyes, when first opened to the light of truth, have not acquired the power of discriminating the just proportions of objects, of distinguishing between the real and the imaginary. Garcilasso was not a convert, indeed, for he was bred from infancy in the Roman Catholic faith. But he was surrounded by converts and neophytes,—by those of his own blood, who, after practising all their lives the rites of paganism, were now first admitted into the Christian fold. He listened to the teachings of the missionary, learned from him to give implicit credit to the marvellous legends of the Saints, and the no less marvellous accounts of his own victories in his spiritual warfare for the propagation of the faith. Thus early accustomed to such large drafts on his credulity, his reason lost its heavenly power of distinguishing truth from error, and he became so familiar with the miraculous that the miraculous was not longer a miracle.

Yet, while large deductions are to be made on this account from the chronicler's reports, there is always a germ of truth which it is not difficult to detect, and even to disengage from the fanciful covering which envelops it; and, after every allowance for the exaggerations of national vanity, we shall find an abundance of genuine information in respect to the antiquities of his country, for which we shall look in vain in any European writer.

Garcilasso's work is the reflection of the age in which he lived. It is addressed to the imagination, more than to sober reason. We are dazzled by the gorgeous spectacle it perpetually exhibits, and delighted by the variety of amusing details and animated gossip sprinkled over its pages. The story of the action is perpetually varied by discussions on topics illustrating its progress, so as to break up the monotony of the narrative and afford an agreeable relief to the reader. This is true of the First Part of his great work. In the Second there was no longer room for such discussion. But he has supplied the place by garrulous reminiscences, personal anecdotes, incidental adventures, and a host of trivial details,—trivial in the eyes of the pedant,—which historians have been too willing to discard, as below the dignity of history. We have the actors in this great drama in their private dress, become acquainted with their personal habits, listen to their familiar sayings, and, in short, gather up those minutiæ which in the aggregate make up so much of life, and not less of character.

It is this confusion of the great and the little, thus artlessly blended together, that constitutes one of the charms of the old romantic chronicle,—not the less true that, in this respect, it approaches nearer to the usual tone of romance. It is in such writings that we may look to find the form and pressure of the age. The worm-eaten state papers, official correspondence, public records, are all serviceable, indispensable, to history. They are the framework on which it is to repose; the skeleton of facts which gives it its strength and proportions. But they are as worthless as the dry bones of the skeleton, unless clothed with the beautiful form and garb of humanity and instinct with the spirit of the age. Our debt is large to the antiquarian, who with conscientious precision lays broad and deep the foundations of historic truth; and no less to the philosophic annalist; who exhibits man in the dress of public life,—man in masquerade; but our gratitude must surely not be withheld from those who, like Garcilasso de la Vega, and many a romancer of the Middle Ages, have held up the mirror—distorted though it may somewhat be—to the interior of life, reflecting every object, the great and the mean, the beautiful and the deformed, with their natural prominence and their vivacity of coloring to the eye of the spectator. As a work of art, such a production may be thought to be below criticism. But, although it defy the rules of art in its composition, it does not necessarily violate the principles of taste; for it conforms in its spirit to the spirit of the age in which it was written. And the critic, who coldly condemns it on the severe principles of art, will find a charm in its very simplicity, that will make him recur again and again to its pages, while more correct and classical compositions are laid aside and forgotten.

I cannot dismiss this notice of Garcilasso, though already long protracted, without some allusion to the English translation of his Commentaries. It appeared in James the Second's reign, and is the work of Sir Paul Rycaut, Knight. It was printed at London in 1688, in folio, with considerable pretensions in its outward dress, well garnished with wood-cuts, and a frontispiece displaying the gaunt and rather sardonic features, not of the author, but his translator. The version keeps pace with the march of the original, corresponding precisely in books and chapters, and seldom, though sometimes, using the freedom, so common in these ancient versions, of abridgment and omission. Where it does depart from the original, it is rather from ignorance than intention Indeed, so far as the plea of ignorance will avail him, the worthy knight may urge it stoutly in his defence. No one who reads the book will doubt his limited acquaintance with his own tongue, and no one who compares it with the original will deny his ignorance of the Castilian It contains as many blunders as paragraphs, and most of them such as might shame a schoolboy Yet such are the rude charms of the original, that this ruder version of it has found considerable favor with readers, and Sir Paul Rycaut's translation, old as it is, may still be met with in many a private, as well as public, library.